An Interpretive Account to Agent-based Social Simulation

Using the investigation of criminal culture as an example application, this edited volume presents a novel approach to agent-based simulation: interpretive agent-based social simulation as a methodological and transdisciplinary approach to examining the potential of qualitative data and methods for agent-based modelling (ABM).

Featuring updated articles as well as original chapters which provide a cohesive and novel approach to the digital humanities, the book challenges the common conviction that hermeneutics and simulation are two mutually exclusive ways to understand and explain human behaviour and social change. Exploring how methodology benefits from taking cultural complexities into account and bringing these methods together in an innovative combination of qualitative-hermeneutic and digital techniques, the book unites experts in the field to connect ABM to narrative theories, thereby providing a novel tool for cultural studies.

An innovative methodological contribution to narrative theory, this volume will be of primary benefit to researchers, scholars, and academics in the fields of ABM, hermeneutics, and criminology. The book will also appeal to those working in policing, security, and forensic consultation.

Martin Neumann is Research Associate at the Department of Language, Culture, History and Communication of the University of Southern Denmark, Denmark.

An Interpretive Account to Agent-based Social Simulation

Using Criminology to Explore
Cultural Possibilities

Edited by Martin Neumann

Routledge
Taylor & Francis Group

LONDON AND NEW YORK

First published 2024
by Routledge
4 Park Square, Milton Park, Abingdon, Oxon OX14 4RN

and by Routledge
605 Third Avenue, New York, NY 10158

Routledge is an imprint of the Taylor & Francis Group, an informa business

British Library Cataloguing-in-Publication Data
A catalogue record for this book is available from the British Library

Library of Congress Cataloging-in-Publication Data
Names: Neumann, Martin, Dr, editor.
Title: An interpretive account to agent-based social simulation : using criminology to explore cultural possibilities / edited by Martin Neumann.
Identifiers: LCCN 2023014935 (print) | LCCN 2023014936 (ebook) | ISBN 9781032489704 (hardback) | ISBN 9781032493237 (paperback) | ISBN 9781003393207 (ebook)
Subjects: LCSH: Criminal behavior--Research--Methodology. | Social change.
Classification: LCC HV6115 .I58 2024 (print) | LCC HV6115 (ebook) | DDC 364.3072--dc23/eng/20230621
LC record available at https://lccn.loc.gov/2023014935
LC ebook record available at https://lccn.loc.gov/2023014936

ISBN: 978-1-032-48970-4 (hbk)
ISBN: 978-1-032-49323-7 (pbk)
ISBN: 978-1-003-39320-7 (ebk)

DOI: 10.4324/9781003393207

Typeset in Galliard
by KnowledgeWorks Global Ltd.

Contents

List of contributors

Petra Ahrweiler
Johannes Gutenberg University Mainz

Sascha Dickel
Johannes Gutenberg University Mainz

Vanessa Dirksen
Open University of the Netherlands

Bruce Edmonds
Manchester Metropolitan University

Ulf Lotzmann
University of Koblenz

Martin Neumann
University of Southern Denmark

Cornelis van Putten
Dantes Psychology

1 Introduction

An interpretive account of an agent-based social simulation

Martin Neumann

1.1 How the present book developed

The process that culminated in the publication of this book began in November 2012, when I joined the European research project GLODERS for the agent-based modelling (ABM) of the global dynamics of extortion racket systems, which ran from 2012 to 2015. GLODERS aimed to apply theoretical concepts to develop agent-based simulation models of the norm dynamics not only between criminal organizations and societies but also within criminal organizations. It was a follow-up to another European Union funded project, EMIL, which ran from 2006 to 2009. EMIL attempted to simulate theoretically the dynamics of norm innovation. When I joined the research group on information systems at the University of Koblenz, the members had just finalized the European Union funded project OCOPOMO, which attempted to develop a new bottom-up approach to policy modelling. We then attempted to apply the new tools the team had developed to GLODERS, modelling and simulating norm dynamics within criminal groups and organizations, for which we secured extensive data from police investigations. The subjects were a group of drug dealers who had allegedly been amongst the best Ecstasy cooks in Europe. The puzzle was why they started fighting with each other. At a certain point, their internal relations were characterized by extortion, extreme violence, and even murder, which were counterproductive for their business model. The goal of the project was to develop an agent-based model to comprehend the group's behaviour and address the central research question: why could they not carry on manufacturing and selling drugs?

The question was an interpretive one, based as it was on the concept of understanding. As such, it followed the classical sociological tradition of Max Weber, George Herbert Mead, and others. The tools developed during the OCOPOMO project (see Scherer et al. 2013; Lotzmann and Wimmer, 2013, 2015), which were based on the ideas of Scott Moss and Maria Wimmer, facilitated our attempt to find an answer. During the OCOPOMO project, the team designed a specific modelling *grammar* (denoted as condition–action sequences). To our surprise, at the end of the GLODERS project, we realized we had created a new style of ABM. In collaboration with ethnographers and

DOI: 10.4324/9781003393207-1

hermeneutic social scientists, it has since been further explored and developed. However, findings are scattered across various journals and book publications, which have made it more difficult for people to grasp the methodology. The present volume explains in detail the entire research process (including its epistemological foundations) by means of an ABM case study. It also offers suggestions for future applications.

Based on an investigation of a criminal subculture, the book outlines a novel research methodology for ABM to trace the simultaneous emergence of a social and cultural structure. It challenges the widely held conviction that hermeneutics and simulation are two mutually exclusive ways of understanding and explaining human behaviour and social change by combining empirical research and technologies of the artificial. It reveals the potential of bringing together these methods in an innovative combination of qualitative-hermeneutic and digital techniques. The book explicates the research process through an ex-ante or what-if analysis. It contributes to the ABM literature by developing narrative scenarios and investigating the meaningfulness of counterfactuals by a hermeneutic interpretation of simulation results. This connects ABM to narrative theories (Gibson, 2022; Walter-Smith et al., 2020), thereby providing a novel tool for use in cultural studies.

The methodology is based on two important innovations. The first is the development of narratives as simulation results rather than – as is usually the case – numerical time series. Its origins lie in the tools that were developed during the aforementioned OCOPOMO project. The concept of traceability is relevant in this context. In particular, the significance of textual outputs has been recently recognized in studies such as "Justified stories with agent-based modelling for local COVID-19 planning" (Bedham et al., 2021). The innovation proposed herein may be described as the generation of meaningful stories based on an ethnographic approach for formulating agent rules.

The second innovation is its hermeneutic interpretation of the results of narrative simulations. While many agent-based models have referred to qualitative evidence, interpretive methods – which allow for understanding (Verstehen) agents in the Weberian sense – have never been applied in agent-based research. Dissecting the meaningfulness of counterfactual scenarios again makes ABM suitable for use in cultural studies.

1.2   ABM as a new style of scientific reasoning

Since the publication of Joshua Epstein and Robert Axtell's *Growing Artificial Societies: Social Science from the Bottom-up* (1996) and Robert Axelrod's *Complexity of Cooperation* (1997), ABM has become an important area of research in social sciences. The methodology was consolidated in *Simulation for the Social Scientist* (Gilbert and Troitzsch, 2005), *Agent-Based Models* (Gilbert, 2008), *Agent-Based Computational Sociology* (Squazzoni, 2012), *Introduction to Computational Social Science* (Cioffi-Revilla, 2014), and *Agent-Based and Individual-Based Modelling* (Railsback and Grimm, 2019). Several journals are dedicated to agent-based social simulation, most notably the *Journal of Artificial Societies and Social Simulation* and *Computational and Mathematical Organization Theory*. Articles applying agent-based social simulation have appeared in several social science journals, for example, *The Journal for Mathematical Sociology, American Political Science Review*, and *Mind and Society*, as well as in journals covering artificial methods such as *Autonomous Agents and Multi-Agent Systems, Artificial Intelligence and Law*, and the *Journal of Simulation*. ABM is, therefore, a well-established research methodology in social sciences.

Simulations of the behaviour of many individual actors in civil wars, protest movements, the formation of public opinion, and multilateral negotiations can be carried out using agent-based models. The term "agent" in this context is a generic one for the independent actors modelled in each case. They might be persons, parties, constitutional bodies, or whole states. Technically speaking, agents are software units that act autonomously in a virtual environment to achieve their own goals (Wooldridge, 1999). They are characterized by the following:

- Reactivity, that is, the ability to perceive the environment and react to changes within it. In many cases, an adaptation to environmental requirements takes place, so such systems are *adaptive*.
- Proactivity, that is, the ability to act purposefully in pursuit of one's plans.
- Sociality, that is, the ability to interact with other agents in a virtual environment.
- Bounded rationality, that is, they may have limited information about their environment (perhaps as a result of forgetting) or may be restricted in terms of calculating possible actions. Thus, actions may need to be based on heuristic reasoning rather than optimization.

These characteristics, which mirror certain aspects of human interaction, can be used to study social phenomena in a virtual lab. ABM allows researchers to examine the effects of heterogeneity or networks and the ways micro-level behaviour generates social patterns and dynamics. It also makes it possible to study the bidirectional dynamics of the micro and the macro, which is a source of social uncertainty and unpredictability (Squazzoni et al., 2013). A classic example is the Schelling model (1971), where agents live in a checkerboard grid world. They are *red* or *blue*, have skills and properties that define their goals, and perceive their neighbours as similar or dissimilar. Their degree of satisfaction depends on how many are of the same colour as themselves. If they are dissatisfied with their neighbours, they can increase their satisfaction by moving. In the end, the actions of individual agents lead to a world in which neighbourhoods are either red or blue. The Schelling model is one of the best-known examples of agent-based simulation (cf. Neumann and Lorenz, 2020). A second example is provided by Robert Axelrod (1984), who studied the evolution of cooperation. The author created agents who used different strategies to compete against each other in the manner of a prisoner's dilemma, except that the agents could meet repeatedly. The evolution of the agents' strategies could then be studied. The simplest strategies were those of cooperation or defection. The still quite simple strategy tit-for-tat cooperates on the first move, and from then on always cooperates or defects if the other player did it in his previous move. The "Tit-for-Tat" strategy turned out to be a very successful strategy in simulation experiments (see Galan and Izquierdo, 2005). Another classic instance of the study of social phenomena using agent-based models involved the emergence of equilibrium prices through local interaction between heterogeneous agents (Epstein and Axtell, 1996). Thus, agent-based models typically generate social regularities on a macro level through individual interactions on a micro level. Often, these social macrophenomena are denoted as emergent as they are not (or at least not directly) programmed into the model code; rather, they result from the interactions of agents.

ABM can be described as a new style of scientific reasoning (Hacking, 1985). Certain techniques can be used to determine whether scientific statements are true or false. Following Foucault's method of discourse analysis, the philosopher Ian Hacking (1985) refers to these techniques as a form of scientific reasoning. Examples include laboratory science, statistical reasoning, or agent-based computer simulations. Only through scientific reasoning can scientific statements attain objectivity because such reasoning creates specific sentences, classifications, and objects. Moreover, scientific reasoning creates specific forms of scientific explanations. In the case of ABM, these are described as generative explanations (Epstein, 2006): a social macrophenomenon such as ethnic segregation, cooperation, or equilibrium prices is generated, or grown, by interactions between individual heterogeneous agents. This provides a candidate explanation because the simulation demonstrates how the rules of the interaction might generate the phenomenon to be explained. It is a candidate explanation because other constellations on the micro level of interacting agents might generate the same phenomenon; this is an example of how ABM as a form of scientific reasoning creates its own style of explanation: "if you didn't grow it, you didn't explain it" (Epstein, 2006: 8).

While early agent-based models were mostly theoretical, recent ones tend to be more empirically orientated or based on domain theory. Broadly, three different uses of modelling can be distinguished (Epstein, 2008): (a) explanatory models in theoretical research; (b) descriptive models with a more applied focus; and (c) participatory models in which researchers and stakeholders develop a model together as a community of inquirers. In the first case, ABM is used as a virtual laboratory for experimenting with theories (Dowling, 1999). Growing macro-level phenomena by local interactions of agents at the micro level (Epstein, 2006) enables researchers to explore the implications of social science theories (Edmonds et al., 2019) and make nomothetic, law-like statements. On the other hand, the value of description cannot be underestimated (Edmonds et al., 2019). While models for theoretical exposition make universal claims, descriptive models represent empirical cases in space and time and are thus idiographic tools. Typically, descriptive models employ more complex micro-level rules informed by the case in hand and are used as scenario analytical tools (Ahrweiler et al., 2015). Finally, agent-based simulations may include stakeholders who provide input into the formalization of rule and fact bases and comment on intermediate results. Simulated scenarios can then be used as a communication tool in social practice (Neumann and Troitzsch, 2019). These participatory models have policy or real-world rather than purely scientific purposes (Barreteau et al., 2014) and as such are problem-solving tools.

ABM has been used primarily to investigate social structures rather than culture. However, the methodology benefits from taking cultural complexity into account. *Perspectives on Culture and Agent-Based Simulations: Integrating Cultures*, edited by Virginia Dignum and Frank Dignum (2014), was an early example of this approach. Meanwhile, a considerable amount of research has been conducted on modelling norms (e.g., Conte et al., 2014) and institutions (Ghorbani et al., 2013). Social norms are a standard of acceptable behaviour in groups. Because the validity of norms (i.e., what is acceptable) is anchored in cultural values, their study is naturally closely related to the study of culture. Normative agent-based simulation models can be assigned to one of two categories – models inspired by evolutionary game theory and models of cognitively richer agents with a background in artificial intelligence and cognitive science – though the distinction is not clear-cut (Neumann, 2008). Typically, models of normative agents are theoretical; they are used to study mechanisms of norm spreading or adoption, not how norms are legitimized, so the focus is on social structure rather than on culture or sense-making. This remains an open issue in relation to ABM.

In the past decade, the use of qualitative data has attracted increasing attention, as was evidenced by the formation of a special interest group of the European Social Simulation Association (ESSA) for the integration of qualitative and quantitative evidence into ABM and the inclusion (in 2015) of a section dedicated to "qualitative evidence to inform the specification of agent-based models" in the *Journal of Artificial Societies and Social Simulation*. Qualitative methods are often applied in participatory modelling approaches used in socio-ecological research (e.g., land use planning; Étienne, 2014). The potential of qualitative data for ABM has been examined in several articles, including "Getting away from numbers" (Yang and Gilbert, 2008), "'An ethnographic seduction': How qualitative research and agent-based models can benefit each other" (Tubaro and Casilli, 2010), or "From participants to agents: Grounded simulation as a mixed-method research design" (Dilaver, 2015). What is missing, however, is an interpretive account of the use of qualitative data in ABM.

1.3 The present book's objective and model

Although this book provides technical details of the research process, it is not designed to be an ABM (e.g., Railsback and Grimm, 2019) or a mixed-method textbook (e.g., Kukartz, 2014). By outlining a novel approach to sociocultural research and a new style of scientific reasoning, it follows Hacking (1985), Epstein and Axtell (1996), and Axelrod (1997) for developing a new style of scientific reasoning (Hacking, 1985). It both grows an *artificial culture* in the manner of the generative social sciences and makes an innovative methodological contribution to narrative theory (e.g., Puckett, 2016; Gibson, 2022) through the use of ABM.

The role model for the book is Joshua Epstein's (2006) *Generative Social Science*, a collection of previously published articles. Epstein's book is more than the sum of its parts, and it is hoped that this holds true in the present case, where a series of articles, some published, some unpublished, go into detail about the different stages of the methodology that has been developed by the contributors over the past decade. The authors describe discrete elements of the research process, but while each chapter can be read independently, the overall process and the advantages to be gained by following the approach only become apparent at the end.

Epstein's (2006) work makes the claim for ABM as a novel and powerful technique enabling a new standard of explanation for social sciences where phenomena *grown* in an artificial society. The present book has a narrower focus in that it presents an emergent methodology. An emergent methodology can be characterized as a reaction to existing methods that are not sufficient to answer open research questions (Schreier, 2017). The present book proposes a mixed-method approach (Saetra, 2017). While qualitative data are being used more and more in ABM, extending the qualitative approach to an interpretive one has yet to be explored. It is hoped that our methodology will enable researchers to apply ABM to the field of digital humanities and policy modelling. In the case of the criminological example used herein, the stakeholders (such as the police investigators) are part of a virtual experience. The goal is to stimulate abductive reasoning and generate hypotheses about possible courses of meaningful action, as well as factual and counterfactual scenarios, with the methodology instantiating a virtual Sherlock Holmes. The narrative formulation of the scenarios makes it possible to trace back knowledge claims to what Geertz (1983) calls *the intelligible frame*.

1.4   Overview of the chapters

As has been noted, each chapter can be read independently, but it should be borne in mind that they all build on each other in a logical sequence; only when all the articles have been read does the overall methodology reveal itself.

1.4.1   *Epistemological underpinnings*

The traditional philosophy of history emphasized the difference between nomothetic and idiographic science. While the former seeks universal laws in the manner of the mathematical ideal, the latter attempts to understand historical individuals using hermeneutical methodologies, thus deciphering the meaningfulness of the social world. As has been noted, these scientific approaches have often been regarded as dichotomous, with the computerized technology of agent-based social simulation leaning towards nomothetic science. The chapter draws on the philosophical underpinnings of hermeneutics (e.g., Dilthey, Windelband, Rickert, and Weber) and the work of the progenitors of agent-based simulation (e.g., Axelrod, Epstein, and Squazzoni), challenging the view that hermeneutics and simulation are mutually exclusive approaches. In brief, the chapter will outline the epistemological foundations of the interpretive account of an agent-based social simulation outlined in this book.

1.4.2 From the field to a model, or from agent to action

This chapter uses the example of crime research to explain the first step in the methodological process: from the data to the model, by grounding agent rules on ethnographic data analysis. The application of computational tools in crime research typically entails the removal of the *intelligible frame* of criminal behaviour and, hence, meaningful evidence. Ethnography is a microscopic research tradition geared towards the preservation of contextualized meaning deemed essential for the exploration of the variety of prospective alternative scenarios and, by extension, plausible futures. Using empirical material from a qualitative study of the transit trade of cocaine in the Netherlands, the chapter examines the complementarity and potential integration of the research traditions of ethnography and ABM. It explores the compatibility of the formal languages of both domains and the mutual benefit of stitching together these ostensibly distinct methods. The ethnographic approach to social simulation categorizes the what-if relations of conventional ABM into condition–action sequences, which will facilitate *thick description* and ground ABM in meaningful evidence.

1.4.3 Methodological underpinnings: Growing criminal culture

Agent-based social simulation is well known for generative explanations. Following the theory of thick description, we extend the generative paradigm to interpretative research in cultural studies. This chapter describes the growing of virtual cultures. Relying on qualitative data to develop agent rules, the methodological process combines several steps: qualitative data analysis enables concept identification, which in turn results in the development of a conceptual model of the relationship between the concepts. The software tool CCD and the simulation platform DRAMS are used to trace the empirical evidence. Traceability enables the interpretation of simulations by generating a narrative storyline of the simulation. Thereby simulation enables a qualitative exploration of textual data. The whole process generates a thick description of the subject of study, which in the present case is criminal culture. The simulation is characterized by a socio-cognitive coupling of agents' reasoning regarding the state of the mind of other agents. This reveals how participants make sense of the phenomenology of a situation from their perspective. This methodology is described in more detail in the following two chapters.

1.4.4   Example 1: Conceptual model of the collapse of a criminal enterprise

This chapter presents an example of the development of a conceptual model based on qualitative data analysis, again using crime research. It demonstrates the added value of the methodology of simultaneously growing cultural and social structures for agent-based research and our understanding of cultural dynamics. The chapter investigates the collapse of a network of criminals involved in drug trafficking and money laundering. The analysis is based on several police investigations involving numerous interrogations. First, the data were loaded into MaxQDA, a qualitative text analysis tool. Passages were then annotated and coded according to the concepts derived from the data. The concepts represented classes of objects, events, or actions that had significant properties in common. Finally, the CCD tool was used to build a model of the relationships between the concepts.

1.4.5   Example 2: A simulation model for generating narrative scenarios. A simulation model of intra-organizational conflict regulation

This chapter follows directly from the previous one, where the qualitative analysis of textual data from police investigations into a criminal network was transformed into a conceptual model. The model was then transformed and formalized into a simulation model, as described in the present chapter. The results of simulation experiments with the model are presented and transformed into narrative scenarios that rely on the traceability of rules invoked during a simulation run to the textual evidence. This chapter closes with a theoretical reflection on the insights that can be gained from growing culture as demonstrated here and in Example 1. One of the objectives here is to show how the approach can be applied to all manner of empirical and generative research.

1.4.6   The hermeneutics of social simulation

This chapter connects two methodological worlds, addressing a problem that has been under-researched in the field of social simulation. It uses hermeneutic sequence analysis for the interpretation of ABM, constructing scenarios where specific social constellations are played out. The simulation model refers back to the one described in the previous chapters. The results are formulated as narrative scenarios that are subjected to a sequence analysis. The chapter shows how hermeneutic sequence analysis can be used for structural generalizations and the validation of agent-based models. In the present case, a digital hermeneutics is developed that combines social simulation with social meaning, as was proposed in Chapter 2.

1.4.7 Transdisciplinary reflection: The impact on stakeholders

This chapter describes the stakeholders in the modelling process, demonstrating how practical skills and theoretical knowledge are intertwined. The central aim of the simulation is to generate counterfactual scenarios. An example of a narrative is provided, and typical scenarios are described. These explore complex and non-transparent situations in the form of a virtual experience from the perspective, or cultural horizon, of the criminals. While the factual criminal acts are transparent to the police, the possible alternative courses of action are not. The field of possibilities crucially depends on how meaning is negotiated. The goal is to stimulate abductive reasoning to generate hypotheses about the possible courses of action or intervention strategies.

1.4.8 Concluding reflections: Triangulating ethnography and objective hermeneutics with ABM

This chapter summarizes and reflects on the research process, in particular the integration of the methods. The process in question starts with the qualitative data analysis of unstructured textual data in natural language. The first step is to generate a thick description of the field under study and decipher the subjective worldview of the agents. (The reader may recall an example provided by Geertz: is an eye movement an involuntary twitch or a conspiratorial signal?) Qualitative content analysis is used as the basis for the implementation of a simulation model. The final stage involves a qualitative analysis of the various scenarios, whereby objective hermeneutics are used to decipher the latent meaning of structures. Although the scenarios are counterfactual cases, because they are generated from empirical evidence, they can be described as the horizon of possibilities that are hidden in the cultural matrix, potential pathways opened up by the cultural frame of the field. They enable the construction of the *ideal type* of the culture's latent meaning structures. Thus, the simulation enables the triangulation of two qualitative methods – ethnography and objective hermeneutics – that are traditionally seen as opposite poles in the domain of qualitative research. From the perspective of computational social science, both are necessary and mutually dependent: ethnographic analysis is needed to generate the narratives that can then be interpreted. In turn, hermeneutics is needed to confirm the meaningfulness of the ethnographic analysis.

1.4.9 Outlook to potential further applications

Finally, some suggestions are made for possible future applications of the methodology – one of which could be modelling narrative identities – and how it might be generalized.

Finally, some suggestions are made for possible further application of this methodology. An example of a potentially fruitful application in modelling narrative identities is briefly sketched. These notes will be a brief outlook of potential future research for stimulating ideas on how the methodology can be generalized.

1.5   Theoretical objective: Reconciling interpretive and analytical sociology

In theoretical terms, the central objective of the book is to reconcile interpretive and analytical sociology and demonstrate how both domains benefit from formalizing a Weberian understanding. The methodological innovation outlined involves the generation of narrative scenarios that are subsequently interpreted to grasp their meaning. It is hoped that the approach will be further explored not only by the editor of the present volume and its contributors but also by a wider community of scholars. It is crucial that the methodology is adapted by other research groups and developed independently. While ABM has, and will continue to be, conducted without the interpretive strategy described herein – and ethnographic research and hermeneutics have, and will continue to be, conducted without digital technologies – the goal of this book is to establish a research technique that can be included in the toolbox of social science methodologies. The editor invites other researchers to participate in this project.

For the purpose of replicability, this book uses a single case study to describe the research process. Each step is described sequentially and framed by its epistemological foundations. In addition, the editor provides some pointers for the practical reasoning that is supported by this approach, as well as reflections on the specific approach to mixed methods suggested by it. However, the use of one example (i.e., criminal culture) across all chapters comes at a price. For instance, because it was intended that each chapter could be read independently, Chapters 7 and 8 refer back to a model extensively described in Chapters 5 and 6. While the brief descriptions in Chapters 7 and 8 are not sufficient to fully understand the model, readers may be aware of an element of repetition. However, Chapters 7 and 8 use the example to illustrate the aspects of the methodology that are not touched on in the extensive description of the model, that is, the interpretation of simulation results (Chapter 7) and the abductive reasoning process in the transdisciplinary application of the model (Chapter 8). That said, and as has been noted, the methodology could be used in other applications such as research on narrative identities (McAdams, 2001), political culture, and inter- and intrastate conflict; however, other applications are conceivable as well.

Finally, a note on the language used in this book. Developing the methodology of interpretive ABM was only possible through inter- and transdisciplinary collaboration between scholars and practitioners from widely divergent backgrounds, and this is reflected in the different kinds of languages and styles of reasoning. For instance, some chapters were written with an ethnographer and others with a software engineer. One chapter was co-written by a former police officer with whom we developed the model. The technical knowledge claims in the various domains have been adhered to; all fields have their own language and take certain things for granted. My role as the editor was partly that of an interlocutor, with the result that each chapter differs in terms of writing style and technical language. Partly this is compensated by the fact that I am a co-author of all chapters. This ensures that the language remains considerably coherent. In consequences, a potentially new style of scientific reasoning seemed to emerge. It is assumed that readers will come from different backgrounds, so this might be problematic for those who are familiar (or unfamiliar) with one particular style of reasoning. A list of key terms of the different scientific disciplines has, therefore, been included to support the readers who are not familiar with one or the other domain language. Have fun!

References

Ahrweiler, P., Schilperoord, M., Pyka, A. and Gilbert, N. (2015) 'Modelling research policy: Ex-ante evaluation of complex policy instruments', *Journal of Artificial Societies and Social Simulation* 18(4). https://jasss.soc.surrey.ac.uk/18/4/5.html

Axelrod, R. (1984) *The evolution of cooperation*. New York: Basic Books.

Axelrod, R. (1997) *Complexity of cooperation. Agent-based models of competition and cooperation*. Princeton: Princeton University Press.

Barreteau, O., Bousquet, F., Étienne, M., Souchère, V. and d'Aquino, P. (2014) 'Companion modelling: A method of adaptive and participatory research', in Étienne, M. (ed.) *Companion modelling*. Dordrecht: Springer, pp. 13–40.

Bedham, J., Barbrook-Johnson, P., Caiado, C. and Castellani, B. (2021) 'Justified stories with agent-based modelling for local COVID-19 planning', *Journal of Artificial Societies and Social Simulation*, 24(1). https://www.jasss.org/24/1/8.html

Cioffi-Revilla, C. (2014) *Introduction to computational social science: Principles and applications*. New York: Springer.

Conte, R., Andrighetto, G. and Campenni, M. (eds.) (2014) *Minding norms: Mechanisms and dynamics of social order in agent societies*. Oxford: Oxford University Press.

Dignum, V. and Dignum, F. (eds.) (2014). *Perspectives on culture and agent-based simulations: Integrating cultures*. Cham: Springer.

Dilaver, O. (2015) 'From participants to agents: Grounded simulation as a mixed-method research design', *Journal of Artificial Societies and Social Simulation*, 18(1). https://www.jasss.org/18/1/15.html

Dowling, D. (1999) 'Experimenting on theories', *Science in Context*, 12(2), pp. 261–273.

Edmonds, B., et al. (2019) 'Different modelling purposes', *Journal of Artificial Societies and Social Simulation*, 22(3). https://www.jasss.org/22/3/6.html

Epstein, J. (2006) *Generative social science. Studies in agent-based computational modelling*. Princeton: Princeton University Press.

Epstein, J. (2008) 'Why model?', *Journal of Artificial Societies and Social Simulation*, 11(4). https://www.jasss.org/11/4/12.html

Epstein, J. and Axtell, R. (1996) *Growing artificial societies: Social science from the bottom-up*. Cambridge, MA: MIT Press.

Étienne, M. (2014) *Companion modelling: A participatory approach to support sustainable development*. Dordrecht: Springer.

Galan, J. and Izquierdo, L. (2005) 'Appearances Can Be Deceiving: Lessons Learned Re-Implementing Axelrod's 'Evolutionary Approach to Norms'. *Journal of Artificial Societies and Social Simulation* 8(3). http://jasss.soc.surrey.ac.uk/8/3/2.html

Geertz, C. (1983) *Local knowledge: Further essays in interpretive anthropology.* New York: Basic Books.

Gibson, A. (2022) *Towards a postmodern theory of narrative.* Edinburgh: Edinburgh University Press.

Gilbert, N. (2008) *Agent-based models.* London: Sage.

Gilbert, N. and Troitzsch, K. (2005) *Simulation for the social scientist.* London: Open University Press.

Ghorbani, A., Bots, P., Dignum, V. and Dijkema, G. (2013) 'MAIA: A framework for developing agent-based social simulations', *Journal of Artificial Societies and Social Simulation,* 16(2). https://www.jasss.org/16/2/9.html

Hacking, I. (1985) 'Styles of scientific reasoning', in Rajchman, J. and West, C. (eds.) *Post-analytic philosophy.* New York: Columbia University Press, pp. 145–165.

Kukartz, U. (2014) *Mixed-methods. Methodologie, Forschungsdesigns Und Analysever-fahren.* Wiesbaden: Springer VS.

Lotzmann, U. and Wimmer, M. (2013) Evidence traces for multi-agent declarative rule-based policy simulation. In: *2013 IEEE/ACM 17th International Symposium on Distributed Simulation and Real Time Applications.* Delft: IEEE, pp. 115–122.

McAdams, D. (2001) 'The psychology of life stories', *Review of General Psychology,* 5(2), pp. 100–122.

Neumann, M. (2008) 'Homo socionicus: A case study of simulation models of norms', *Journal of Artificial Societies and Social Simulation,* 11(4). https://jasss.soc.surrey.ac.uk/11/4/6.html

Neumann, M. and Lorenz, J. (2020) 'Agentenbasierte simulation in der politikwissenschaft', in Wagemann, C., Goerres, A. and Siewert, M. (eds.) *Handbuch Methoden der Politikwissenschaft.* Wiesbaden: Springer VS, pp. 595–618.

Neumann, M. and Troitzsch, K. G. (2019) 'Social simulation', in Atkinson, P., Delamont, S., Cernat, A., Sakshaug, J. and Williams, R. (eds.). *SAGE Research Methods Foundations.* doi: 10.4135/9781526421036764890. https://methods-sagepub-com.elibrary.iimnagpur.ac.in/foundations/social-simulation

Puckett, K. (2016) *Narrative theory. A critical introduction.* Cambridge: Cambridge University Press.

Railsback, S. and Grimm, V. (2019) *Agent-based and individual-based modelling: A practical introduction.* Princeton: Princeton University Press.

Saetra, H. (2017) 'Exploring the use of agent-based modeling (ABM) in mixed methods research', *Barataria: revista castellano-manchega de ciencias sociales,* 22, pp. 15–31.

Schelling, T. (1971) 'Dynamic models of segregation', *Journal of Mathematical Sociology,* 1, pp. 143–186.

Scherer, S., Wimmer, M., Lotzmann, U., Moss, S. and Pinotti, D. (2015) 'An evidence-based and conceptual-driven approach for agent-based policy modelling', *Journal of Artificial Societies and Social Simulation,* 18(3). https://www.jasss.org/18/3/14.html

Scherer, S., Wimmer, M. A. and Markisic, S. (2013) 'Bridging narrative scenario texts and formal policy modelling through conceptual policy modelling', *Artificial Intelligence and Law,* 21(4), pp. 455–484.

Schreier, M. (2017) 'Kontexte qualitativer Sozialforschung: Arts-based research, mixed methods und emergent methods', *Forum Qualitative Sozialforschung/Forum Qualitative Social Research,* 18(2). Art. 6. https://www.qualitative-research.net/index.php/fqs/article/view/2815/4095

Squazzoni, F. (2012) *Agent-based computational sociology*. Chichester: Wiley.

Squazzoni, F., Jager, W. and Edmonds, B. (2013) 'Social simulation in the social sciences. A brief overview', *Social Science Computer Review*, 32(3), pp. 279–294.

Tubaro, P. and Casilli, A. (2010) 'An ethnographic seduction': How qualitative research and agent-based models can benefit each other', *Bulletin of Sociological Methodology*, 106(1), pp. 59–74.

Walter-Smith, A., Jones, M., Shanahan, E. and Peterson, H. (2020) 'The stories groups tell: Campaign finance reform and the narrative networks of cultural cognition', *Quality and Quantity*, 54(2), pp. 645–684.

Wooldridge, M. (1999) 'Intelligent agents', in Weiss, G. (ed.) *Multi agent systems: A modern approach to distributed artificial intelligence*. Cambridge, MA: MIT Press, pp. 27–77.

Yang, L. and Gilbert, N. (2008) 'Getting away from numbers', *Advances in Complex Systems*, 11(2), pp. 175–185.

2 Epistemological foundations

Petra Ahrweiler and Martin Neumann

2.1 Objectives

Coping societal problems is often in need of understanding strategies, hopes, or fears of the involved actors. Examples range from lifetime transitions, cultural diversity, to criminal investigations. Examining such problems is the particular strength of interpretative research approaches. While many different interpretive research methods exist in the social sciences such as grounded theory, ethnography, a range of discourse analytical methods, or objective hermeneutics, we will refer in this chapter to these methods as hermeneutical approaches. These emphasize less the search for universal laws but rather examine the details of specific contexts. A famous example by Clifford Geertz describes two boys rapidly contracting the eyelids of their right eyes. In one, this is an involuntary twitch, perhaps because a sand corn has hit his eye; in the other, it is a conspiratorial signal to a friend. Thus, interpretation is needed which puts the observation in context. On the other hand, in particular policy-related issues benefit from a "social laboratory" that allows for experimentally assessing "potential" futures. While such a scenario-based approach is not the classical domain of the more diagnostic, hermeneutic approaches, this is the specific strength of social simulation approaches. In particular, agent-based simulation is a relatively new technology which enables to model the actions and interactions of autonomous agents for simulating their effects on the system as a whole. Thus, it would be beneficial to make use of the strength of both approaches. However, it is a common conviction that hermeneutics and simulation are two mutually exclusive ways of research belonging to different epistemological camps of sociological explanations, as expressed already in Dilthey's famous dichotomy of explaining and understanding.

The central objective of this book is to challenge this conviction by outlining an epistemologically sound mixed-methods approach to combine the strength of interpretive, hermeneutical approaches and agent-based modelling (ABM). This book will reveal the potential of bringing together these methods in an innovative combination of qualitative-hermeneutic and digital techniques for a mixed-methods approach to provide a sound foundation of integrating methods from hermeneutics and social simulation; to translate this

DOI: 10.4324/9781003393207-2

framework into methodological requirements; and to realize these requirements with an agent-based simulation platform. This approach relies on classical social theory, namely the work of Max Weber who described sociology as "cultural science". While there exist attempts at formalizing sociological theory such as agent-based models of aspects of Luhmann's theory (Dittrich et al., 2003) or Simmel (Benvenuto, 2000; Cederman, 2005), the approach of this project is different: it will not simulate a certain theory but rather will rely on Weber's methodological concepts of "understanding" and "ideal type".

As a proof of concept, the book refers to criminal culture as the running example. Understanding criminal culture calls for a contextualized hermeneutic interpretation of a world outside the state monopoly of violence which fosters specific codes of conduct, a criminal culture. Understanding this culture potentially enables more targeted interventions, whereas simulation allows for investigating scenarios which provide virtual experiences for criminal investigators. These features make criminal culture a fruitful and practically useful case for exploring the potential of an interpretive account to ABM. Simulation will reveal sense-making agents that are able to interpret situational encounters in the light of different and changing cultural expectations. Thus, the simulation allows agents to grow culture (i.e., patterns to interpret and react accordingly to courses of actions of other agents) in course of a simulation run. The different scenarios will then be able to explore the horizon of cultural possibilities. Thereby an attempt is made to a computational study of culture.

2.2   State of the art

2.2.1   Understanding in the social sciences

"Qualitative methods" is an umbrella term, covering a wide array of disparate approaches. For instance, discourse analytical methods, often associated with the work of Michel Foucault, analyse significant semiotic events. With a background in cultural anthropology, participant observation aims to get intimate familiarity with distinct groups of individuals by close involvement in their cultural environment. Biographical research attempts at deciphering narratives of a life story. Grounded theory claims to generate theory by qualitative data analysis, often based on assumptions from symbolic interactionism. Correspondingly, the objective of thick description is to get access to the subjective meaning attributed to situational encounters by people engaged in the field. This concept traversed to various disciplines such as general sociology, psychology, education research, or business science (Denzin, 1989; Ponterotto, 2006). Objective hermeneutics, on the other hand, attempts to work out latent meaning structures of a living environment and thus objective rather than subjective meaning structures.

These are by no means exhaustive examples of qualitative methods.[1] However, they have in common that they involve interpretative methods attempting at deciphering the meaning of the social world as meaning shapes the space of plausible (and implausible) follow-up actions. The central element of an interpretative approach to the social world is an attempt to comprehend how participants in a social encounter perceive a particular concrete situation from within their world view. Instead of observing from the outside, interpretation attempts to comprehend social interaction from inside the social actors. This refers to the notion of culture which has a significant role in determining meaning structures of the social world. Resembling Wittgenstein's theory of language games, culture can be characterized as public symbolic action. Analysing such action calls for a microscopic diagnosis of specific situations. For this reason, interpretative methods go along with a focus on analysing case studies rather than searching for universal laws. These features of qualitative methods are often framed in opposition between so-called idiographic and nomothetic science. This dichotomy is based on the history of science, specifically the philosophy of history, to characterize a distinction between social and natural science as no meaning is inherent in the natural world. This suggests a review of the historical legacy of this scientific divide.

The disparity between the nomological, mathematically based natural sciences and history has always been an important topic in the philosophy of science. Already Kant distinguished between (natural) scientific knowledge and historical knowledge. The philosophers of the Southwest School of Neo-Kantianism accepted Kant's distinction about legitimate knowledge claims but tried to find a sound foundation of historical knowledge. Wilhelm Windelband (1848–1915) in his "History and Natural Science" (Geschichte und Naturwissenschaft) and Heinrich Rickert (1863–1936) in his "The Limits of Concept Formation in the Natural Science" (Die Grenzen naturwissenschaftlicher Begriffsbildung) established the notions of "nomothetic" and "idiographic" research, denoting law finding and individualistic, descriptive research, respectively, as appropriate but distinctive methods for the natural and historical sciences following Kant's original distinction. However, they did not accept that historical knowledge had an inferior cognitive status.

In the wake of Friedrich Schleiermacher, Willhlem Dilthey (1833–1911), German philosopher and cultural historian, often referred to as the "father of hermeneutics", attempted at explaining historical phenomena by understanding its meaning (Sinngehalt) and essence (Wesen). Dilthey's "Introduction to the Human Sciences" (1970) is a systematic foundation of humanities to ensure their methodological and epistemological autonomy. To him, "understanding" (Verstehen) of the "historicality" of social phenomena was central to the human sciences and hermeneutics the adequate method to achieve this goal as outlined in his works on "Hermeneutics and the Study of History".

Based on these predecessors, Max Weber's aim was to reconstruct human actions scientifically according to the significance and meaning assigned to them in history and culture by a method called "understanding" (Verstehen). An acting individual assigns meaning and significance to their actions according to their culture and history, socialization and educational background, etc. Each "subjectively assigned meaning" forms a single case. Investigating them in detail gives us an understanding of the regularities that we observe in the social reality. As Weber puts it: "The aim is to understand the social reality that surrounds us in its peculiar character – on the one hand, the contemporary framework and cultural meanings of all the single phenomena we observe now, and on the other hand, the reasons for their historical path that led to their special characteristics" (Weber, 1968a: 170f.). However, Weber distinctively disagreed with his contemporaries that interpretation stands in contrast to causal explanations as he defined sociology as "... a science which attempts the interpretive understanding of social action in order thereby to arrive at a causal explanation of its course and effects" (Weber, 1922: 3). Thus, Weber argued that interpretation and understanding is a precondition for causal explanation. As meaning shapes action, understanding meaning provides the basis for a causal explanation of the causes and effects of social action.

Cultural significance and meaning are not only important to explain social phenomena but are also the general selection mechanism that all social knowledge production relies on for its object formation. Weber claimed that studying cultural phenomena is every time a young science. Following Kant's argument that the "object per se" cannot be perceived but just its appearance for us, objects for the humanities are only available for the study if they have cultural meaning and significance. Everything else is just noise. The mechanisms of object formation guarantee that the humanities are not concerned with a fixed combination of raw material but with a constant formation process of permanently changing objects that has the effect of making each of the objects individual.

Following the same line of reasoning, more recent objective hermeneutics, developed by Ulrich Oevermann, states that this constant flow of changing social objects is available to us as "text": we "manage to perceive the basically autonomous everyday practice only in its textual expression. Directly accessing the level of social reality, which exists outside of this textuality, unmediated experiencing everyday practice itself under conditions of crisis, is scientifically impossible for us. We have to rely methodologically on the mediation by textuality" (Oevermann, 1986: 49).

Hermeneutics believes that this textuality is universal, which makes it so successful: we are "concerned with meaningful objects. Both, these objects themselves and the empirical access to them, need to be made explicit by a mode of communication .... This is why we always deal with texts, which are organized by rule-based structures of meaning – and re-constructing these texts also follows explicable rules" (Sutter, 1997: 305). The textual structure of actions can be read as expressions of a general framework of rules. According to objective hermeneutics, meaning structures are generated by a system of "generative rules". Following Chomski, such a system can generate an infinity of results by a finite number of generative rules. Expanding on the idea of objective hermeneutics, representatives of hermeneutic ontology (cf. Dahlstrom, 2010) understand the very process of understanding social "facts" as an interpretative helix that is a continuous operation of reflecting on the conditions of an interpretation whereby these conditions itself are changed. Hence, hermeneutic ontology stresses the historicity of interpretation. "This historical character encompasses the interpreter (interpretans), the experience, the event, object, text, etc. to be interpreted (interpretandum), and the concepts and proto-concepts by means of which they are interpreted (modi interpretandi)" (Dahlstrom, 2010: 410). Hermeneutic ontology much like historical ontology (cf. Hacking, 2004) and historical epistemology (cf. Daston, 1994) gives short shrift to concepts of timeless and universal knowledge.

Including a hermeneutic perspective is therefore crucial for refining social simulation approaches (see below) and in consequence for arriving at a comprehensive investigation of social phenomena. On the other hand, for instance, Gläser and Laudel claim that "the crucial and, unfortunately, so far unanswered question is how to identify social mechanisms from descriptions of social phenomena provided in the texts we analyze" (Gläser and Laudel, 2013: 6). For investigating this question, simulation provides a useful tool, in particular by enabling counterfactual analysis, as "the most powerful synthesis of forms of knowledge comes through posing and responding to historically counterfactual questions and situations" (Griffin, 1993: 1100). In fact, already Max Weber referred to a counterfactual theory of causality. It has to be analysed if another course of events would have been "objectively possible". Counterfactually it can be examined what course of events would have to be expected in the case of varied preconditions. Thus, Weber has provided an elaborated conceptual framework for the analysis of social mechanisms and only current digital hermeneutics offers the technological possibility for fully making use of this approach. Thus, merging agent-based simulation with hermeneutics enables to realize Weber's dictum of merging understanding and causal explanation.

2.2.2 Social simulation

In fact, ABM has a number of properties that coincide with the account of a thick description: ABM studies the interaction of individual agents on a microscopic level (Squazzoni et al., 2014), in relation between cognition and interaction (Nardin et al., 2016). Likewise, simulation is ultimately based on algorithms and is thus a rule-based approach which reflects the claim of objective hermeneutics of dissecting generative rules for latent meaning structures. Nevertheless, a mixed-methods approach, combining hermeneutics and agent-based social simulation, has not been tried out so far. A substantial reason can be found in the epistemological background: computational simulation models seem to belong to the world of epistemological realism, to mathematics, formalization, and digitalization, to nomological knowledge where single cases are just representations of a class of phenomena, to quantitative methods and codifiable knowledge, and to a hard science approach in the realm of "social engineering".

Technically, ABM is an approach for studying social phenomena by computational technologies. Agents are software units that are capable of acting autonomously in a virtual environment. Autonomous action means that the actions performed by individual agents are not controlled top-down by a central processing unit, but that agents decide for themselves. The central processing unit may only give the floor to a certain agent at a certain time, either in every time step in a certain order or in an event-oriented manner in which each event generates a series of dependent future events. In agent-based simulation models, many of these software units act and interact with each other in their virtual environment. In order to act autonomously, agents need to possess certain characteristics that can be denoted as intelligent (Wooldrige, 1999). These features already exhibit certain analogies to human actors in social groups. Furthermore, the analogy is extended by features of the agents that are also typical for humans in society (Epstein, 2006), such as the following:

- *Heterogeneity:* In agent-based models, it is possible to represent agents individually (instead of representing human beings by a "representative agent", which is more often than not modelled as a *homo oeconomicus*), which implies that different agents usually have different properties.
- *Bounded rationality:* Agents may have limited information about their environment or may have restricted capacities for calculating possible actions or forget less recent information. Thus, actions need not be directed at optimizing but rather can be based on heuristic reasoning.

Note, however, that an agent can be everything that may operate as an actor (having properties as a unit and having behaviour) such as a human being, but also collective actors such as organizations, households, or states which are also heterogeneous and having restricted capacities for rational decision-making. Using ABM enables us to relate the behaviour of individual agents and their interactions to the properties of the structure of a system (Epstein and Axtell, 1996; Macal and North, 2009). ABM enables investigating long-term causal chains in dynamic environments, non-intended multi-level feedbacks, and emerging macro-level parameters. It is possible to trace the system's behaviour to the combination of individual action points and decisions on the actor level and the reverse way back how changes of the systems level affect the individual behaviour of the agents.

It has to be noted that different modelling approaches exist. The so-called KISS (keep it simple stupid) principle (Axelrod, 1997) advocates simple agents with only a few properties. The basic assumption is to generate complex dynamics from simple rules that can be found in early approaches of agent-based social simulation (Epstein and Axtell, 1996). These approaches resemble the first development of cellular automata such as the game of life (Langton, 1986) in the 1980s but are still much used in a socio-physics framework for studying effects of isolated theories or mechanisms, such as signalling (Scheutz and Schermerhorn, 2004), opinion polarization (Hegselmann and Krause,

2002), or segregation processes (Troitzsch, 2017). The epistemology of this approach follows the positivistic epistemology of nomological science aiming at the detection of universal laws and principles.

However, a large community is using agents based on an artificial intelligence approach with complex cognitive architectures such as so-called Belief-Desire-Intention (BDI) structures (Wooldridge, 1999; Balke and Gilbert, 2014), BOID (Beliefs-Obligations-Intentions-Desires (Broersen et al., 2001) or BDOING (Beliefs, Desires, Obligations, Intentions, Norms and Goals (Dignum et al. 2002), or other sophisticated design principles, for instance, for normative reasoning (Neumann, 2010; Conte et al., 2014, Hollander and Wu, 2011). Agents can be equipped with many properties with individual and changing knowledge bases and a multitude of behavioural options for interaction in a dynamic environment. Though ABM is used in many scientific disciplines meanwhile, ABMs of this type are mostly found in the humanities and the social sciences due to their capacity to mimic complex human and social behaviour and the two-way dynamics of how the structural properties feed back on individual behaviour (Conte et al., 2014). Thus, this type of modelling is specifically appropriate for investigating the responsiveness between the micro-level agent behaviour and the macro level of a system's behaviour: cognitive complexity is needed to study the social causality, namely the dynamics of a two-way process, from the micro level to the macro level and vice versa. Agents need to reason about their social environment to let their behaviour be directed by a social level. A simple reactive behaviour is useful to model low level actions, but when simulating humans who need to decide between many different options, a higher level of thought is required. As noted by Balke and Gilbert (2014) and Sun (2007), adding cognition to agents is a way to tackle this issue. Emphasis on cognitive complexity is associated with the so-called EROS (enhancing realism of simulation) principle (Jager, 2017) that attempts at grounding modelling assumptions as much as possible on the theories found in the scientific disciplines of the respective target system. Simulation results in turn can inform the empirical theories, thus cycling from theory to simulation and back (Conte, 2009). It is argued (Jager, 2017) that for agent-based simulation in particular, psychological theory in the agents' formalization is relevant to capture behavioural phenomena in simulation models.

In line with the emphasis on complex agents is also the so-called KIDS (keep it descriptive stupid) principle (Edmonds and Moss, 2005) suggesting to inform the agents' design by as much descriptive empirical evidence as possible. In the recent past, a growing interest can be observed to include qualitative data in the model (Yang and Gilbert, 2008; Edmonds, 2015a). Narrative textual data provides evidence for the formulation of agent rules. In the computational framework, this can be integrated with any other kind of information, e.g., from theory or quantitative sources. The generation of qualitative evidence may be more or less based on procedures developed in qualitative research such as transcribing and coding the data. This descriptive approach is particularly useful in participatory modelling (Barreteau et al., 2003), often used for exploratory purposes. Exploratory simulation takes into consideration scenario analysis for studying "what-if" questions. This becomes particularly relevant for the assessment of interventions. Intervening measures shape the social dynamics in unforeseeable ways because they are not executed in isolation. A scenario analysis of complex simulation models allows to take into consideration a multitude of variables and to estimate the relevance of their consequences. The investigation of potential pathways enables the detection of chances and options but can also function as an early warning signal to avoid undesirable developments. In a participatory setting, a simulation can examine many alternative scenarios in vitro, before deciding what kind of policy should be introduced in vivo. This kind of research is closely related to the epistemology of case study research (Flyfbjerg, 2006), emphasizing that in the social world, context and context variation is more relevant than the search for universal laws. This can be denoted as idiographic oriented modelling, where the aim is to understand and explain a special case, the history of an individual formation. The purpose of the research is to comprehend specific single features of social phenomena and a detailed description of the history and context of them. Single cases are of interest for their own sake, not only as representatives of features that are constant or generalizable over time. On the contrary, the ever-changing context is the most important determinant for each observable. The modeller acts like an anthropologist or ethnographer, reconstructing a social field in a permanently changing cultural context, where "we do not have direct access, but only that small part of it which our informants can lead us into understanding" (Geertz, 1973: 20).

Including qualitative evidence need not result in interpretative research but can just be an additional source to justify modelling assumptions. Once specified by whatever evidence, a simulation model can be run, and the results measured. This is called cross-validation (Moss and Edmonds, 2005). However, such an approach need not result in an understanding of agents' behaviour but generates quantitative output data. To mention two examples, emotions and context are central elements of human social behaviour and thus might play a central role for interpretative sense-making. Whereas emotions refer to the cognitive complexity of the agents' design, including context refers to the complexity of the interaction structure represented by the model. Following Damasio and Sutherland (1994), Bourgais et al. (2018) argue that emotions are strongly related to human decision-making and are an integral part of reasoning. As emotions are regarded as relating situations to appraisal (Frijda et al., 1989), they are a central element of creating valued meaning structures. However, computational representations of emotions are still in their infancy even though some agent architectures exist such as DETT (Van Dyke Parunak et al., 2006), EMA (Gratch and Marsella, 2004), or GAMA (Bourgais et al., 2016). At the same time, context is relevant for interpreting situational encounters and, in turn, selecting behaviour. Expert skills are less characterized by knowledge of general rules but by the capability of easily transferring between contexts (Dreyfus et al., 1986). Context needs to be approached from a narrative account that is only rarely modelled (Bhawani, 2004; Fieldhouse et al., 2016; Lotzmann and Neumann, 2017). Edmonds suggests the framework of a CSNE approach (Edmonds, 2015b). However, for achieving a fully interpretative, hermeneutic social simulation, still further research is necessary. However, in contrast to traditional quantitative research methods such as linear regression, in principle agent-based social simulation provides more appropriate tools for dealing with context as agents are situated in a virtual environment that changes during a simulation, also due to the actions of the agents themselves.

2.3 The benefit of integrating the two approaches

By integrating qualitative-hermeneutic techniques and agent-based simulation, we challenge the state of the art concerning both the possibilities of experimental settings in the humanities and the limitations of scenario analysis. In the first instance, the challenge to the current state of the art can be exemplified by the orientation to the future of the different scientific approaches. Grunwald (2014) distinguishes between "scenario-based" and "hermeneutic" approaches when looking at three methods of providing orientation on the future (Table 2.1).

As it is well known, the classical and still dominant view on science is the claim that a statement is only of scientific validity if it implies a prognosis. Prognosis is still the "gold standard" for ensuring scientific validity. This orientation to future is intimately connected to scientific realism, assuming that there is only one reality which can be investigated by scientific observation, and in consequence its future state can be predicted. Closely related to prognosis is Carl Popper's notion of falsification of scientific theories: if a prognosis

Table 2.1 The different approaches to future

	Prognostic	*Scenario based*	*Hermeneutic*
Approach to the future	One future	Corridor of sensible futures	Open space of futures
Spectrum of futures	Convergence as ideal	Bounded diversity	Unbounded divergence
Preferred methodology	Quantitative, model based	Quantitative or qualitative	Narrative
Used knowledge	Causal and statistical	Participatory models, knowledge of stakeholders	Associative knowledge, qualitative arguments
Role of normative issues	Low	Depends on case	High
Provided orientation	Decision-making support, optimization	Robust action strategies	Self-reflection and contemporary diagnosis

made by a scientific theory turns out not to be valid, the theory is falsified. The converse concept is statistical significance, stating that a certain distribution of relative frequencies is unlikely to have occurred given the null hypothesis, i.e., by chance. While being an important criterion for many practical purposes, as for instance, clinical tests of new drugs, philosophy and history of science have challenged this view by showing that it overlooks important preconditions for making valid prognostic statements. To mention just one example, Thomas Kuhn's historical investigation of research paradigms showed that scientific progress is not made by falsifying single hypotheses but rather by the fruitfulness of a research paradigm for making new observations. Paradigms themselves are immune to falsification as they are secured by a bundle of auxiliary assumptions. Therefore, the contemporary landscape of science is characterized by a pluralism of orientations to the future. Scenario-based orientations to the future typically are oriented to a bounded diversity of sensitive futures. To mention just two examples of bounded diversity: the sensitivity of Meadow's classical world model to a variation of economic or population growth and the vulnerability of particular banks to economic stress tests of the banking sector. This orientation to future still assumes a reality which exits independent from the observer but follows the assumption of critical realism that reality can be discovered only impartially by an observer. In turn, it admits a bounded diversity of "possible" futures. On the other hand, interpretative research typically emphasizes the social construction of "reality" as well as scientific "knowledge". For instance, history tells as much about the values of the historian as about history. Interpretation remains a dialogue between the researcher and the researched subject. While a lot of research has identified quality criteria for qualitative research (Creswell and Miller, 2000; Cho and Trent, 2006), these criteria rarely provide an orientation towards future. As Grunwald states, "we cannot learn anything about future developments, but in the sense of a 'hermeneutic turn' we can learn something for and about our present situation" (Grunwald, 2014: 282). Hermeneutics seem to be trapped in "self-enlightenment" and the present. Thus, the contemporary scientific landscape is characterized by a pluralism of scientific paradigms. Nevertheless, the scientific discourse is also characterized by rather closed communities of the diverse paradigms that remain rather unrelated and mutual exchange *between* these paradigms can only rarely be found.

It follows that orientation to future cannot be detached from the epistemological foundations of the diverse scientific approaches. Thus, for integrating hermeneutic and social simulation, it is crucial to dissect the epistemological orientations of the different scientific accounts that determine the standards for what counts as a scientific realm. The gold standard of science is offering a "scientific" explanation of a phenomenon, while it is less clear what exactly characterizes such an explanation. The analytical sociologist Hedström (2006) distinguishes three types of explanation: deductive-nomological, statistical, and mechanistic explanations. The deductive-nomological model proposed by Hempel and Oppenheim (1948) argues with logic. An event or phenomenon

Table 2.2 The different types of explanation

	Deductive-nomological explanations	Statistical explanations	Mechanistic explanations
Principles of an explanation	Subsumption under a law	Identifying a statistical relation	Specifying a social mechanism
Central factors of an explanation	No restrictions, except that the factor has a law-like relation to the event to be explained	No restrictions, except that the factor needs to be relevant for the event to be explained	Entities and activities that are relevant for actions and the way how they are related to each other

is explained if it can be logically deduced from two elements: the starting or boundary conditions and a universal law. Statistical explanations aim at identifying factors that increase the probability of the event to be explained. Mechanistic explanations neither search for universal laws nor statistical regularities between variables. Rather, a mechanistic explanation builds on identifying entities and processes that generate the phenomenon to be explained. Following Hedström, the epistemological orientation of ABM follows the standards of a mechanistic explanation as the interactions of agents generate a particular phenomenon in the course of a simulation (Table 2.2).

Hedström argues that a hermeneutics of a thick description does not provide an explanation at all by emphasizing that – like typologies – a thick description is merely a description. However, this conviction does not take into account that understanding motivations, fears, and strategies of actors is essential for comprehending the why and how of particular actions. Understanding is essential for the negotiation of meaning that determines potential futures. For instance, in the example whether an eye movement is an involuntary twitch or a conspiratorial signal, understanding the motivation (e.g. to give a secret signal) is the key for explaining potential follow-up actions. This is in line with Weber's argument that understanding and causal explanation go hand in hand in the cultural sciences. Nevertheless, while research on the quality of qualitative explanations has found several criteria for ensuring the quality of the research, these criteria differ significantly from the quality criteria of quantitative research. In the following, just two criteria shall be highlighted: members checking (Creswell and Miller, 2000) and transformational validity (Cho and Trent, 2006). Members checking shifts the validity process from the researcher to the subjects of the research by letting them confirm the credibility of the research findings. Transformational validity goes a step further. Building on the constructivist paradigm that "truth finding" is questionable if "truth" is deciphered as a social construct, the transformational validity of research procedures is seen in empowering members of the field to transform their living conditions.

This leads to the pragmatics of scientific explanations: for instance, the final criterion for the effectiveness of medical tests of drugs is if these are effectively healing diseases, thereby transforming social reality. In medical tests, the complexity of the real world in contrast to controlled laboratory environments can be captured by large statistical data sets, i.e., a statistical concept of an explanation. However, often such data sets are not at hand, for instance when investigating global climate change, but nevertheless the complexity of the real-world environment has to be taken into account by research procedures subject to assessment by accounts of transformational validity. In particular, participatory simulation has in common with this kind of research that it enables taking complexity into account. However, simulation reduces the risk associated with research procedures undertaken directly in the field by offering a virtual environment similar to a "social laboratory", but nevertheless preserving the transformational aspiration. Models and simulations are second-order constructions of modellers (cf. Latour and Woolgar, 1979), however, in contrast to "analogous model construction" laid out as an algorithm, i.e., codified, explicit, observable, and testable. Simulation experiments aim at understanding the micro dynamics at the actor level that lead to structure on the macro level and at using scenario modelling as a worksite for our own reality constructions. With hermeneutically rich social simulation, scenario analysis becomes more than an event corridor between "best case" and "worst case". The spectrum of experimental scenarios becomes more than bounded diversity. By putting interpretation in motion with an agent-based framework, scenario analysis enables an exploration of the cultural horizons and thus opens hermeneutic research towards an orientation to the future. The project will investigate the chances and limitations of a tool offering this environment.

2.4   The scientific potential of the new research methodology

Certainly, this research process cannot replace research based on representative and quantitative input data. For instance, how many people are poor in a certain country at a certain time or how crime rates change is important information that cannot be provided by this approach. However, the research process enables an endogenous development of scenarios, not by pre-defined cases of, e.g., externally varying certain variables such as economic or population growth, whereas the narrative scenarios provide sensitivity to context. Thereby the research process allows for an identification of the possibility of critical junctures hidden within a cultural matrix. Such research becomes important when understanding of motivations and negotiations of meaning as causal factors for social action becomes relevant. Throughout this book, the example of criminal culture is used to exemplify the insights that can be gained by an approach which takes this into account. However, research following this paradigm is certainly not restricted to this case. Further examples may include the following:

- Understanding heuristics for action under conditions of uncertainty that cannot be deduced from rational choice theory or numerical utility functions and exploring its possible effects. This includes cases from strategic decision-making (e.g., human resource management or the development of international relations) to deviant behaviour such as heuristics for criminal decision-making.
- Values, value change, and value conflicts: a traditional example is the impact of protestant ethics on economic behaviour and attitudes. Also, various forms of corruption and possible anti-corruption strategies, the emergence of a culture of legality in Sicily, or the transition towards ecologically sustainable behaviour include value dimensions that fall into the category of value change.
- Identities, identity change, and identity conflicts. This includes examples such as becoming familiar with a foreign culture, ethnic conflicts, tension between protestant and catholic inhabitants of Northern Ireland, or specific eastern German identity in Eastern Germany. Identities have a crucial role also in the processes of othering and polarization. How can such identities change?
- Identity change may be regarded as a specific case of cultural change. The code of conduct that constitutes a specific criminal culture used in this book is but one example. We will see how the negotiation of meaning (and potential misunderstandings) decisively shapes the course of conduct. Other examples may include, for instance, political culture in the processes of a transformation from authoritarian regimes to democratic societies and vice versa which may or may not go along with changing mentalities and how this affects the institutional change of the macro level. Hungary of Hong Kong may serve as examples.

2.4.1   *The benefit for hermeneutics*

The research programme outlined throughout the book attempts to realize the potential of Max Weber's research programme of "interpretive understanding of social action in order to thereby arrive at a causal explanation of its course and effects" (Weber, 1922: 3). While mostly Weber's study on protestant ethics is seen as a proof of concept of his methodology, a lot of Weber's methodological writing remained on a conceptual, programmatic level. In particular, his reference to counterfactual causality has not been realized in his research practice. This can be systematically realized by the development of counterfactual scenarios with the digital technologies of agent-based social simulation. This opportunity could not be foreseen by Weber. However, exploration of the counterfactual scenarios enables to realize Weber's dictum that "for studying the real causal links, we construct unreal" (Weber, 1968b: 287).

In fact, they provide information about critical junctures hidden within a cultural matrix. In developing his counterfactual theory of causality, Weber discusses claims made by contemporary historians that the battle of Marathon was decisive as it decided between theocratic or intellectually oriented development of the Western World (Weber, 1968b: 288). Agent-based social simulation provides a computational technology for a systematic exploration of thought experiments (cf. Levy, 2008).

The research process further develops Weber's methodological approach by describing for the first time a formal procedure for "composing" ideal types. While Weber provides several hints about the scientific goal of ideal types and that they are "composed" at the end of a research process, these hints are firstly scattered throughout his work and secondly and most important clear methodological advice of how to arrive at an ideal type during a research process is missing. While he provides some examples such as "medieval town economy" or most prominent "protestant ethics" and some hints such as "one-sided increase of one or more aspects" (Weber, 1968a: 191), this is quite sparse as advice for other researchers to use this concept for their own. For this reason, it also remains unclear in Max Weber's studies how to qualify a certain terminus as an ideal type or not. In particular, Chapter 6 attempts to provide a step towards reducing methodological vagueness by proposing a research process that is intersubjectively transparent and replicable.

Hermeneutics may benefit from the research process outlined in the book by realizing Max Weber's goal of arriving at a causal analysis of the course and effects of social action by providing an interpretative understanding of this social action. Thus, the book suggests a research process for integrating interpretative research and the analysis of social mechanisms. Since Max Weber, this stream of research remained rather under explored. Gläser and Laudel claim that "the crucial and, unfortunately, so far unanswered question is how to identify social mechanisms from descriptions of social phenomena provided in the texts we analyze" (Gläser and Laudel, 2013: 6). However, it is essential for studying social and historical dynamics to arrive at a comprehension of mechanisms, i.e., not only understanding whether the contraction of an eyelid is a twitch or a conspirational signal but also how this leads to what kind of possible actions. Thus, understanding is in fact essential for identifying social mechanisms.

The analysis of social mechanisms is more important as the historical origin of hermeneutics has been the study of history. History is about processes and dynamics. Agent-based social simulation is a tool that enables the investigation of dynamics. Typical tools for interpreting are the various forms of qualitative content analysis (Mayring, 2000; Gläser and Laudel, 2013). However, as qualitative content analysis is based on the analysis of a document, the basis for the analysis is static, even though sequence analysis as a particular form of qualitative content analysis aims at identifying the temporal order in the text (see Chapter 6). Therefore, hermeneutics benefits from an integration of both methodologies. While on the one hand, conceptual modelling for identifying the interaction structures can benefit from sequence analytical methods for identifying phases of the interaction structures (Kübler-Ross, 2009), on the other hand also qualitative content analysis can benefit from organizing the interpretation in a conceptual model. In the next step, hermeneutically rich agent-based social simulation enables to analyse the dynamics implied by the interaction structures for investigating potential scenarios. In sum, the research process outlined here suggests opening hermeneutic towards orientation to future.

The modelling will also support the development of cross-connections between categories found in the qualitative content analysis. In coding processes which are based on grounded theory, a related procedure is sometimes called axial coding, even though axial coding follows a different approach than investigating interaction structures. However, often an investigation of the relation between categories remains underdeveloped.

The scenario-based approach of agent-based social simulation also provides support for procedures of exhaustive inference. The objective of such procedures is an exploration of the horizon of possibilities hidden in the data. This is often done by involving groups of several interpreters to explore the variability of possibilities. For such a procedure, the production of scenarios by virtual machines increases the power of an exhaustive inference of the cultural horizon hidden by exploring the counterfactual question of what could have happened.

Finally, even scholars from the humanities question the knowledge claims of their approach. For instance, Sutter criticizes the validity claim of objective hermeneutics via an ontology of rules (Sutter, 1997: 309–314) due to its assumption that there is a general approach to rule construction and text interpretation. Digitalizing hermeneutic procedures means in the first instance to reflect on and describe the interpretation activity itself, its axioms, and processes. From here, the validity claims of the approach can again be reviewed, and the extension of its applicability can be established, first of all by algorithmically explicating the ontology of rules. In the next step, the development of narrative scenarios provides a new procedure for assessing the rule's credibility by providing a means for assessing whether the rules are able to produce storylines that "produce for the readers the feeling that they have experienced, or could experience, the events being described in a study" (Creswell and Miller, 2000: 129) such as a sense of verisimilitude (Ponterotto, 2006).

2.4.2   *The benefits for social simulation*

Computational simulation models seem to belong to the world of epistemological realism, to mathematics, formalization and digitalization, to nomological knowledge where single cases are just representations of a class of phenomena, to quantitative methods and codifiable knowledge, and to a hard science approach in the realm of "social engineering". Many scholars of the humanities "despise the products of modellers ... and feel something like the lust for rokoko or art deco, which you sometimes experience when looking at modern office buildings" (Mayntz, 1967: 26).

However, it is obvious that the more is known empirically about the micro dynamics on the actor level, the better informed can be the agent design and calibration and the more a computer simulation will resemble everyday experience. To make simulations useful as a "social laboratory", computational agents need to be provided with the knowledge, the behaviours, intentions, strategies, as well as hopes and fears, the options of empirical actors to choose and to interact. This means that actors and their interactions need to be understood before they can be modelled as agents. For this purpose, a qualitative-hermeneutic approach is needed for "rich" social simulations. Interpretive research focuses cognitive interest on action-generating latent meaning structures. Conceptualization of actions and realized actions are mutually responsive. What is needed to inform agents in social simulations is the matrix of conceptual action orientations of empirical actors (Elzinga, 1997), which can only be distilled through qualitative methods of interpretative humanities. Agent-based models as production algorithms for social phenomena need to make use of qualitative approaches from the humanities and social sciences for calibration and validation purposes. For the model, it is not enough to be informed about what it should entail or to know whether and how variables correlate. The model needs additional qualitative insight into the actors, their orientations, and logics – may they be rational or irrational. This means modelling needs to "understand" the agents in the old Weberian sense for designing the agents and their interactions. This is what qualitative research such as participatory observation, case studies, or interviews can provide and inform the model about behaviours, processes, strategies, and contexts of actors. In turn, a narrative analysis puts simulation models into context which is essential for understanding observed behaviour. Counterfactual scenarios describe context variation and thus allow transferring between contexts (Flyfbjerg, 2006), which is essentially what characterizes human experts (Dreyfus et al., 1986). This enables backward tracing as well, i.e., the tracing of processes and circumstances that give rise to a particular phenomenon like the diagnosis of an airplane crash in which the causal chain that ultimately resulted in the event may be traced back to the small defect of a valve. This is hardly possible with abstract models of a nomological approach to modelling seeking to identify universal laws but is a unique feature of an idiographic approach to simulation. In Chapter 3, the preconditions of a more descriptive, micro-level approach for the model development are described which preserves contextualized meaning. Subsequently, Chapters 4 and 5 provide a concrete example which is picked up in Chapter 7 that dives into the details of such abductive reasoning.

Agents in agent-based social simulations feature individual connections between the conceptual and action level of human behaviour: agents in simulations act according to their conceptual action orientations that can be elaborated by agent designs from artificial intelligence (such as BDI architectures). Here qualitative-hermeneutic methods come into play by providing information about behaviours, processes, strategies, and contexts of actors. These methods add further dimensions to the rules of the simulation such as culture, or identity, to mention only a few aspects. All these are relevant for actions. Thus, they allow for "understanding" agents in the old Weberian sense. Thereby, the concept of "understanding" provides a boundary object as an epistemological building block for the mixed-methods approach combining interpretive research and ABM. Such boundary objects are inherent in both methods which makes them appropriate as hints for integration. The function of boundary objects has been described for qualitative research and computational methods (Star, 1989). Another boundary object for the mixed-methods approach is the universal textuality (cf. Oevermann, 1986; Sutter, 1997), which seems to be an element of both approaches. In particular objective hermeneutics reads the textual structure of actions as an expression of a framework of rules. This is what agent-based simulations, which computationally mimic human actions, are based on: textuality (computer code) and rules (algorithms) for their agents.

Last but not least, Gilbert and Ahrweiler (2009) argue that the current debate within the social simulation community about the epistemological status of their subject has many connections with the debates above about the character of knowledge in the humanities and the appropriate epistemological and methodological assumptions on which humanities should rest. Current models in social simulation cover a whole continuum of epistemological options. Though there are many models characterized by an interest in the most abstract and general features of the social world and mathematically tractable axioms and theorems that surround them, there is an equally large class of models characterized by an interest in the particular and single features of social phenomena and the detailed descriptions and history that contextualize them.

For idiographic oriented modellers, the aim is to understand and explain a special case, the history of an individual formation. The idiographically oriented area in social simulation is characterized by an interest in the particular and singular features and the detailed description and history that contextualize them. Single cases are of special interest for their own sake – not only as a representative of features that are constant or generalizable over time. On the contrary, the ever-changing context, i.e., the exact time and location, is the most important determinant for each observable. The modeller acts like an anthropologist and ethnographer, reconstructing a social field in a permanently changing cultural context where "we do not have direct access, but only the small part of it which our informants can lead us into understanding" (Geertz, 1973: 20). Since object formation is part of the procedure, a constructivist approach to knowledge production is implied in this approach to social simulation (Gilbert and Ahrweiler, 2009). An interpretative approach allows us software models, which are closely connected to the "action text".

Note

1 Among the many qualitative methodologies, in this book we specifically combine ethnographic methodologies in the semiotic tradition going back to Charles Sanders Peirce and Charles Herbert Mead with hermeneutic elements in the tradition of philosophy of history by means of agent-based modelling. Of course, this is not to say that agent-based simulation cannot be usefully combined with other qualitative methodologies.

References

Axelrod, R. (1997) *The complexity of cooperation: Agent-based models of competition and collaboration*. Princeton: Princeton University Press.

Balke, T. and Gilbert, N. (2014) 'How do agents make decisions? A survey', *Journal of Artificial Societies and Social Simulation*, 17(4 https://www.jasss.org/17/4/13.html

Barreteau, O. et al. (2003) 'Our companion modeling approach', *Journal of Artificial Societies and Social Simulation*, 6(1). http://jasss.soc.surrey.ac.uk/6/2/1.html

Benvenuto, S. (2000) 'Fashion: Georg Simmel', *Journal of Artificial Societies and Social Simulation*, 3(2). http://jasss.soc.surrey.ac.uk/3/2/forum/2.html

Bhawani, S. (2004) '*Adaptive knowledge dynamics and emergent artificial societies. Ethnographically based multi agent simulations of behavioural adaption to agro-climatic systems*', Doctoral thesis, University of Kent, Canterbury UK.

Bourgais, M., Taillandier, P. and Vercouter, L. (2016). An agent architecture coupling cognition and emotions for simulation of complex systems. In *Social Simulation Conference* Sep 2016, Rome, Italy.

Bourgais, M., Taillandier, P., Vercouter, L. and Adam, C. (2018) 'Emotion modelling in social simulation: A survey', *Journal of Artificial Societies and Social Simulation*, 21(2). http://jasss.soc.surrey.ac.uk/21/2/5.html

Broersen, J., Dastani, M., Hulstijn, J., Huang, Z. and van der Torre, L. (2001). The BOID architecture: Conflicts between beliefs, obligations, intentions and desires. In *Proceedings of the Fifth International Conference on Autonomous Agents* (pp. 9–16). New York: ACM.

Cederman, L. E. (2005) 'Computational models of social forms: Advancing process theory', *American Journal of Sociology*, 110(4), pp. 864–893.

Cho, J. and Trent, A. (2006) 'A validity in qualitative research revisited', *Qualitative Research*, 6(3), pp. 319–340.

Conte, R. (2009) 'From simulation to theory (and backwards)', in Squazzoni, F. (ed.) *Epistemological aspects of computer simulation in the social sciences*. New York: Springer, pp. 29–47.

Conte, R., Andrighetto, G. and Campenni, M. (2014) *Minding norms: Mechanisms and dynamics of social order in agent societies*. Oxford: Oxford University Press.

Creswell, J. and Miller, D. (2000) 'Determining validity in qualitative research', *Theory into Practice*, 39(3), pp. 124–130.

Dahlstrom, D. O. (2010) 'Hermeneutic ontology', in Poli, R. and Seibt, J (eds.) *Theory and application of ontology: Philosophical perspectives*. Springer, pp. 395–415.

Damasio, A. and Sutherland, S. (1994) 'Descartes' error: Emotion, reason and the human brain', *Nature*, 372(6503), pp. 287–287.

Daston, L. (1994) 'Historical epistemology', in James K. Chandler, Arnold Ira Davidson and Harry D. Harootunian (eds.) *Questions of evidence: Proof, practice and persuasion across disciplines*. University of Chicago Press, pp. 282–289.

Denzin, N. K. (1989) *The research act: A theoretical introduction to sociological methods.* 3rd edn. New Jersey: Prentice Hall.

Dignum, F., Kinny, D. and Sonenberg, L. (2002) 'From desires, obligations and norms to goals', *Cognitive Science Quarterly*, 2(3–4), pp. 407–430.

Dilthey, W. (1970 [1907]) *der Aufbau der geschichtlichen Welt in den Geisteswissenschaften.* Frankfurt a.M: Surkamp.

Dittrich, P., Kron, T. and Banzhaf, W. (2003) 'On the scalability of social order. Modelling the problem of double and multiple contingency following Luhmann', *Journal of Artificial Societies and Social Simulation*, 6(1). http://jasss.soc.surrey. ac.uk/6/1/3.html

Dreyfus, H., Dreyfus, S. and Athanasio, T. (1986) *Mind over machines. The power of human intuition and expertise in the era of computer.* New York: Free Press.

Edmonds, B. (2015a) 'Using qualitative evidence to inform the specification of agent-based models', *Journal for Artificial Societies and Social Simulation*, 18(1). http:// jasss.soc.surrey.ac.uk/18/1/18.html

Edmonds, B. (2015b) 'A context- and scope-sensitive analysis of narrative data to aid the specification of agent behaviour', *Journal of Artificial Societies and Social Simulation*, 18(1). http://jasss.soc.surrey.ac.uk/18/1/17.html

Edmonds, B. and Moss, S. (2005) 'From KISS to KIDS – An "anti-simplistic" modelling approach', in Davidsson, P. et al (eds.) *Multi agent based simulation 2004.* Springer, lecture notes in artificial intelligence, 3415. Berlin: Springer, pp. 130–144.

Elzinga, A. (1997) 'The science-society contract in historical transformation: With special reference to epistemic drift', *Social Science Information*, 36(3), pp. 411–445.

Epstein, J. (2006) *Generative social science. Studies in agent-based computational modelling.* Princeton: Princeton University Press.

Epstein, J. and Axtell, R. (1996) *Growing artificial societies.* Cambridge: The MIT Press.

Fieldhouse, E., Lessard-Phillips, L. and Edmonds, B. (2016) 'Cascade or echo chamber? A complex agent-based simulation of voter turnout', *Party Politics*, 22(2), pp. 241–256.

Flyfbjerg, B. (2006) 'Five misunderstandings about case-study research', *Qualitative Inquiry*, 12(2), pp. 210–245.

Frijda, N. H., Kuipers, P. and Ter Schure, E. (1989) 'Relations among emotion, appraisal, and emotional action readiness', *Journal of Personality and Social Psychology*, 57(2), pp. 212–228.

Geertz, C. (1973) 'Thick description: Toward an interpretive theory of culture', In: Geertz, C. (ed.), *The interpretation of cultures: Selected essays.* New York: Basic Books, pp. 3–30.

Gilbert, N. and Ahrweiler, P. (2009) 'The epistemologies of social simulation research', in Squazzoni, F. (ed.) *Epistemological aspects of computer simulation in the social sciences.* Berlin/New York: Springer, pp. 12–28.

Gläser and Laudel (2013) Life with and without coding: Two methods for early-stage data analysis in qualitative research aiming at causal explanations. *Forum Qualitative Research*, 14(2) Art. 5. https://www.qualitative-research.net/index.php/fqs/ article/view/1886

Gratch, J. and Marsella, S. (2004) 'A domain-independent framework for modeling emotion', *Cognitive Systems Research*, 5(4), pp. 269–306.

Griffin, L. (1993) 'Event structure analysis and causal interpretation in historical sociology', *American Journal of Sociology*, 98(5), pp. 1094–1133.

Grunwald, A. (2014). 'Modes of orientation provided by future studies: Making sense of diversity and divergence', *European Journal of Futures Research* 2(1), p. 30. https://doi.org/10.1007/s40309-013-0030-5

Hacking, I. (2004) *Historical ontology.* Harvard University Press.

Hedström, P. (2006) *Dissecting the social. On the principles of analytical sociology.* Cambridge: Cambridge University Press.

Hegselmann, R. and Krause, U. (2002) 'Opinion dynamics and bounded confidence: Models, analysis and simulation', *Journal for Artificial Societies and Social Simulation* 5(3). http://jasss.soc.surrey.ac.uk/5/3/2.html

Hempel, C. and Oppenheim, P. (1948) 'Studies in the logic of explanation', *Philosophy of Science*, 15(2), pp. 135–175.

Hollander, C. and Wu, A. (2011) 'The current state of normative agent-based systems', *Journal for Artificial Societies and Social Simulation*, 14(2). http://jasss.soc.surrey.ac.uk/14/2/6.html

Jager, W. (2017) 'Enhancing the realism of simulation (EROS): On implementing and developing psychological theory in social simulation', *Journal of Artificial Societies and Social Simulation*, 20(3). jasss.soc.surrey.ac.uk/20/3/14.html

Kübler-Ross, E. (2009) *Death: The final stage.* New York: Touchstone book.

Langton, C. G. (1986) 'Studying artificial life with cellular automata', *Physica D*, 22(1–3), pp. 120–149.

Latour, B. and Woolgar, S. (1979) *Laboratory life. The social construction of scientific facts.* New York: Princeton University Press.

Levy, J. (2008) 'Counterfactuals and case studies', in Box-Steffensmeier, J., Brady, H. and Collier, D. (eds.) *The oxford handbook of political methodology.* Oxford: Oxford University Press, pp. 627–643.

Lotzmann, U. and Neumann, M. (2017) 'A simulation model of intra-organizational conflict regulation in the crime world', in Elsenbroich, C., Gilbert, N. and Anzola, D. (eds.) *Social dimensions of organized crime. Modeling the dynamics of extortion rackets.* Cham: Springer, pp. 177–213.

Macal, C. M. and North, M. J. (2009) Agent-based modeling and simulation. In: *Winter Simulation Conference*, Austin, TX, pp. 86–98.

Mayntz, R. (1967) 'Modellkonstruktion: Ansatz, Typen und Zweck', in Mayntz, R. (ed.) *Formalisierte Modelle in der Soziologie.* Neuwied und Berlin: Luchterhand, pp. 11–32.

Mayring, P. (2000) 'Qualitative content analysis', *Forum Qualitative Social Research*, 1(2). http://www.qualitative-research.net/index.php/fqs/article/view/1089

Moss, S. and Edmonds, B. (2005) 'Sociology and simulation. Statistical and qualitative cross-validation', *American Journal of Sociology*, 110(4), pp. 1095–1131.

Nardin, L. G., Andrighetto, G., Conte, R., Székely, A., Anzola, D., Elsenbroich, C., Lotzmann, U., Neumann, M., Punzo, V. and Troitzsch, K. G. (2016) 'Simulating protection racket. A case study of the Sicilian mafia', *Autonomous Agents and Multi-Agent Systems*, 30(6), pp. 1117–1147.

Neumann, M. (2010) 'A classification of normative architectures', in Takadama, K., Cioffi-Revilla, C. and Deffuant, G. (eds.) *Simulating interacting agents and social phenomena.* New York: Springer, pp. 3–18.

Oevermann, U. (1986) 'Kontroversen über sinnverstehende Soziologie. Einige wiederkehrende Probleme und Mißverständnisse in der Rezeption der "objektiven Hermeneutik"', in Aufenanger, S. and Lenssen, M. (eds.) *Handlung und Sinnstruktur. Bedeutung und Anwendung der objektiven Hermeneutik.* München: Kindt, pp. 19–83.

Ponterotto, J. G. (2006) 'Brief note on the origins, evolution, and meaning of the qualitative research concept thick description', *The Qualitative Report*, 11(3), pp. 538–549.

Rickert, H. (1929) *Die Grenzen der naturwissenschaftlichen Begriffsbildung. Eine logische Einleitung in die historischen Wissenschaften.* 5. verb. Aufl. Tübingen: Mohr.

Scheutz, M. and Schermerhorn, P. (2004) 'The role of signalling action tendencies in conflict resolution', *Journal for Artificial Societies and Social Simulation*, 7(1). http://jasss.soc.surrey.ac.uk/7/1/4.html

Squazzoni, F., Jager, W. and Edmonds, B. (2014) 'Social simulation in the social sciences. A brief overview', *Social Science Computer Review*, 32(3), pp. 279–294.

Star, S. L. (1989) 'The structure of ill-structured solutions. Boundary objects and heterogeneous distributed problem solving', in Gasser, L. and Huhns, M. N. (eds.) *Distributed artificial intelligence.* Volume II. London, San Mateo: Pitman, Morgan Kaufmann, pp. 37–54.

Sun, R. (2007) 'Cognitive social simulation incorporating cognitive architectures', *IEEE Intelligent Systems*, 22(5), pp. 33–39.

Sutter, T. (1997) 'Rekonstruktion und doppelte Kontingenz. Konstitutionstheoretische Überlegungen zu einer konstruktivistischen Hermeneutik', in Sutter, T. (ed.) *Beobachtung verstehen, verstehen beobachten. Perspektiven einer konstruktivistischen Hermeneutik.* Opladen: Westdeutscher Verlag, pp. 303–336.

Troitzsch, K. G. (2017) 'Axiomatic theory and simulation: A philosophy of science perspective on Schelling's seggregation model', *Journal for Artificial Societies and Social Simulation*, 20(1). http://jasss.soc.surrey.ac.uk/20/1/10.html

Van Dyke Parunak, H., Bisson, R., Brueckner, S., Matthews, R. and Sauter, J. (2006). A model of emotions for situated agents. In *Proceedings of the Fifth International Joint Conference on Autonomous Agents and Multi-agent Systems* (pp. 993–995). ACM.

Weber, M. (1922) *Wirtschaft und Gesellschaft.* Tübingen: Mohr.

Weber, M. (1968a) 'Die Objektivität sozialwissenschaftlicher und sozialpolitischer Erkenntnis', in Winckelmann, J. (ed.) *Gesammelte Aufsätze zur Wissenschaftslehre.* Tübingen: Mohr, pp. 146–204.

Weber, M. (1968b) 'Objektive Möglichkeit und adäquate Verursachung in der historischen Kausalbetrachtung', in Winckelmann, J. (ed.) *Gesammelte Aufsätze zur Wissenschaftslehre.* Tübingen: Mohr, pp. 266–290.

Windelband, W. (1915) 'Geschichte und Naturwissenschaft', in Windelband, W. (ed.) Praeludien 2, Tuebingen, pp. 136–160.

Wooldrige, M. (1999) 'Intelligent agents', in Weiß, G. (ed.) *Multi agent systems: A modern approach to distributed artificial intelligence.* Cambridge, MA: MIT Press, pp. 27–77.

Yang, L. and Gilbert, N. (2008) 'Getting away from numbers: Using qualitative observation for agent-based modeling', *Advances in Complex Systems*, 11(2), pp. 175–185.

3 The use of ethnographic social simulation for crime research*
From the field to the model

Vanessa Dirksen, Martin Neumann, and Ulf Lotzmann

3.1 Introduction

The previous chapter outlined the epistemological foundations of the overall re-search process of an interpretive account to agent-based modelling (ABM) that is proposed in this book. This chapter will now set forth the conceptual foundations of the very first step of the overall research process: for the output to better approximate the real world, we propose basing the input of the model on qualitative empirical evidence rather than on "reductionism-based abstraction" (Zackery et al., 2016: 40). While such evidence-based modelling is hardly novel (Moss, 2008), in so doing, we advance the notion of "meaningful evidence". To achieve this goal, we develop a specific take on social simulation in this chapter. For this purpose, we rely here on the theoretical and methodological framework of ethnography for the phase of developing conceptual models.

In terms of anticipation community, the kind of simulation advocated here resembles what Li Vigni (2020) calls the "future co-construction community" of complexity science. First, our approach to simulation may be positioned as a form of participatory modelling as it hinges on the sense-making of stakeholders in the field, i.e., when both the input *and* the output of the model are concerned. For illustrating the novel methodology for simulation, we refer here to applications in crime research in general and cocaine trafficking in particular. Relevant stakeholders are a variety of police investigators knowledgeable on the topic of cocaine trafficking. Second and in line with Li Vigni's notion of the future co-construction community, our approach to simulation aims for "the production of different scenarios, allowing for the opening and exploring the space of the possible" (Chateauraynaud and Lehtonen in Li Vigni, 2020: 5). The scenarios generated by the methodology for simulation modelling we propose in this chapter explore the space of prospective actions from an emic perspective (Heemskerk, 2003), i.e., the perspective of the cocaine trader as inferred from their interactions (cf. Collins, 2009).

---

* This chapter is based on the article Dirksen, V., Neumann, M., Lotzmann, U. (2022) From agent to action: the use of ethnographic social simulation for crime research that has been published in the special issue on simulation and dissimulation in the journal Futures, vol. 142.

DOI: 10.4324/9781003393207-3

That being said, evidence making in policing is taking on a new form at a time in which large data sets and new data infrastructure are increasingly available to police investigation and increasingly involve the application of the so-called novel methods and techniques of big data analytics (Chan and Bennett Moses, 2016). Though these methods and techniques will undoubtedly uncover new patterns and relationships (i.e., correlations) between variables, they do not necessarily generate *meaningful* ones. For instance, in the United States there is a public debate on whether the use of machine learning in criminal justice and predictive policing fosters racial discrimination (Angwin et al., 2016; Flores et al., 2016). Algorithms as such cannot account for meaningful concepts such as discrimination. Following Greene (2014: 202), we refer to this as a "meaning gap" in policing research; that is, "in our zeal to pursue the more 'scientific' aspects of research on the police, we have often settled for statistical results-absent contextual meaning; resulting in the pursuit of Durkheim's social facts without the associated social interpretation" (Amoore and Piotukh, 2015).

Apart from a tendency towards uncritical techno-enthusiasm, responses to the recent drug-related killings in the Netherlands[1] show proof of an overall proclivity for decontextualization and hence risk failing to capture the complex nature of the social organization of the drug trade (Molijn, 2020). For a thorough understanding of the "tricks of the trade", however, grasping the complex organizing principles at play is crucial. Indeed, doing so allows for intervention in the actual *modus operandi* prevailing in organized crime. In the era of big data and algorithmic decision-making, we therefore advocate *small data* research (Kitchin and Lauriault, 2014), especially for areas in which tracing back knowledge claims to the "intelligible context" (Geertz, 1983) is of utmost importance. In so doing, we follow the interpretive turn in social theory, emphasizing the explication of meaningful (i.e., cultural) patterns rather than the search for cultural rules and laws of behaviour in the understanding of social practices. In simulation and computational social sciences, this is, to date, still rare. However, a focus on small data research in a big data world does not suffice. Instead, we agree with Crawford (2013) that "we must ask how we can bring together big data approaches with small data studies – computational social science with traditional qualitative methods (…) Then we can move from the focus on merely big data towards something more three dimensional: data with depth".

Our research objective is twofold. On the one hand, we aim to contribute to understanding how the social sciences in general and policing in particular can and should incorporate the "new" methods and techniques of computational social science (Mützel, 2015) so as to generate meaningful insights into particular social worlds. On the other hand, we aim to understand how these methods may be developed further in order to better accommodate the particularities and objectives of the qualitative research tradition. Such an undertaking may be characterized in terms of what Marres (2012) refers to as the *redistribution of methods*, and more specifically in terms of what

Blok and Pedersen (2014) term *complementary social science*, stitching together computational and ethnographic methods. In this chapter, it is the stitching together of ABM and qualitative research in which we are interested. When stitching together ABM and qualitative research, we will in this chapter be concerned with the input side of the integration. In developing the novel methodology, we concentrate here on the very first phase of the simulation modelling process, i.e., the formulation of the initial assumptions ("rules") of a conceptual model.

Similarly to laboratory experimentation, ABM allows for an *ex-ante* investigation of alternative scenarios and of the likely implications of interventions by way of "what-if" questions: what happens if the conditions of the simulation are changed? In this chapter, we will demonstrate that this feature of "conditionalizing social phenomena" by means of "what-if" analyses is *the* essential characteristic of ABM, making it highly suited for the experimental study of crime patterns such as those prevailing in the cocaine transit trade. A point of added value of social simulation for crime research and policing concerns the fact that in this context we are typically confronted with missing, confidential, and flawed data. Due to the "what-if" analyses ABM affords, simulation potentially helps to fill in the blanks, so to speak. A failure to fill in the blanks provides an indicator for further data gathering (Eck and Liu, 2008).

Although we contend that the method of agent-based social simulation may be of value to crime research, we argue for a different approach to ABM simulation from the one commonly taken. Just as investigations of complex forms of crimes – such as cocaine trafficking in the Netherlands – ask for the generation of contextualized meaning (Sampson, 2013), in this chapter we argue for a qualitative take on social simulation. To do this, we will first discuss the body of knowledge representing the state of knowledge with respect to the use of ABM in crime research in general and the qualitative take on ABM in particular. Next, we will introduce the exploratory study of the distributive trade of cocaine in the Netherlands (Dirksen et al., 2021) conducted by one of this chapter's authors, on the basis of which we will develop a particular form of qualitative ABM that we call *ethnographic social simulation*. We will then explore the extent to which the research traditions of ethnography and ABM are compatible, and how the qualitative research tradition of ethnography is the most appropriate given the nature of the topic under investigation as well as providing the best fit with ABM's formal language. The chapter will end by specifying the requirements to mutually accommodate ("stitch together") ethnography and ABM modelling.

3.2 Background: Criminological agent-based modelling

Application of ABM in criminological research and police investigation is, to date, still relatively rare (Groff and Birks, 2008). This stands in contrast to the application of computational, artificial intelligence (AI)-based technologies used in predictive policing and criminal justice.[2] Notwithstanding the dangers of uncritical application by, for instance, the use of analogies (Chattoe-Brown, 1998), the spurious formalization of theories (Scholz et al., 2021), or overly simplified representations of the target system (Edmonds, 2020),[3] ABM has a number of characteristics that potentially benefit crime research. First, simulation is inherently dynamic and hence allows for studying the processes and mechanisms involved in the organization of complex forms of crime. Second, as agents act in a virtual environment, ABM may cover explicit spatial representations. This is interesting for the identification of so-called crime hotspots (Weisburd et al., 2017) in, for example, environmental criminology (Brantingham and Brantingham, 2004; Bosse and Gerritsen, 2008; Birks and Davies, 2017; Groff et al., 2019) and predictive policing (Perry, 2013). Third, ABM is explicitly aimed at modelling interactions, e.g., interaction between agents under whatever guise, human and non-human, as well as with the environment. This enables, for instance, the investigation and disruption of criminal networks (Duijn et al., 2014; Lettieri et al., 2017; Duxbury and Haynie, 2019). Finally, ABM allows the modelling of heterogeneous agents (Axtell, 2000). This means that agents may acquire different skills, or at different times take on different roles, enabling for instance the study of social capital in criminal groups, i.e., how actors with different specialized competences interact in criminal networks and how their individual skills together contribute to the execution of specific criminal activities (Duijn et al., 2014; Duijn, 2016). Another example pertains to simulating the changing characteristics of agents over time, such as growing into and aging out of crime (Cornelius et al., 2017). These features of ABM have also been used to investigate burglary (Malleson et al., 2010) and extortion (Nardin et al., 2016).

In an attempt at classifying the use of ABM in contemporary criminological research, we start with one of the most well-known distinctions in agent-based research: between simple and complex models. This is sometimes denoted as the difference between the "keep it simple, stupid" (KISS; Axelrod, 1997) and the "keep it descriptive, stupid" (KIDS) approaches to modelling (Edmonds and Moss, 2005). In a similar vein, Ahrweiler and Gilbert (2009) speak of the difference between nomothetic and idiographic models associated with the knowledge claims of mathematics and history, respectively. The former strand of ABM research attempts at building relatively simple models at a high level of abstraction. The objective of such simulation models is to yield generalizable results that reflect the nomothetic knowledge claim of law-like statements. This is in the tradition of quantitative social research and is often associated with theoretical research in evolutionary game theory. The idiographic strand of ABM research attempts at "understanding and explaining a special case" (Ahrweiler and Gilbert, 2009: 22) in as much detail as possible. Such models are typically more complex. Although such models have more internal validity in representing an individual case, their simulations yield less generalizable results. This is close to the tradition of qualitative social research.

There is no clear-cut distinction between the two styles of modelling. Rather the various forms of models should be seen in a continuum from less to more complex. Nonetheless, the classification of simple and complex models is useful for the characterization of the state of knowledge on ABM in criminological research. Traditionally, criminological models are relatively simple (exceptions include Groff, 2008; Wang et al., 2008) and attempt at generating complex patterns from simple rules (Malleson et al., 2010; Birks et al., 2012; Groff et al., 2019). The aim of these kinds of simulation experiments is to reveal general insights formulated in the form of law-like statements (Birks et al., 2012). Today, criminological ABM research is closer to the tradition of quantitative research and the field has yet to see the development of qualitative ABM models for the in-depth investigation of specific crime phenomena. This is despite the fact that, in general, there has been growing interest in the inclusion of qualitative evidence for specifying the agent rules of agent-based models (Edmonds, 2015).

The two modelling styles not only reflect differences in epistemology, but modelling purposes too. In line with the typology developed by Edmonds et al. (2019), the modelling purpose of abstract, generic models may be best understood as theoretical exposition, i.e., providing insight into the implications of a single mechanism. Such modelling attempts of the theoretical exposition type include the question of what would be the consequence if this or that mechanism were in place. By providing small building blocks of a general theory that are tested in isolation, modelling efforts of this kind allegedly contribute to cumulative knowledge (Townsley and Birks, 2008). Adding building blocks increases the complexity and hence creates a cumulatively growing body of theoretical knowledge. For instance, a model might apply a game theoretical framework and add an additional assumption (e.g., of homophily) to the general theoretical framework. The simulation experiment could then explore how adding the assumption of homophily to the general game theoretical framework changes the behaviour of the model at large. Such cumulative knowledge builds on the assumption that the individual theoretical building blocks are unrelated and do not have any interdependent effects. The purpose of many criminological ABMs may best be classified as theoretical exposition. For instance, the purpose of a model of burglary may be described as investigating the effects of theoretical building blocks taken from routine activity theory on patterns of burglary (Malleson et al., 2010).

As we contend, however, the requirements of safeguarding context specificity as described in the introduction call for a descriptive approach that is not covered by simple and abstract generic models. Typically, providing a detailed description of context-specific circumstances in the social world reveals complex, interacting systems in which various feedback loops between the interacting parts of the system commonly exist (i.e., the existence of interdependent effects between the small building blocks), hindering cumulative research, starting from simple assumptions. In Section 3.4, we will discuss what kind of modelling approach is hence sought in the case of crime research in general and for the investigation of the cocaine transit trade in particular. Prior to doing so, we will first introduce the empirical findings on the basis of which our first modelling attempt was done.

3.3   Context: The distributive trade of cocaine in the Netherlands

In this section, we will describe the exploratory qualitative study of the distributive trade of cocaine in the Netherlands (Dirksen et al., 2021) that was taken as the point of departure for the development of the methodology of ethnographic simulation modelling. For outlining the conceptual foundations of the model development process, this material has an exemplary function only. Understanding the nature of the research topic and the kinds of data encountered on the input side of the model aids in exploring the various options for qualitative social simulation in crime research.

The exploratory qualitative study of the distribution of cocaine via the Netherlands abroad was conducted by one of this chapter's authors in collaboration with two police researchers of the Dutch National Police. The distributive trade of cocaine is a form of transit crime which refers to the level of trade between import and retail.[4] It is a form of "organized crime that is geared toward border-crossing trafficking" (Kruisbergen et al., 2012: 42). Although quite a lot is known about the import of cocaine in the Netherlands, the transit of cocaine via the Netherlands remains a blind spot. The study aimed to shed light on the underlying organizing principles (Powell and DiMaggio, 1991) of the workings of the Dutch distribution hub in cocaine. The term "organizing principles" refers to both the coordination mechanisms and the structures of association of the transit networks involved, i.e., both the content and the form of such relations. After all, understanding the basis on which relations in the trade are developed and maintained is a prerequisite for understanding the development of any kind of criminal network in terms of its prospective structure (Malm et al., 2010; Rostrami et al., 2017).

During the course of the study conducted from June 2017 to July 2018, a wide variety of primary and secondary data were collected and analysed, including digital and traditional data obtained from both internal and external police sources. First, police information databases (from 2013 to 2016) were analysed (the big data source of the study). For reasons of confidentiality and because in this chapter we only use the data to exemplify the *kind* of empirical material encountered in policing, we will not specify the volume and nature of these data sources. It suffices to say that it provided information on ways of working together, and the interactions and relationships between the subjects involved in the transit trade. In this chapter, this source is referred to as "internal police information". Second, a total of 22 semi-structured interviews with investigating officers from the Netherlands and neighbouring countries were conducted. Third, a small qualitative questionnaire was distributed among 24 of the participating country members of the cocaine and heroin task force of the European Multidisciplinary Platform Against Criminal Threats (EMPACT). Fourth, a content analysis of recent media outlets as well as of various research reports of European law enforcement agencies on cocaine trafficking was undertaken.

The research findings of the exploratory qualitative study first and foremost provided evidence of a supply-driven dynamic prevalent in the market for cocaine, rather than this being solely demand-driven. Considering the recent history of the cocaine market, which saw a drastic albeit stabilized increase in the supply of cocaine especially from the year 2013, this outcome might not be entirely surprising. Due to developments in South America at that time and the respective increasing production of cocaine (especially in Colombia), Europe is currently facing what might rightly be referred to as an oversupply of cocaine (UNODC, 2020). What *is* striking, however, is that to date, the market for cocaine has yet to be studied from a supply-side perspective. In the police, the market for cocaine has traditionally been – and still is – regarded as demand-driven. Paying attention to the supply side of the market instead changes the entire outlook of its organizational dynamics and prospective development. One reason for this is that the mechanisms of trust and reputation building (i.e., coordination mechanisms) in a supply-driven market are wholly different from the organizing principles in a demand-driven market. One example includes word-of-mouth-based forms of *transitive trust*. Typical instances include inferences such as the following: A has faith in the transportation if B has faith in the customer.

This brings us to the second key finding of the exploratory study: the growing importance of reputation in the establishment of new trading relations. This is an effect of the first finding. That is to say, an overly supply-driven market for cocaine forces people to look outside their own established networks and work with others with whom they are unfamiliar, with the aim of entering new markets to get rid of their "stash" (Kruisbergen et al., 2012: 18). Put in terms of social network theory (Granovetter, 1973), in a demand-driven market, exchange relations tend to rely on so-called strong ties between criminals. In a supply-driven market, however, establishing new contacts is done by way of tapping into weak ties. This means that accessing new markets is done on the basis of introduction and reputation instead of strong ties fed by trust.

To further our understanding of the consequences of the market for cocaine being increasingly supply-driven for the prospective development of the trade, social simulation is proposed. To be precise, what we aim to explore by way of social simulation is how exactly demand and supply meet in a supply-driven market. In social network theory's terms, demand and supply meet at the junction between strong and weak trading relations. To explore this, various types of social simulation as discussed in Section 3.2 could be utilized. For instance, one could think of taking a more traditional and theory-driven perspective, such as from the stance of supply chain management, and simulate different decoupling points between demand and supply at the various levels of the trade. This could be done to understand the possible consequences of decoupling for issues like risk-taking, storage of overstock, conflict resolution, and the price-quality relation, and hence the kind of coordination required. A second line of study by way of social simulation, which also represents the more top-down or theory-driven approach, might include simulating the cocaine supply chain under the market forces (Porter, 1979) in which decoupling may be opted for by a distributor. It is assumed here that situations of overstock influence how the "supply chain manager" chooses risk mitigation strategies that are strikingly different from those under conditions of stock-out supply. In order to understand the transit trade in depth, however, we argue for a third line of investigation zooming into how people engage in (new) trading relations with each other under conditions of oversupply of cocaine. Such a descriptive account (Moss, 2008) tends to avoid the uncritical application of potentially misleading theories as could be the case in the other, more top-down approaches to ABM. As we contend, focusing on the how, when, and with whom people make new contacts will reveal the cultural logic of the trade, essential for formulating *embedded* interventions. Hence, the specific research question for our social simulation experiment is: How do trading relations come about and are sustained in a supply-driven market for cocaine?

3.4   An ethnographic account of agent-based modelling

3.4.1   *The suitability of ethnography for the study of cocaine trafficking*

In the previous section, we showed why our study calls for ABM simulation. In this section, we will describe why and how we see ourselves urged by the nature of the topic at hand to stitch together ABM with the ethnographic research procedure. First, we will demonstrate the suitability of ethnographic research for the study of complex organized crime, as exemplified by the topic described above. Next, we will explore the extent to which the formal languages of ethnography and ABM are compatible as well as mutually beneficial. This is ultimately done to understand why and how the methods may be stitched together.

As we have already argued, studying the cocaine transit trade requires an in-depth investigation of the dynamics of trust and reputation building at the microscopic level of how co-offending contacts are made, sustained, and broken. Of the qualitative research traditions, we contend that interpretive ethnography is best equipped for this task. First, ethnography aims at accessing the symbolic world through the observation of (local) practices. It departs from asking "what the devil is going on" (Geertz, 1973: 26) to grasping the meaning of that behaviour. Geertz's (1973: 26) thick description is the ethnographer's instrument for arriving at such meanings in context, accounting for what he refers to as the "intelligible frame", asserting that "human nature is only specified and made intelligible by the particular context (i.e., symbolic systems) in which it is found" (Schwandt, 2014: 41).

In the case of the cocaine trade, "gaining a working familiarity with the frames of meaning within which [people] enact their lives" (Geertz, 1999: 11), i.e., their symbolic doings, is, like member checking, not an option. In line with what is referred to as trace ethnography (Geiger and Ribes, 2011),[5] we are, however, able to infer this meaning from their "texts", i.e., practices

of communication and communication of practices, as captured by the confiscated communication data. Such captured communication is to be seen as
interrelated actions that may generate symbolic meaning, as actions undertaken by actors become symbolic in the context of other actors interpreting
their doings and reacting and responding accordingly. Therefore, meaning is
an emergent property of linguistic practices; that is to say, it is negotiated between actors and groups of actors. By observing how actions and actors relate
to each other, and hence negotiate meaning, the ethnographer interprets the
interpretations of the actors involved (referred to as the double hermeneutic,
Giddens, 1987).[6] A typical feature of the interpretive paradigm is abductive
reasoning which involves going "from partial information to a probable general scenario" (Bennato, 2021: 211). In ethnographic simulation modelling,
inferring meaning from what traders say and do (i.e., arriving at a probable
scenario) is done with the help of a large variety of domain experts in the field
in the various phases of the research procedure. The multiplicity of interpretations is subsequently built into the model by way of annotations attached
to the various condition-action sequences of the model. As such, the ethnographic simulation modeler is building "explications upon explications upon
explications" (cf. Munk et al., 2022: 11), hence elucidating the various layers
of meaning. This is how we arrive at intersubjective meaning intersubjectively
so to speak.

3.4.2   ABM as a framework for ethnographic research

In fact, even though ethnography has rarely been used in building agent-based
models, it has a close resemblance to ABM. In a similar vein, scholars have
noted the resemblance between ethnography and machine learning (Elish
and Boyd, 2018) as well as between ethnography and game theory (Chattoe-
Brown, 2011). The resemblance between ethnography and ABM is most
striking in the method of ethnography as described by cognitive anthropologist James Spradley. Spradley's (1980) ethnography focuses on extensively describing types of settings, types of actors, and the types of actions conducted
in those settings. It shows a close resemblance and high compatibility with the
formal language of ABM, in which agents (as representatives of actors) and action rules (as representatives of actions) executed within a virtual environment
(as representatives of the settings) are at the centre of the formalism.

Heavily relying on a wide variety of semantic relationships (for instance of
inclusion, such as "X is a kind of Y"), Spradley shows how to move from a
rich description of "what is going on here?" to the meaning of that behaviour.
Or, stated differently, by way of describing the types of actors and the types
of activities involved in the diversity of settings, it allows one to go from a description of the social situation to understanding a cultural scene. Here, a social
situation is defined in terms of "the stream of behavior (activities) carried out
by people (actors) in a particular location (place)" (Spradley, 1980: 86).
The cultural scene, then, refers to "the patterns of behavior, artifacts, and

knowledge that people have learned or created and refers to an organization of things, the meanings given by people to objects, places, and activities" (Spradley, 1980: 86). The move from social situation to the cultural scene is in contemporary forms of trace ethnography made by means of inferring meaning from linguistic practices rather than through the native's points of view of Geertz's thick description. Taking a specific paradigmatic stance (i.e., a semiotic one) may certainly also limit the ethnographic investigation: while Geertz is often believed to be too contextual, the limitation of Spradley's account is that it disregards the historical background of the symbolic social world (Van Maanen, 1980). However, both limitations are compensated for by microscopic descriptive ABM's promise to compare *across* (rather than *within*) cases.

The social situation is observable for the ethnographer in a similar way as virtual agents on the computer screen are observable for the agent-based modeller. The social situation may also be directly translated into any modelling style of ABM. To illustrate this, we will focus on a social situation from our exemplary empirical material, i.e., the one of "making and executing a deal", and show that the features of ABM described in the second section of this chapter are compatible with an ethnographic investigation of this situation. The first point to note in this regard is that making and executing a deal involves interaction between at least two actors. Thus, a modelling attempt needs to be able to differentiate between different "acting units" such as "supplier" and "buyer". In fact, modelling the interactions of heterogeneous actors is at the core of the agent-based approach to modelling, as agents are software units that are able to act autonomously and interact with each other also. This feature is a basic but crucial characteristic of ABM for representing the making and execution of a deal in a specific social setting.

Focusing on the different ways in which deals are made, executed, and broken, modelling the distribution of cocaine in the Netherlands may (in line with Spradley's semantic analysis) begin with the observation that making and executing a deal occurs in various *types of settings*: (1) physical and virtual; (2) open and closed; (3) places where the making of the deal goes together with the exchange of the merchandise, and places where the making of the deal and the execution of the deal occur at different points in time and in different locations. The latter depends, among other factors, on the size of the trade and whether or not the deal is made on a dark net marketplace. This focus of ethnography on the various types of making and executing a deal occurring in spaces – be they physical or virtual – is compatible with two basic features of ABM. It corresponds, first, to the spatial aspect of ABM. The software units operate in a virtual space that can easily be adapted to different empirical circumstances, such as by geographic information system (GIS) maps of the physical world, or a network topology of the dark net. Second, the potential delay between making and executing a deal specifically highlights the simple fact that social processes happen in time. Including a temporal dimension is a central feature of running a simulation.

Furthermore, the exploratory research showed that there are numerous *types of actors* involved in making and executing a deal in a particular setting, such as offloaders, transporters, distributors, street dealers, and vendors. We will exemplify the use of "types of actors" by zooming in on the various kinds of activities coded in our data analysis as "logistics service provision", including activities involved in the actual transportation and in organizing the required shipping documents, to the alignment of demand and supply of cocaine in the Netherlands. Accordingly, the type of actor "logistic service provider" may include the respective roles of the transporter, the coordinator, and the supply chain manager (Dirksen et al., 2018). Representing this heterogeneity of actors can take advantage of the fact that each software unit of an ABM can be individually designed. Typically, templates are used to represent the particular role of, for instance, a transporter, a coordinator, or a supply chain manager. However, no principle limits of differentiation exist. Representing the heterogeneity of actors by ABM is a strong advantage of this modelling approach.

In addition, not only are the various roles traders may attain be specified in terms of what people do, but also in terms of what people know (or better yet, what they themselves say they know as well as what other people say they know). In the word-of-mouth (WoM) forms of reputation building prevalent in a supply-driven market, points of recommendation or the inferred traits of the "good" distributor include but are not limited to the following: knowing which type of deck charge to choose; knowing how to get through border controls; being able to arrange the right paperwork and shipping documents; having corrupt or bribable contacts in the harbour; and being able to arrange for storage as required (Dirksen et al., 2018).

Representing reputation-building mechanisms in ABM (Paolucci and Sabater, 2006) in the cocaine trade requires first that the history of interaction is to be taken into account to infer, for instance, what is to be regarded as a "good distributor" based on past experiences. Second, inferring traits such as being a good transporter requires a cognitive representation of the history of interaction in the ABM model (which is missing in modelling approaches based on differential equations, for example). For this purpose, it is possible to exploit the feature of ABM that intelligent agents may have a memory and acquire new skills and knowledge in the course of the interaction history, i.e., broadly speaking, that they are able to learn. As a result, we could model the transporter growing into the role of supply chain manager under conditions of an overly supply-driven market for instance.

3.5 The thick conditional: From agent to action-based modelling

3.5.1 *From "what-if" relations to "condition-action" sequences*

In this section, we will describe how in ethnographic simulation modelling, thick description is accommodated by way of adding a more fine-grained and microscopic layer to the "what-if" relations of ABM (Lotzmann and Neumann, 2017). For this purpose, we refer to the approach and formal language of the consistent conceptual description (CCD) (Wimmer, 2011) and associated software (Scherer et al., 2015) used for the development of the new methodology. Such software is a tool for conceptual modelling that specifies the *logic* of a model before running a simulation by a so-called CCD. The tool was originally developed for the purpose of a research project to enable regional governments to improve their policy performance (Wimmer, 2011). One example was the evaluation of options for different energy sources for heating (Scherer et al., 2013). CCD provides a specific grammar for the description of processes through alternating appearances of situational conditions and responsive actions in a temporal sequence. These are plotted as a flow diagram, or in other words, as condition-action sequences (Lotzmann and Neumann, 2017). The descriptions (of the conditions and the actions) are linked with the empirical evidence found in the data that justify these elements (Scherer et al., 2015). As the sequences of conditions and actions take on the form of a flow diagram, at first sight the conceptual modelling of CCD software seems similar to the causal loop diagrams developed in the tradition of system dynamics modelling (Voinov et al., 2018). However, condition-action sequences differ from causal loop diagrams in that they specify the general logic of "what-if" relations (which can also be found in causal loop diagrams) to a social framework of *situated actions*. CCD software thus facilitates a microscopic and action-oriented approach. Deciphering sequences of situational conditions and subsequent actions, which in turn provide new situational conditions that trigger further new subsequent actions, follows a scheme of analysis already formulated by Max Weber (1968: 279, own translation): namely to "disassemble the given as far in its components until each of these can be inserted in the rules of experience to see by rules of thumb which achievement it would have yielded individually".

While CCD software is a multipurpose tool that may be applied in various approaches to ABM, it is specifically well suited to develop what we call the *thick conditional*, referring to the inclusion of microscopic descriptions in ethnographic modelling. In terms of formal language, this can be achieved by specifying the "what-if" relations of traditional simulation modelling into condition-action sequences. Prior to showing what condition-action sequences may look like in the case of the distributive trade of cocaine in the Netherlands, we will first demonstrate how to make use of condition-action sequences in contrast to the "what-if" relations of traditional approaches to ABM (summarized in Table 3.1).

Table 3.1 Characteristics of "condition-action" and "what-if" relations

Condition-action	What-if
1. Facilitates micro-level analysis	Micro, meso, and macro levels
2. Diachronic relation	Synchronous relation possible
3. Social mechanism with concrete actions	Not necessarily concrete actions
4. Actor-oriented	No concrete actors needed

CCD allows one to "capture" ethnographic, descriptive observations, as *first*, condition-action sequences correspond to the micro level of the *web of actions and interactions*, that is, actors reacting in a particular manner to the conditions produced by the actions of other actors. From this, the negotiation of meaning within groups may be inferred. "What-if" relations, on the other hand, do not necessarily correspond to the micro level of (inter)actions but to the meso and macro levels as well, e.g., by relating inflation rates to unemployment rates in classical macroeconomics. Notably, condition-action sequences are always "what-if" relations, but "what-if" relations are not necessarily condition-action sequences, for instance, in the case of relations between macroeconomic variables that do not specify situated actions.

Second, condition-action sequences denote a diachronic relation, i.e., a temporal, chronological relation, in the sense of "it first needs to rain to open an umbrella". "What-if" relations, on the other hand, can also be logical relations that are not necessarily of a temporal order. For instance, the macroeconomic relation between inflation and unemployment rates denotes a synchronous relation. These are parallel processes, meaning that the one does not (necessarily) lead to the other, but rather goes alongside it.

Third, condition-action sequences are social mechanisms (Hedström and Ylikoski, 2010) that may have various instantiations. When it rains (a condition), it becomes likely that an actor opens an umbrella (an action). The sequence can be instantiated in various circumstances, at different times, and in different places. However, an instantiation of the sequence is always a specification to a specific context: a condition is a situation, and a responsive action is an action to that particular situation. It needs to rain at a specific point in space and time for the sequence to be realized.

Fourth, in contrast to causal loop diagrams, these sequences are about actors, be they generic in the sense of the *type* of actor or the *type* of non-human actors undertaking actions in specific situations. In the case of "what-if" relations, this is not necessarily the case, as the example of macroeconomics shows: inflation is not an actor, nor is underemployment. Thus, the condition-action sequences support the specification of different *types* of actions rather than merely different (stereo)types of actors, moving ABM from an actor to an action orientation, fully in line with the ethnographic tradition as described in the previous section. The ethnographic focus on the *variety* of roles people acquire tends to characterize actors in terms of what traders *do* and *know* instead of in terms of superficial traits of personal data such as age, gender, ethnicity, and group affiliation. Hence, the ethnographic take on ABM provides the answer to both the prevalent offender orientation ("catching blokes") in policing and the stereotyping and bias inherent to conventional ABM in crime (e.g., Groff and Badham, 2021). This, however, is not to say that our methodology is without bias. Implicit bias in our study is inherent in the kinds of data sources used; the required selection of data made from these large data sets so as to conduct a qualitative data analysis as well as in the choice for the interpretive ethnographic paradigm. Alike the traditional ethnographer, the ethnographic simulation modeller accepts the conditionality and partiality of the interpretive knowledge claim (cf. Lichterman, 2017).[7]

3.5.2   *Illustrations*

In this section, we will illustrate the ways in which the "what-if" relations of conventional ABM are to be translated into the more microscopic level of condition-action sequences. As we argued in Section 3.3, focusing on the varying mechanisms of trust and reputation building under conditions of supply and demand would help in better understanding the complexity of the transit trade in general and, ultimately, will bring us closer to comprehending the prospective directions (or scenarios) in which the market could develop. This leads us to define the following two general "what-if" relations: (1) What if the market for cocaine is supply-driven and counterfactual; (2) what if the market for cocaine is demand-driven? In this section, we will show how the formal language of condition-action sequences typical for the CCD approach to social simulation may be applied to the qualitative findings of the exploratory study and how they relate to the aforementioned "what-if" relations. We will illustrate how the formal language of condition-action sequences accommodates the more fine-grained social instantiation of the aforementioned "what-if" relations.

As we argued, the level of condition-action sequences is the level required for ABM to generate a more in-depth understanding of how trading relations are established and maintained in the distributive trade of cocaine. The notion of a supply-driven market has a trickle-down effect so to speak on the condition-action sequences related to trust and reputation building in the trade. Or rather, by way of ethnographic simulation modelling, the transition from a demand- to a supply-driven market may be inferred from the various kinds of reputation-building regimes at the microscopic level, i.e., as an *emergent* property, not so much an *a priori* condition. To illustrate this, we will focus on a condition-action sequence typical for an overstock market: "getting rid of the stash" as an instantiation of an overstock market.

A typical condition-action sequence for a supply-driven market for cocaine is one in which traders do not know how to get rid of their "stash" and will consequently try to get in touch with co-offending traders or potential customers through the connections of their connections. As we have already demonstrated, whereas the existing trade (the demand-driven trade) largely relies on strong and homogeneous relations, the new trade (being supply-driven) resorts to exploiting weak links so as to tap into new markets. Fig. 3.1 shows our first attempt at modelling the condition-action sequences involved in "getting rid of the stash". This modelling attempt concerns an actor – a cocaine trader – having to take action in order to sell his stock of merchandise and thus make a profit. The actor is a seasoned cocaine trader, with already

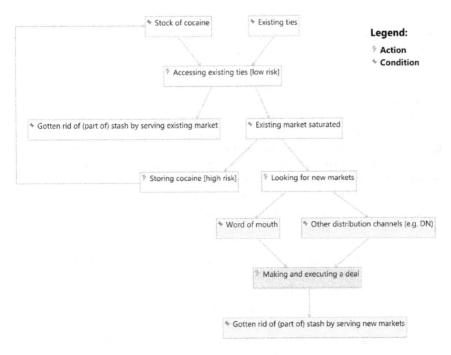

Figure 3.1 Conceptual model "getting rid of the stash" (bird's-eye view)

established trading relations (i.e., strong ties). In this modelling excerpt, the bases on which these strong ties came into being are not taken into account.

As the model shows, the actor will first serve the already established contacts, i.e., the existing ties and the already established market. If the deal is executed successfully, no further action is needed. If the existing market (of strong ties) is saturated, the actor will seek to establish new trading contacts so as to access new markets. After all, a supply-driven market dynamic entails no longer being able to rely on already existing markets and trading relations, but having to find new outlets for the abundant supply of cocaine where a profit can still be made. While in search of new markets (and hence new trading partners), the actor will have to temporarily store the stash of cocaine, which means an increased risk of being detected and caught by the police. New trading relations are established on the basis of reputation. As the exploratory study shows, in a supply-driven market, reputation is often established by way of recommendation, that is, by WoM more than by the direct experience of proven ability or history of interaction (track record of accomplishments in the past). Other options for entering new markets might include the use of the dark net. It should be noted, however, that the role of the dark net in the distributive trade of cocaine is treated as a black box in the model, as whether or not crypto markets do in fact serve as a means to tap into new markets was not within the scope of the exploratory study.

The remainder of the diagram concerns "making and executing a deal" (marked in grey), which is elaborated in Fig. 3.2.

Whereas Fig. 3.1 displays a bird's-eye view, providing a rather general overview, Fig. 3.2 shows how the model displayed in Fig. 3.1 should be extended to include the level of detail required for ethnographic simulation modelling. In ethnographic simulation modelling, all extensions have to be incorporated into one model. By way of illustrating this, Fig. 3.2 zooms in on the deeper microscopic level of a specific element of Fig. 3.1: the condition-action sequences involved in the "making and executing a deal". Hence, Fig. 3.2 displays only some of the complexity that remains invisible in the bird's-eye view of Fig. 3.1, as it does not show all possible extensions.

Figure 3.2 displays the condition-action sequence of making and executing a deal. This entails "accessing new contacts on the basis of reputation" (fourth level of the diagram), eventually leading up to the condition "gotten rid of the stash". As the figure shows, making new contacts (required for entering new markets) involves the increased risk of being exposed as it necessarily involves (more) communication and information exchange, as one does not yet know if the co-offending trading partner can be trusted. Factors decisive for taking the "leap of faith" and waiving those risks include speaking the same language, complementary competencies, access to valuable contacts such as to the harbours of Rotterdam or Antwerp, and (favourable) prices. Once new contacts are established, the terms of the deal have to be negotiated. In cases of smaller amounts of cocaine, executing a deal ("cash for stash") occurs concurrently and in the same setting as making the deal (negotiating the terms). In cases of larger amounts of cocaine, such direct exchange is impossible and here the execution of the deal is lapsed in time. Such indirect exchange lapsed in time needs extra "security mechanisms", as relations of trust resulting from that initial contact are not established overnight. Other forms of commitment (i.e., other ways of making sure people live up to their end of the deal) have to be installed, other than a feeling of trust anchored in strong ties and past experience of interaction. Such "forms of guarantee" include requesting a down payment as well as various forms of intimidation or threat of sanction if people do not "deliver". In addition to financial sanction and violent retaliation, this may comprise various forms of blaming and shaming, hence the manipulation of reputation by a third party. An alternative form of commitment includes the above-mentioned transitive form of trust. If commitment is secured and all the actors involved stick to their end of the bargain, the transaction is executed, and the trader has gotten rid of the stash successfully.

Altogether, Fig. 3.2 illustrates how there are various branching points at the microscopic level that can decisively influence the outcomes of transactions. It clearly shows how there are "multiple variations of relations, varying as a result of a varied explicit circumstances" (Fuller, 2017: 41) that cannot be sufficiently dissected by the bird's-eye view (Fig. 3.1).

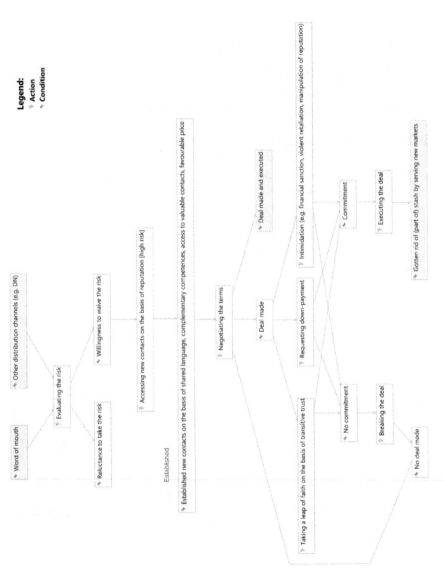

Legend:
↯ Action
✦ Condition

Figure 3.2 Conceptual model "making and executing a deal"

3.5.3   *What does ABM add to ethnography?*

In the same way as Heemskerk (2003) argues that "anthropology and scenario planning will benefit from cross-fertilization" (p. 932), we contend that ethnography and ABM are mutually beneficial (Tubaro and Casilli, 2010). In the previous section, we saw how a focus on roles and actions moves ABM from being agent-based to more action-based. In this section, we described how combining ethnography and ABM allows the latter to act at a more microscopic level of analysis and, hence, allows for "a richer variety of possible futures" (Heemskerk, 2003: 932). The question that now begs an answer is what then does ABM add to ethnography?

First, adding "what-if" relations embedded in the various condition-action sequences potentially lifts ethnography out of the micro scene level of analysis and helps in understanding how those micro-mechanisms may lead to the emergent macro-phenomenon (Zackery et al., 2016). ABM then aids in dissecting how macro-phenomena emerge from micro-situations. Here, the distinction between micro and macro is one of action and structure (Knorr-Cetina, 1981). The ethnographer by means of ABM arrives at (multiple) generalized patterns of meaning, however, still embedded in situated action (i.e., not abstracted from the "what is going on" in a particular social situation). That is what we refer to as the *thick conditional*.

Second, whereas the outcome of ethnography is per definition a static representation, "freezing societies in time" (Fabian, 1983), ABM may be used to attain a process view in the coding of data, rendering the ethnographic representation dynamic. Extrapolating insights into how people make, break, and sustain their new partnerships under conditions of an increasingly supply-driven market introduces such a dynamic (for instance with respect to growing into new roles as well as transitioning between different regimes of reputation building). Hence, putting ABM and ethnography together means accounting not only for sociocultural logic but also for sociocultural *change* (Heemskerk, 2003).

Third, ethnographic ABM enables backward tracing as well. That is to say, not only in the model development phase as described in this chapter, but also for the analysis of the simulation outcomes, ethnographic ABM enables the tracing of processes and circumstances that give rise to a particular phenomenon. Here, the ethnographic approach to modelling becomes relevant, as only the ethnographic diagnosis of micro scenes enables a tracing of the processes involved in the field. This is a unique feature of the more descriptive micro-level approach to simulation modelling preserving contextualized meaning. In the case of an ethnographic social simulation of the cocaine transit trade in the Netherlands, this may aid in revealing the cultural logic of reputation building under the various degrees of supply- and demand-driven markets for instance.

3.6   Concluding remarks and future work

This chapter has shown that an ethnographic foundation of the formulation of the rules of an agent-based social simulation has the following three advantages for crime research. First, ethnographic social simulation, through the mud of observations of intersubjective doings and knowings in a micro setting, enables the crime researcher to arrive at meaningful evidence and at an understanding of group-level organizing principles. Ethnographic social simulation adds the explication of meaning to the generative explanations of agent-based social simulation (Epstein, 2006) and, hence, connects ABM to the interpretive paradigm in social theory. This stands in contrast to the increased reliance in policing and crime research on large-scale abstractions based on statistics and a focus on individual trajectories into crime. With Heemskerk (2003), we are here "not arguing for a replacement of statistical models but rather for the use of ethnographic data to enrich thinking about the future" (p. 934). Second, by combining ethnographic research (with an eye to intersubjective meaning and the intelligible context of knowledge claims) with agent-based social simulation (equipped to explore how various scenarios might potentially and realistically evolve), ethnographic social simulation enables us to move microscopic understanding to the emergent macro level of the (criminal) phenomenon. Third, due to the inclusion of time series in ABM, ethnographic simulation modelling is characterized by a focus on processes, i.e., a dynamic instead of a static representation. Due to these features, ethnographic simulation modelling enables the extrapolation of trends as well as back tracing to the conditions that instantiated particular (reputation-building) mechanisms and, hence, network formations. Altogether, we contend that ethnographic social simulation may very well result in what we referred to in the introduction as "data with depth". Especially in view of the increasing availability of big data in policing and crime research, in the form of confiscated encrypted communication, such a methodology combining the best of interpretive social science and formalist approaches of the computational sciences is called for. Altogether, this will provide an insight into possible prospective futures. Notably, the aim of the approach outlined in this chapter is not *predicting* but *understanding*, i.e., understanding on the basis of a large variety of plausible stories generated by ABM, including counterfactual ones.

This chapter has outlined the conceptual foundations of developing conceptual models based on meaningful evidence by connecting the interpretative ethnography of Geertz with ABM to safeguard the quality of the ethnographic work done in ethnographic simulation modelling. Thus, in this chapter, we reflected on theory in ethnographic simulation modelling which implies reflecting on the work of interpretation done so as to arrive at meaning in the *input* of a conceptual model as the very first basis of an interpretive account to ABM. The next chapter will go into the technical details of how to implement such an approach on a computational level.

Notes

1 Such as the liquidation of the lawyer of one of the crown witnesses in the Marengo trial in September 2019.
2 Examples include software for calculating the risk of recidivism applied in many US states (Angwin et al., 2016). In this field, computational technologies are already applied on a commercial level.

3 See Edmonds et al. (2019) for a comprehensive discussion of the problems and pitfalls of various modelling purposes.
4 Import trade concerns the import of cocaine from abroad; retail concerns the supply of cocaine to the end consumer.
5 "Trace ethnography extends forms of documentary ethnography to environments that are not amenable to simple observation: for instance, online environments in which collaboration is facilitated through digital 'traces' of action like logs and records, which may seem like incomprehensible markup to outsiders but are deeply meaningful to community members" (Thomer and Wickett, 2020: 1).
6 The ethnographic paradigm adhered here belongs to the semiotic paradigmatic stance of Geertz (thick description) and Spradley (semantic analysis). The implicit assumption of Geertz's thick description is that meaning is derived from the native's point of view. The implicit assumption of Spradley's semantic analysis is that meaning may be inferred from people's linguistic practices (Van Maanen, 1980).
7 Ethnographic simulation modelling, relying heavily on stakeholder interpretation, asks for a broader notion of researcher reflexivity than is common in ethnography. This broader understanding of reflexivity may be referred to as "interpretive reflexivity" (Lichterman, 2017) and includes being transparent about the established rapport with the various domain experts as well as about their respective social positions.

References

Ahrweiler, P. and Gilbert, N. (2009) 'The epistemologies of social simulation research', in Squazzoni, F. (ed.) *Epistemological aspects of computer simulations in the social sciences.* Berlin: Springer, pp. 12–28.
Amoore, L. and Piotukh, V. (2015) 'Life beyond big data: Governing with little analytics', *Economy and Society,* 44(3), pp. 341–366.
Angwin, J., Larson, J., Mattu, S. and Kirchner, L. (2016) Machine bias: There's software used across the country to predict future criminals. And it's biased against blacks. *ProPublica,* 23 May. Retrieved from: www.propublica.org/article/machine-bias-risk-assessmentsin-criminal-sentencing (last accessed 10 February 2021).
Axelrod, R. (1997) *The complexity of cooperation: Agent-based models of competition and collaboration.* Princeton: Princeton University Press.
Axtell, R. (2000). Why agents? On the varied motivations for agent computing in the social sciences. *Center on Social and Economic Dynamics,* Working Paper No. 17, November 2000.
Bennato, D. (2021) 'The digital traces' diamond. A proposal to put together a quantitative approach, interpretive methods, and computational tools', *Italian Sociological Review,* 11(4S), pp. 207–224.
Birks, D. and Davies, T. (2017) 'Street network structure and crime risk: An agent-based investigation of the encounter and enclosure hypothesis', *Criminology,* 55(4), pp. 900–937.
Birks, D., Stewart, A. and Townsley, M. (2012) 'Generative explanations of crime: Using simulation to test criminological theory', *Criminology,* 50(1), pp. 221–254.
Blok, A. and Pedersen, M. A. (2014) 'Complementary social science? Quali-quantitative experiments in a Big Data world', *Big Data & Society,* 1(2), pp. 1–6.
Bosse, T. and Gerritsen, C. (2008). *Agent-based simulation of the spatial dynamics of crime: On the interplay between criminal hotspots and reputation.* Proceedings of the 7th conference on autonomous agents and multiagent systems, volume 2, Estoril, Spain, 12–16 May 2008, 1129–1136.

Brantingham, P. and Brantingham, P. (2004) 'Computer simulation as a tool for environmental criminologists', *Security Journal*, 17(1), pp. 21–30.

Chan, J. and Bennett Moses, L. (2016) 'Is big data challenging criminology?', *Theoretical Criminology*, 20(1), pp. 21–39.

Chattoe-Brown, E. (1998) 'Just how (un)realistic are evolutionary algorithms are as representations of social processes?', *Journal of Artificial Societies and Social Simulation*, 1(3), https://www.jasss.org/1/3/2.html

Chattoe-Brown, E. (2011) 'Combining ethnography and game theory using simulation: A critique and development of "can norms account for strategic interaction?" by S. Gezelius', *Sociology*, 46(2), pp. 339–353.

Collins, R. (2009) 'The micro-sociology of violence', *The British Journal of Sociology*, 60(3), pp. 566–576.

Cornelius, C., Gore, R. and Lynch, C. (2017) 'Aging out of crime. Exploring the relationship between age and crime with agent-based modelling', in Zhang, Y. and Madey, G. (eds.) *SpringSim ADS 2017, Proceedings of the agent-directed simulation symposium*. San Diego: Society for Modeling and Simulation International, pp. 1–12.

Crawford, K. (2013). The hidden biases in big data. *Harvard Business Review*. Retrieved from http://blogs.hbr.org/2013/04/the-hidden-biases-in-big-data (accessed 28 January 2020).

Dirksen, V., Van der Leest, W. and Vermeulen, I. (2021) 'Netwerken van netwerken in transit. De doorvoer van cocaïne via Nederland', *Tijdschrift voor Criminologie*, 63(2), pp. 129–145.

Duijn, P. A. C. (2016) '*Detecting and disrupting criminal networks: A data driven approach*', PhD thesis, Universiteit van Amsterdam, Amsterdam.

Duijn, P. A. C., Kashirin, V. and Sloot, P. M. (2014) 'The relative ineffectiveness of criminal network disruption', *Scientific Reports*, 4, p. 4238.

Duxbury, S. and Haynie, D. (2019) 'Criminal network security: An agent-based approach to evaluating network security', *Criminology*, 57(2), pp. 314–342.

Eck, J. and Liu, L. (2008) 'Contrasting simulated and empirical experiments in crime prevention', *Journal of Experimental Criminology*, 4, pp. 195–213.

Edmonds, B. (2015) 'Using qualitative evidence to inform the specification of agent-based models', *Journal of Artificial Societies and Social Simulation*, 18(1). https://www.jasss.org/18/1/18/18.pdf

Edmonds, B. (2020) 'Co-developing beliefs and social influence networks – Towards understanding socio-cognitive processes like Brexit', *Quality & Quantity*, 54(2), pp. 491–515.

Edmonds, B., Le Page, C., Bithel, M., Chattoe-Brown, E., Grimm, V., Meyer, R., Montanola-Sales, C., Ormerod, P., Root, H. and Squazzoni, F. (2019) 'Different modelling purposes', *Journal of Artificial Societies and Social Simulation*, 22(3). https://www.jasss.org/22/3/6.html

Edmonds, B. and Moss, S. (2005) 'From KISS to KIDS – An 'anti-simplistic' modelling approach', in Davidsson, P., Logan, B. and Takadama, K. (eds.) *Multi-agent based simulation 2004*. Berlin: Springer, pp. 130–144.

Elish, M. C. and Boyd, D. (2018) 'Situating methods in the magic of big data and AI', *Communication Monographs*, 85, pp. 57–80.

Epstein, J. (2006) *Generative social science: Studies in agent-based computational modelling*. Princeton: Princeton University Press.

Fabian, J. (1983) *Time and the other: How anthropology makes its object*. New York: Columbia University Press.

Flores, A. W., Bechtel, K. and Lowenkamp, C. T. (2016) 'False positives, false negatives, and false analyses: A rejoinder to machine bias: There's software used across the country to predict future criminals. And it's biased against blacks', *Federal Probation*, 80(2), pp. 38–46.

Fuller, T. (2017) 'Anxious relationships: The unmarked futures for post-normal scenarios in anticipatory systems', *Technological Forecasting and Social Change*, 124, pp. 41–50.

Geertz, C. (1973) *The interpretation of cultures: Selected essays.* New York: Basic Book, pp. 3–30.

Geertz, C. (1983) *Local knowledge: Further essays in interpretive anthropology.* New York: Basic Books.

Geertz, C. (1999). A life of learning: Charles Homer Haskins Lecture for 1999. *American Council of Learned Societies: Occasional Paper* 45. Charles Homer Haskins lecture.

Geiger, R. S. and Ribes, D. (2011) 'Trace ethnography: Following coordination through documentary practices', in *2011 44th Hawaii international conference on system sciences.* New York, NY: IEEE, pp. 1–10.

Giddens, A. (1987) *Social theory and modern sociology.* Cambridge: Polity Press.

Granovetter, M. (1973) 'The strength of weak ties', *American Journal of Sociology*, 78, pp. 1360–1380.

Greene, J. R. (2014) 'New directions in policing: Balancing prediction and meaning in police research', *Justice Quarterly*, 31(2), pp. 193–228.

Groff, E. (2008) 'Characterizing the spatio-temporal aspects of routine activities and the geographic distribution of street robbery', in Liu, L. and Eck, J. E. (eds.) *Artificial crime analysis systems.* Hershey, PA: IGI Global, pp. 226–251.

Groff, E. and Badham, J. (2021) 'Examining guardianship against theft', in Gerritsen, C. and Elffers, H. (eds.) *Agent-based modelling for criminological theory testing and development.* London: Routledge, pp. 71–103.

Groff, E. and Birks, D. (2008) 'Simulating crime prevention strategies: A look at the possibilities', *Policing*, 2(2), pp. 175–184.

Groff, E., Johnson, S. and Thornton, A. (2019) 'State of the art in agent-based modelling of urban crime: An overview', *Journal of Quantitative Criminology*, 35(1), pp. 155–193.

Hedström, P. and Ylikoski, P. (2010) 'Causal mechanisms in the social sciences', *Annual Review of Sociology*, 36, pp. 49–67.

Heemskerk, M. (2003) 'Scenarios in anthropology: Reflections on possible futures of the Suriname Maroons', *Futures: The Journal of Policy, Planning and Futures Studies*, 35(9), pp. 931–949.

Kitchin, R. and Lauriault, T. (2014). Towards critical data studies: Charting and unpacking data assemblages and their work. *The Programmable City Working Paper 2*, pp. 1–19.

Knorr-Cetina, K. (1981) 'The micro-sociological challenge of macro-sociology: Towards a reconstruction of theory and methodology', in Knorr-Cetina, K. and Cicourel, A. V. (eds.) *Advances in social theory and methodology: Toward an integration of micro- and macro-sociologies.* London: Routledge, pp. 1–47.

Kruisbergen, E. W., Van de Bunt, H. G. and Kleemans, E. R. (2012) *Georganiseerde Criminaliteit in Nederland. Vierde Rapportage op Basis van de Monitor Georganiseerde Criminaliteit.* Den Haag: Boom Lemma.

Lettieri, N., Malandrino, D. and Vicidomini, L. (2017) 'By investigation, I mean computation', *Trends in Organized Crime*, 20(1/2), pp. 31–54.

Li Vigni, F. (2020) 'Five anticipation communities in complex systems science. Complexity science and its vision of the future', *Futures: The Journal of Policy, Planning and Futures Studies*, 120, p. 102551.

Lichterman, P. (2017) 'Interpretive reflexivity in ethnography', *Ethnography*, 18(1), pp. 35–45.

Lotzmann, U. and Neumann, M. (2017) 'Simulation for interpretation. A methodology for growing virtual cultures', *Journal of Artificial Societies and Social Simulation*, 20(3), p. 13. https://www.jasss.org/20/3/13.html

Malleson, M., Evans, A. and Jenkins, T. (2010) 'An agent-based model of burglary', *Environment and Planning B: Planning and Design*, 36(6), pp. 1103–1123.

Malm, A., Bichler, G. and Van De Walle, S. (2010) 'Comparing the ties that bind criminal networks: Is blood thicker than water?', *Security Journal*, 23, pp. 52–74.

Marres, N. (2012) 'The redistribution of methods: On intervention in digital social research, broadly conceived', *The Sociological Review*, 60(1), pp. 139–165.

Molijn, C. (2020). Interview: We hebben een spin in het web weten te traceren. Jil Coster van Voorhout, socioloog en jurist. *NRC Handelsblad*, 3 January. Retrieved from: https://www.nrc.nl/nieuws/2020/01/03/we-hebben-een-spin-in-het-web-weten-te-traceren-a3985657/ (last accessed 26 February 2021).

Moss, S. (2008) 'Alternative approaches to the empirical validation of agent-based models', *Journal of Artificial Societies and Social Simulation*, 11(5). http://jasss.soc.surrey.ac.uk/11/1/5.html.

Munk, A., Olesen, A. and Jacomy, M. (2022) 'The thick machine: Anthropological AI between explanation and explication', *Big Data & Society*, 9(1). https://journals.sagepub.com/doi/full/10.1177/20539517211069891

Mützel, S. (2015) 'Facing Big Data: Making sociology relevant', *Big Data & Society*, 2(2), pp. 1–4.

Nardin, G., Andrighetto, G., Conte, R., Székely, Á, Anzola, D., Elsenbroich, C., Lotzmann, U., Neumann, M., Punzo, V. and Troitzsch, K. G. (2016) 'Simulating protection rackets: A case study of the Sicilian mafia', *Autonomous Agents and Multi-Agent Systems*, 30(6), pp. 1117–1147.

Paolucci, M. and Sabater, J. (2006) 'Introduction to the special section on reputation in agent societies', *Journal of Artificial Societies and Social Simulation*, 9(1) https://www.jasss.org/9/1/16/16.pdf

Perry, W. L. (2013) *Predictive policing: The role of forecast in law enforcement operations*. Santa Monica: RAND.

Porter, M. E. (1979) 'How competitive forces shape strategy', *Harvard Business Review*, 57(2), pp. 137–145.

Powell, W. and DiMaggio, P. (eds.) (1991) *The new Institutionalism in Organizational Analysis*. Chicago: University of Chicago Press.

Rostrami, A., Mondani, H., Liljeros, F. and Edling, C. (2017) 'Criminal organizing applying the theory of partial organization to four cases of organized crime', *Trends in Organized Crime*, 21(4), pp. 315–342.

Sampson, R. (2013) 'The place of context: A theory and strategy for criminology's hard problems', *Criminology*, 51(1), pp. 1–31.

Scherer, S., Wimmer, M. A., Lotzmann, U., Moss, S. and Pinotti, D. (2015) 'An evidence-based and conceptual model-driven approach for agent-based policy modelling', *Journal of Artificial Societies and Social Simulation*, 18(3). https://www.jasss.org/18/3/14.html

58   *Vanessa Dirksen, Martin Neumann, and Ulf Lotzmann*

Scherer, S., Wimmer, M. A. and Markisic, S. (2013) 'Bridging narrative scenario texts and formal policy modelling through conceptual policy modelling', *Artificial Intelligence and Law*, 21(4), pp. 455–484.

Scholz, G., Eberhard, T., Ostrowski, R. and Wijermans, N. (2021) 'Social identity in agent-based models—Exploring the state of the art', in Ahrweiler, P. and Neumann, M. (eds.) *Advances in social simulation, proceedings of the 15th social simulation conference*. Cham: Springer, pp. 59–64.

Schwandt, T. (2014) *The Sage dictionary of qualitative inquiry*. London: Sage.

Spradley, J. (1980) *Participant observation*. New York: Holt, Rinehart and Winston.

Thomer, A. K. and Wickett, K. M. (2020) 'Relational data paradigms: What do we learn by taking the materiality of databases seriously?', *Big Data & Society*, January–June, pp. 1–16.

Townsley, M. and Birks, D. J. (2008) 'Building better crime simulations: Systematic replication and the introduction of incremental complexity', *Journal of Experimental Criminology*, 4, pp. 309–333.

Tubaro, P. and Casilli, A. (2010) 'An ethnographic seduction: How qualitative research and agent-based models can benefit each other', *Bulletin of Sociological Methodology*, 106(1), pp. 59–74.

UNODC (United Nations Office on Drugs and Crime) (2020) *World Drug Report 2020. Vol. 3: Drug Supply*. United Nations publication.

Van Maanen, J. (1980) 'Participant observation by James P. Spradley; the ethnographic interview by James P. Spradley', *Administrative Science Quarterly*, 25(3), pp. 526–530.

Voinov, A., Jenni, K., Gray, S., Kolagani, N., Glynn, P. D., Bommel, P., Prell, C., Zellner, M., Paolisso, M., Jordan, R., Sterling, E., Schmitt-Olabisik, L., Giabbanelli, P., Sun, Z., Le Page, C., Elsawaho, S., BenDor, T. J., Hubacek, K., Laursens, B. K., Jettert, A., Basco-Carrera, L., Singer, A., Young, L., Brunacini, J. and Smajgl, A. (2018) 'Tools and methods in participatory modelling: Selecting the right tool for the job', *Environmental Modelling and Software*, 109, pp. 232–255.

Wang, X., Liu, L. and Eck, J. E. (2008) 'Crime simulation using GIS and artificial intelligent agents', in Liu, L. and Eck, J. E. (eds.) *Artificial crime analysis systems*. Hershey, PA: IGI Global, pp. 209–225.

Weber, M. (1968) 'Objektive Möglichkeit und adäquate Verursachung in der historischen Kausalbetrachtung', in Winckelmann, J. (ed.) *Gesammelte Aufsätze zur Wissenschaftslehre*. Tübingen: Mohr, pp. 266–290.

Weisburd, D., Braga, A. A., Groff, E. R. and Wooditch, A. (2017) 'Can hot spots policing reduce crime in urban areas? An agent-based simulation', *Criminology*, 55(1), pp. 137–173.

Wimmer, M. A. (2011). Open government in policy development: From collaborative scenario texts to formal policy models. *Lecture Notes in Computer Science (Including Subseries Lecture Notes in Artificial Intelligence and Lecture Notes in Bioinformatics)*, 6536 LNCS, 76–91.

Zackery, A., Shariatpanahi, P., Zolfagharzadeh, M. M. and Pourezzat, A. A. (2016) 'Toward a simulated replica of futures: Classification and possible trajectories of simulation in futures studies', *Futures: The Journal of Policy, Planning and Futures Studies*, 81, pp. 40–53.

4 A framework for simulation in interpretive research*

Growing criminal culture

Martin Neumann and Ulf Lotzmann

4.1 Introduction

Epstein's famous postulate "if you didn't grow it you didn't explain it" (Epstein, 2006) of the programme of a generative social science captures in a nutshell the explanatory account of agent-based social simulation. Agent-based models enable to generate macro-social patterns through the local interaction of individual agents (Squazzoni et al., 2014). Classical examples include the segregation of residential patterns in the Schelling model, the emergence of equilibrium prices (Epstein and Axtell, 1996), or local conformity and global diversity of cultural patterns (Axelrod, 1997). Insofar as the scientific investigation observes the phenomena of, e.g. segregation or a pricing process from outside (as macroscopic patterns rather than from the perspective of individual agents), this programme is an explanatory account also in contrast to ethnographic and cultural studies in the classical divide between explanation and understanding in the social sciences (see, e.g. von Wright, 1971; Manninen and Tuomela, 1976). While agent-based modelling (ABM) is used already for long time in ethnographic and archaeological research for investigating, for instance, spatial population dynamics (Mithen, 1994; Kohler and Gumerman, 2000; Burg et al., 2016), it is less used in ethnographic and cultural studies attempting at uncovering hidden meaning attached to the phenomenology of action in foreign cultures. Typically, this is done by interpretative research using qualitative methods such as thick description (Geertz, 1973). Simulation modelling is often regarded as akin to analytical sociology, attempting to reveal causal patterns, i.e. explaining the "cogs and wheels" (Elster, 1989) of processes that bring about social structures. From this perspective, cultural studies provide merely descriptions (as indicated already in the notion of "thick description") or typologies (Hedström, 2005) but have no explanatory power. While the current state of research and theory in social science is often

* This chapter is based on the following article: Lotzmann, U. and Neumann, M. (2017) 'Simulation for interpretation. A methodology for growing virtual cultures', *Journal of Artificial Societies and Social Simulation*, 20(3). https://www.jasss.org/20/3/13.html

DOI: 10.4324/9781003393207-4

described as "hyperdifferentiated" (Turner, 2006), simulation and interpretation are often perceived as opposing poles of the various types of sociological research. This chapter provides the technical foundations to prove the contrary: at least it is possible to use simulation as a tool in a research process that facilitates interpretation. While applying the generative paradigm, the objective is growing artificial culture, i.e. an artificial perspective from within the subjective attribution of meaning to social situations.

The research process was developed during the EU FP 7 project Gloders. As the project involved stakeholders from the police in a participatory modelling process (Barreteau et al., 2003; Nguyen-Duc and Drogul, 2007; Möllenkamp et al., 2010; Le Page et al., 2015) for providing virtual experiences to police officers, the objective of the research process is the cross-fertilization of simulation and interpretation. The example that is used in this chapter is the investigation of criminal culture. Even though criminal culture emerges in Westernized industrial countries (at least the one investigated in this chapter was European), norms and codes of conduct of the "underworld" nevertheless remain alien to the "upper world". As the criminal world remains covert and outside the social order which is secured by the state monopoly of violence, criminal culture might be regarded as foreign to aboriginal cultures which provide the role model of ethnographic research. However, as soon as crime is undertaken collectively, i.e. in the domain of organized crime, the necessity for standards that regulate interactions emerges in the criminal world as well as in the legal society. Thus, criminal culture provides a perfect example for studying the emergence of a self-organized system of social norms; that means culture. The focus of this chapter is on methodology, namely the research process starting from unstructured textual data and ending up in simulation results which can recursively be traced back to the starting point of the research process. Results concerning content are documented elsewhere (Lotzmann and Neumann 2017; Neumann and Lotzmann 2017). The research process entails two perspectives, an analysis and – additionally to the previous chapter – a modelling perspective, which are recursively related to each other.

- Analysis perspective: The process of recovering information within the empirical data from which certain simulation model elements are derived.
- Modelling perspective: The structured process of the development of a simulation model and the performing of simulation experiments based on the empirical data.

Thus, the relation between data, research question, and methodology has to be considered carefully. The development of the research process is closely oriented to the modelling process developed in the EU funded OCOPOMO project (Scherer et al., 2013, www.ocopomo.eu) but has been adapted and extended by an interpretative perspective. While for the modelling perspective the process of conceptual modelling, model transformation, and implementation of declarative rule-based models has been extended by an initial qualitative data analysis (extending the scenario input proposed in OCOPOMO), for the analysis perspective the traceability concept (Scherer et al. 2013, 2015) is utilized for developing virtual narratives that facilitate interpretative research (i.e. referring back to the initial qualitative analysis). This reveals the meaning attributed to the phenomenology of a situation to finally enable growing criminal culture in the simulation lab.

The rest of the chapter is structured as follows: Section 4.2 provides a brief overview of the concept of thick description as the methodology of interpretative research. Next, the research process is described in detail in Section 4.3. This consists of several steps: in Section 4.3.1, it is shown how concepts are identified by qualitative text analysis of police interrogations. Section 4.3.2 outlines how concept identification enables conceptual modelling of the concept relations. Subsequently, in Section 4.3.2.1 an example is provided of how conceptual modelling enables investigating how participants in the field assign meaning to the phenomenology action. Section 4.3.3 shows how a simulation model is derived from the conceptual model and an example of the analysis of a simulation is provided in Section 4.3.3.1. Finally, in Section 4.3.3.2 a narrative storyline of the simulation outlines how simulation facilitates to get in contact with foreign cultures.

4.2 Thick description in cultural studies

An explanatory account to social theory attempts to find general laws in analogy to, e.g. the laws of mechanics, such as laws of power, stratification, or pricing mechanisms. In contrast, a central element of an interpretative approach to the social world is an attempt of comprehending how participants in a social encounter perceive a particular concrete situation from within their worldview. Instead of observing from the outside, interpretation attempts to comprehend social interaction from inside the social actors. As it has been outlined in Chapter 1 after the introduction, it has for long been the subject of many debates how this can be achieved ranging from philosophical speculation, such as Dilthey (1976) who coined the term understanding, to various methods in qualitative empirical research. A particularly famous approach to interpretative research is the concept of thick description. Originally coined by Clifford Geertz as a method for participant observation in ethnographic research, the concept quickly traversed to various disciplines such as general sociology, psychology, or education research (Denzin, 1989; Ponterotto, 2006).

Geertz owes the term thick description to the philosopher Gilbert Ryle (1971). Citing Ryle, Geertz considers "two boys rapidly contracting the eyelids of their right eyes. In one, this is an involuntary twitch; in the other, a conspiratorial signal to a friend. The two movements are, as movements, identical; from an I-am-a-camera, 'phenomenalistic' observation of them alone, one could not tell which was twitch and which was wink, or indeed whether both or either was twitch or wink. Yet the difference, however unphotographable, between a twitch and a wink is vast ..." (Geertz, 1973: 312). This example describes the step from a phenomenology of a situation to the meaning attributed to it. This move from what Geertz, following Ryle, denotes as a step from "thin" to "thick" description has been influential for an interpretative theory of culture. Geertz provides an example of a drama in the highlands of Morocco in 1912 in which different interpretations of a particular sequence of interactions by various ethnic groups (including Berber, Jews, and French imperial forces) generated a chaotic dissolution of traditional social order: one man had been hijacked by a Berber clan. In compensation, he stole the sheep of the clan. However, subsequently he negotiated that a certain amount of sheep was a legitimate compensation for the raid. But when he came back to the town ruled by French forces, they arrested him for theft. The example serves as a demonstration of an interpretative concept of culture. Resembling Wittgenstein's theory of language games, Geertz argues that culture is public symbolic action. In the example above, the reactions of the different cultural groups failed to be meaningful for the other groups because all parties (in particular the French forces) had a different view of the meaning of the action of the other parties. In consequence, it comes to a confusion of tongues (Geertz, 1973). Twinkling or stealing sheep has different meanings in different cultures. Thus, meaning is important for social order because the reaction to what is perceived as a conspiratorial wink is different than to an involuntary eye movement, say because of the sunlight.

The implication for investigating cultures is that anthropology is an interpretation of interpretations. The task of a cultural analysis is signifying and interpreting the subjects of study, may it be criminals, Berber or Frenchmen (Denzin, 1989). This calls for a microscopic diagnosis of specific situations in a manner that enables a reader of a different cultural background to grasp the meaning that the subjects of the investigation attribute to it. The role of theory in the interpretative account of thick description is to provide a vocabulary to get in conversation across cultures (Geertz, 1973). Such a vocabulary should "produce for the readers the feeling that they have experienced, or could experience, the events being described in a study" (Creswell and Miller, 2000: 129). Thus, the objective of a thick description is providing narrative storylines of the field (Corbin and Strauss, 2008). In the following, we will outline a research process for developing artificial narratives that generate virtual experiences. This enables extending the generative paradigm for growing artificial cultures.

4.3   The research process

In fact, agent-based based modelling has a number of properties that coincide with the account of a thick description: ABM studies the interaction of individual agents on a microscopic level (Squazzoni et al., 2014), in relation between cognition and interaction (Nardin et al., 2016). Likewise, qualitative data is increasingly used for the development of agent rules (Edmonds, 2015; Ghorbani et al., 2015; Dilaver, 2015; Fieldhouse et al., 2016). Nevertheless, it is rarely the intention of agent-based research to get into conversation with the agents. In the following, we describe a process of deriving agent rules from interpretative empirical research methods. Applying the rules in simulation experiments enables the investigation of socio-cognitive coupling: individuals reasoning about other individuals' minds by taking into account a shared social context. That means the agents attribute meaning to the observed behaviour of other agents.

This is undertaken here in the example of the investigation of police files documenting intra-organizational processes within a criminal network, leading to the internal collapse of a criminal organization. Studying intra-organizational norms is faced with the problem of cognitive complexity. For an analysis of intra-organizational norms, detailed information about the motivation and subjective perceptions of the individuals involved in this process is necessary. This calls for tools which support less handling of numerical amounts of data but rather detailed interpretative research methods. For this purpose, *first*, MAXQDA (www.maxqda.de) as a standard tool for computer-assisted qualitative data analysis (CAQDAS) has been selected for this particular research question. *Next*, the interface between interpretative research and development of agent rules in formal modelling draws on the tools that have been developed in the OCOPOMO project, more specifically CCD (Scherer et al., 2013, 2015) and DRAMS (Lotzmann and Meyer, 2011), which enable to preserve traceability of agent rules to the empirical evidence base (Lotzmann and Wimmer, 2013). These tools are part of the OCOPOMO toolbox developed in previous research to achieve empirically founded simulation results. Finally, the results of the simulation are traced back to an interpretative framework for dissecting – in this particular case, criminal – culture.

Data basis are police interrogations of witnesses as well as suspects involved in the collapse of the criminal group which provides the case. Police interrogations can be described as situations of dialogical conversation, allowing for an in-depth analysis of subjective meaning attributed to certain situations which brings the empirical analysis very close to the subjective perception of the actors. The aim is to infer hypothetical, *unobservable* cognitive elements from *observable* actions and statements to analyse cognitive mechanisms that motivate action in very confused and opaque situations. Modelling this cognitive complexity provides a challenge for the foundation of model assumptions. The cognitive complexity can be contrasted to numerical complexity, and both require different forms of analysis. For this reason, a procedure has been developed that describes a controlled process from qualitative evidence to agent rules in order to arrive at a thick description of the field. The simulation model is based on a data-driven, evidence-based model. The overall research process is documented in Fig. 4.1.

The figure highlights three elements of the analysis process of the data which provides the foundation for the development of a simulation model. The data analysis is a basically qualitative process which enables to derive detailed model assumptions. The core is the analysis itself, documented in the

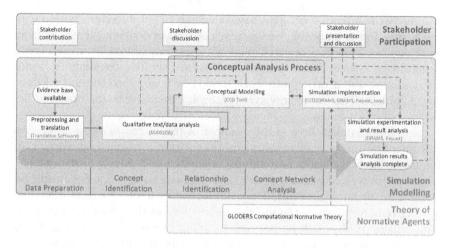

Figure 4.1 Overview of the data analysis process

grey box. The analysis is embedded in a theory of normative agents, developed in prior research in the EMIL project (Conte et al., 2014), and constant stakeholder participation.

The analysis can be grouped into the four processes depicted in Fig. 4.1: data preparation, concept identification, concept relation identification, and concept network analysis. These process steps include various activities which are supported by different software tools. First, data is provided by the stakeholder. This consists of police interrogations of witnesses and suspects. For an analysis of these documents, pre-processing is necessary: data had to be checked for ensuring the protection of privacy, the text was translated, and errors and flaws intruded by certain data pre-processing steps (e.g. OCR, translation) needed to be corrected. Data preparation provides the basis for first identifying concepts in the data.

4.3.1 Concept identification: Qualitative text analysis

In the first step of concept identification, the data was loaded into MAXQDA as a tool for qualitative text analysis (see Corbin and Strauss, 2008). Concepts stand for classes of objects, events, or actions which have some major properties in common. Relevant text passages had to be identified which reveal preliminary concepts, documented in a list of codes. These have been used to annotate further text passages which provide additional information about the concept.

Coding is an iterative process: further text passages give rise to the development of new codes and revision of prior preliminary codes until a stage is reached in which the relevant concepts are identified which should be part of a model of the data. This research design follows an open coding approach. MAXQDA enables to view the text annotations belonging to a certain code. This enables a proof of consistency and an assessment of the dimensions of the concepts.

Following the so-called member checking procedure for ensuring credibility in qualitative research (Lincoln and Guba, 1985; Hammersley and Atkinson, 1995; Creswell and Miller, 2000; Cho and Trent, 2006), these results have been presented to the stakeholder in order to ensure the empirical and practical relevance of the concepts. Thus, while not directly the subjects of the investigation had been involved in the research (i.e. criminals), those actors that the research addresses, namely the police, had been part of the participatory research process.

4.3.2 *Relationship identification: Conceptual modelling*

In order to derive a simulation model from the data, in a second step the coding derived with MAXQDA served as the basis for concept relation identification with the CCD tool, which is a piece of software for creating a conceptual model of the processes that can be found by the analysis of the data (Scherer et al., 2013, 2015). Identifying relations between concepts is a central stage for the process view of a simulation approach. This research makes use of an abstract framework of condition-action sequences (Scherer et al., 2013, 2015; Lotzmann and Wimmer, 2013). The web of interrelated sequences is denoted as an action diagram. The concept of condition-action sequences is an a priori methodological device to identify social mechanisms on a micro level of individual (inter)action. Broadly speaking, a mechanism is a relation that transforms an input X into an output Y. A further condition is a certain degree of abstraction, which becomes evident in a certain degree of regularity, i.e. that under similar circumstances a similar input X* yields similar outputs Y*. In the social world, this is typically an action which relates X and Y (Hedström and Ylkoski, 2010). This is assured by the concept of condition-action sequences. Every process is initiated by a certain condition which triggers a certain action. This action in turn generates a new state of the world which is again a condition for further action. Whereas the data describes individual instantiations, the condition-action sequences represent general event classes. For instance, in our case one condition is denoted as "return of investment available". This triggers an action class denoted as "distribute return of investment". Obviously, this condition-action sequence describes classes of events. Return of investment might be rental income as well as purchasing of companies. This methodology enables controlled generalization from the case. The case, however, provides a proof of the existence of the inferred mechanisms. Note that the data basis of interrogations allows including cognitive conditions (such as "fear for life") and actions (such as "member X interprets aggressive action"). For understanding culture, it is essential to retrieve the unobservable meaning attributed to particular situations which are observable at a phenomenological level.

In terms of the research process, data was loaded into the CCD tool. An actor-network diagram was compiled which entails relevant actors and objects of the domain. These provide the basis for the development of an action diagram of the condition-action sequences describing the processes in the domain. The development of the action diagram had to be undertaken in constant comparison with the concepts identified with MAXQDA in the first research step. CCD provides textual annotations for the identified elements like actors, objects, actions, and conditions which ensure empirical traceability. These are imported from the annotations to the MAXQDA codes. This feature provides a benchmark that all the codes and their relevant dimensions derived with MAXQDA are represented in the condition-action sequences (Neumann and Lotzmann, 2014). Note that this is a recursive process: the action diagram had to be constantly revised until a situation of theoretical saturation (Corbin and Strauss, 2008) was reached. Again, the validity was ensured by members checking, i.e. consulting stakeholders.

Finally, the model of the scenario is embedded in a theory of normative agents. The normative reasoning is put in motion in the simulation by rules working on a dedicated part of the agent memory for storing norm-related information, based on the empirical fact base of this scenario. As the theoretical integration is less important for the research process, we move on with an example of a conceptual model of subjective interpretation of situational phenomenology.

4.3.2.1   *Example: Revealing interpretations*

In the following, an example of a conceptual model will be provided that shows how people under study interpret phenomena. That is how people attribute meaning to the phenomenology of situations. Following Geertz, we provide an interpretation of interpretations. As the example of the sheep raid in the Moroccan highlands discussed by Geertz, the example of our research factually is also an instance of the breakdown of social order. In terms of Gertz, it can be described as a confusion of tongues. For the observer, meaning is most easily transparent in the case when it becomes non-transparent for the participants. However, here we concentrate on the methodological issue to demonstrate how conceptual modelling facilitates the dissection of meaning which is the core business of interpretative research and abstain from presenting the full confusion. A detailed description of the example can be found in the next chapter.

Fig. 4.2 exemplarily describes a part of the CCD action diagram. This example, in particular the action "perform aggressive action against member X", will be used in the following to demonstrate the link between annotations as a result of the empirical analysis outlined above, and the simulation modelling, experimentation, and result analysis. Thus, here we recapitulate the illustrations of the previous chapter with a different example. However, in this chapter, we will go further on and demonstrate how conceptual modelling is transformed into simulation models.

Fig. 4.2 shows an abstract event-action sequence which is derived from the data analysis. The box with a dark grey flag represents an event. The action is represented by a box with a light grey flag. Moreover, in bracket we see the possible type of agents that can undertake the action. The arrow represents the

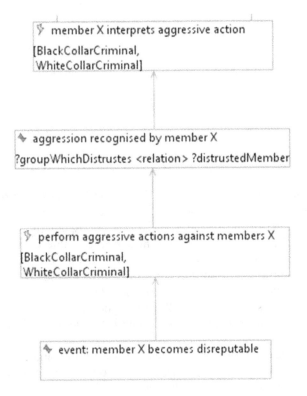

Figure 4.2 Part of CCD action diagram for the initiation of aggression

relation between the event and the action. This is not a deterministic relation. However, the existence of the condition is necessary for triggering the action. Once an action is performed, a new situational condition is created which again triggers new actions. In the figure, the process starts with the event that someone becomes disreputable which triggers the action of performing an act of aggression against this person. When the victim recognizes the aggression, he needs to interpret the motivation. This process of interpretation is displayed in Fig. 4.3.

Two options are considered as possible in the conceptual model. In fact, this is our (i.e. the researchers') interpretation of how the subjects of investigation interpret their experience. However, it is based on a number of instances that had been categorized in the concept identification phase and the credibility has been checked by stakeholder consultation (in terms of validating qualitative research: member checking). Thus Fig. 4.3 shows a branching point in the interpretation: the perceived aggression can be interpreted either as norm enforcement, denoted as the "norm of trust demanded", or as norm deviation, denoted as the "norm of trust violated". At this point, the agents attribute meaning to the phenomenological

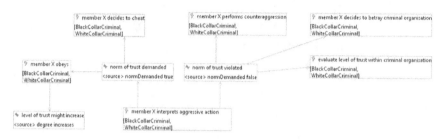

Figure 4.3 Interpretation of aggression

experience of being a victim of aggression. As in Geertz's example of sheep raid, different interpretations are possible. Depending on the interpretation, different action possibilities are triggered. Again this is an abstract cognitive mechanism. However, we show one example of how these abstract mechanisms can be traced back to the data. Starting point is the event that for some reason (out of the scope of the investigation) a member of the organization becomes distrusted (see Fig. 4.2). This initiated a severe aggression as shown in the following annotation[1]:

Annotation (perform aggressive action against member X):"An attack to the life of M."

It remains unclear who commissioned the assassination and for what reason. It shall be noted that it is possible that an attack on the life could be the execution of a death penalty for deviant behaviour. In fact, some years later M. had been killed because he had been accused of stealing drugs. It remains unclear whether this was true or the drugs just got lost for other reasons. However, the murder shows that the death penalty is a realistic option in the interpretation of the attack on his life. However, M. survived the attack which allowed him to reason about the motivation. No evidence can be found in the data about this reasoning. However, it can be found in the data how he reacted.

Annotation (member X decides to betray criminal organization): Statement of gang member V01: "M. told the newspapers 'about my role in the network' because he thought that I wanted to kill him to get the money".

This example allows a reconstruction of possible reasoning, i.e. an interpretation of the field data. First, given the evidence that was available for the police, it is unlikely that this particular member of the organization (V01) mandated the attack. However, the members of the criminal gang had not the time and resources for a criminal investigation as the police would have undertaken. Nevertheless, they had to react quickly in complex situations. In fact, it is not a completely implausible consideration. M. was one of the black collar criminals who invested money in the legal market through the white collar criminals. V01 was a white collar criminal. Thus V01 possessed a considerable amount of drug money which he could have kept for himself if the investor (in this case M.) would be dead. This might be a "rational" incentive for an assassination. Second, it can be noted that M. interpreted the attack on his life not as a penalty (i.e. death penalty) for deviant behaviour from his side.[2] Instead, he concluded that the cause of the attack was based on self-interest (the other criminal "wanted his money"). Thus, he interpreted the attack as norm deviation rather than enforcement (see Fig. 4.3). Next, he attributed the aggression to an individual person and started a counter-reaction against this particular person by betraying "his role in the network". This is an example of an interpretation of how participants in the field make sense of an action from the worldview of their culture. Namely, he interpreted the aggression as a violation of his trust in the gang and reacted by betraying the accused norm violating member. Factually this counter-reaction provoked further conflict escalation. However, for the methodological purpose of demonstrating the research process, we stop at this point (see further empirical detail in the next chapter) and move on to a documentation of how the conceptual model is transformed into a simulation model.

4.3.3 Simulation modelling and experimentation

So far, the exposure of the research process concentrated on the analysis perspective. Now we come to the modelling perspective, as the process of empirical analysis provides the basis for the development of agent rules. The CCD provides an interface to integrate model transformation tools such as CCD-2DRAMS, which supports the semi-automatic transformation of conceptual model constructs into the code of formal models, in this case in declarative code for the distributed rule engine DRAMS. Since DRAMS is implemented in Java, it entails the premises for close integration with Java-based simulation frameworks to extend their functionality. In particular, DRAMS provides abstract agent and model classes to facilitate the integration with RepastJ 3.1 (North et al., 2006). DRAMS as a technological basis for agent behaviour within the simulation model supports both programming and running simulation models and enables traceability of empirical evidence in agent rules and simulation results. According to Lotzmann and Wimmer (2013), a rule engine is a software system that basically consists of the following:

- A fact base, which stores information about the state of the world in the form of facts. A fact contains a number of definable data slots and some administrative information (time of creation, entity that created the fact, durability). The initial fact base builds on the empirical analysis of police interrogations.
- A rule base which stores rules describing how to process certain facts stored in fact bases. A rule consists of a condition part (called left-hand side, LHS) and an action part (called right-hand side, RHS). The rules reflect the actions in the action diagram of the CCD tool.
- An inference engine, which controls the inference process by selecting and processing the rules which can fire on the basis of certain conditions. In the case of DRAMS, this is done in a forward-chaining manner, i.e. trying to draw conclusions from a given fact constellation. The heart of the inference

engine is the data-driven rule schedule, an algorithm deciding which rules to evaluate and fire at each point of time. In order to decide which rules to evaluate for which agent instances, the schedule relies on a data-rule dependency graph.

Calibration of the probabilities in decision points of the agents refers back to the first phase of a qualitative analysis. In the step of the analysis of the textual data, open coding had been created, i.e. annotations of characteristic brief text-elements. These had then been subsumed to broader categories which provide the building blocks of the conceptual model. Their relative frequency is put in use for specifying probabilities. Certainly, these have to be used with caution: first, the categorization entails an element of subjective arbitrariness when subsuming a description of a concrete action under a category such as "outburst of rage", etc. Second, the relative frequencies in data might not be very reliable. As they are based on police interrogations, an event such as an attempted assassination is more likely to be the subject of the interrogation than, e.g. an "outburst of rage". It might well be the case that the respondents did not remember or that the interrogation simply didn't approach the issue. Nevertheless, for instance, the high absolute number of death threats or attempted assassinations compared to other courses of action found in the data provides a hint for the high disposition of violence in the group. Thus given the problem of dark figures inherent in any criminological research, the relative frequencies provide at least a hint to the empirical likelihood of the different courses of action. An example is provided in Table 4.1 of how the likelihood of agents' decisions is informed by the evidence base.

4.3.3.1 Simulation result analysis

This data dependency preserved during the modelling process ensures traceability of the inference such as simulated facts to the data. This facilitates the analysis of simulation results. One of the available analysis tools is the Model Explorer tool, a part of the DRAMS software. Fig. 4.4 shows a screenshot

Table 4.1 Cases from evidence informing the probability for threatening actions

Acts of threat	Severity	Cases in evidence	Inferred probability
Having an eye on you	Low	9	0.264
Outburst of rage	Low	6	0.176
Demanding money in dark forest at midnight	Modest	4	0.118
Death threat	High	11	0.324
Kidnapping	High	3	0.088
Putting a gun into the stomach	High	1	0.030

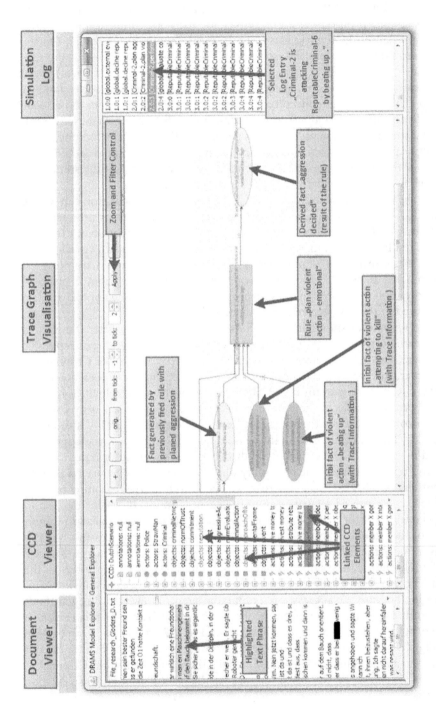

Figure 4.4 Example of exploration of simulation results

of an actual firing of the rule "plan a violent action – emotional", in order to demonstrate a prototypical user interface for analysing simulation results. On the right-hand side, the log files of the simulation run can be found. On the left-hand side, the empirical, textual data is displayed. Both elements, the simulation and the empirical basis, are related by a visualization of the rules fired to transform data into simulation results in the log file and the corresponding CCD elements of the conceptual model. The simulation results can also be written to different kinds of output files, for example, in a dedicated XML format that allows to make the traces persistent. This opens further means for result analysis and presentation to interactively present results together with traces without having to go too much into technical details of the simulation model, which is particularly relevant for stakeholders.

In the following, an example of an interpretation of a simulation run will be provided. Simulation models typically generate outputs such as time series or histograms. Here the output is different: based on the exploration of the simulation results as shown in Fig. 4.4, a simulation run generates a virtual narrative. First, screenshots of an exemplary part of a simulation run are provided (from tick 2 to tick 17 of a simulation run). In the next section, it is shown how the model explorer enables recourse to the open codings of textual data generated in the first step of the qualitative data analysis.

The screenshot shown in Fig. 4.5 displays a scene briefly after the start of the simulation: one randomly selected agent (Criminal 0) became disreputable (indicated by the circle) and had been punished (by Reputable Criminal 1). However, interpreting the aggression, the agent Criminal 0 does not find a norm violation in its event board, the memory of the agent which stores possible norm violations in the past. For this reason, the agent reacts by counter-aggression, namely beating the agent Reputable Criminal 1. This is shown in Fig. 4.5. Fig. 4.6 (left) shows the reasoning of this agent on the aggression faced by the agent Criminal 0. It finds that the offender is not reputable and for this reason excludes the possibility that the aggression had been a punishment. Fig. 4.6 (right) shows the reaction resulting from the reasoning process: namely an attempted assassination of the agent Criminal 0.

The fact that the agent Criminal 0 is still visible on the visualization interface of the model indicates that the attempt has been unsuccessful. For this reason, now the other agent reasons on the aggression as shown in Fig. 4.7 (left). This figure shows that the agent does not interpret the aggression as the death penalty. Potentially the aggression could have been a candidate norm invocation because the aggressor is a reputable agent. However, the agent finds no norm that might have been invoked in its event base. For this reason, it reacts by a further aggression as displayed in Fig. 4.7 (right). As it can be seen in Fig. 4.7 (right), the reaction is again an attempt of an assassination. In this case, the agent Criminal 0 successfully kills the agent Reputable Criminal 1. This is visualized by the disappearance of this agent from the visualization interface.

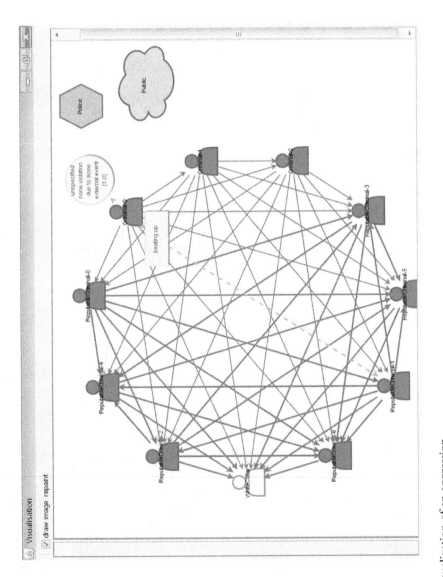

Figure 4.5 Visualization of an aggression

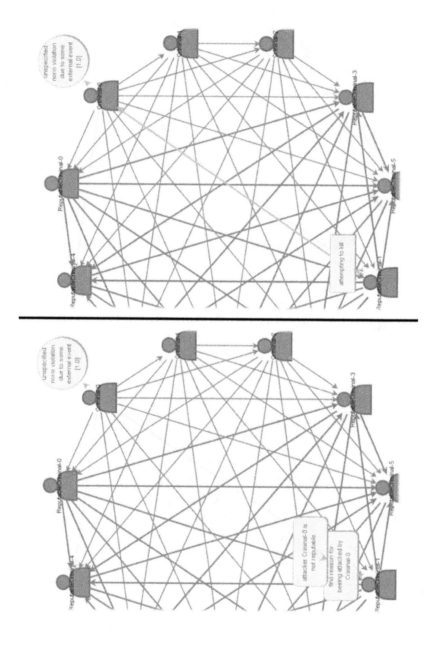

Figure 4.6 Visualization of reasoning on aggression (left) and failed assassination (right)

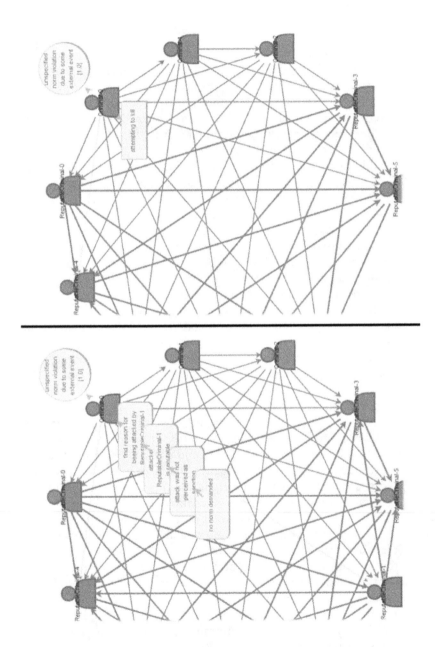

Figure 4.7 Visualization of reasoning on aggression (left) and successful assassination (right)

Here we stop the further elaboration of the simulation run but rather turn to the development of the narrative of this case.

4.3.3.2   *Interpreting simulation: Growing criminal culture*

The simulation runs show how agents act according to rules derived from categories developed by the researchers. This already includes cognitive elements and thus cannot be compared with the "l-am-a-camera" perspective described by Geertz (1973) of a pure phenomenological description of the researcher's observation. Nevertheless, applying the researcher's categories does not suffice for making sense of a culture from the perspective of the worldview of the participants. In terms of the account of a thick description, this still needs to be qualified as a thin description. However, as shown in Fig. 4.4, the rules that are fired during the simulation run can be traced back to open codings of the original textual documents. Following the account of a thick description, a central criterion for sustaining the credibility of a cultural analysis is a sense of verisimilitude (Ponterotto, 2006) which means that the reader gets a feeling to could have experienced the described events (Denzin, 1989). In the same vein, Corbin and Strauss (2008) introduce the notion of a storyline that provides a coherent picture of a case as the theoretical insight of a qualitative analysis.

For this reason, in the description of the scenarios, the rules are now traced back to the original annotations in order to develop narratives of the simulation runs; i.e. the scenarios are a kind of *collage* of the empirical basis of the agent rules. Thus text passages of the police interrogations are decomposed and rearranged according to the rules fired during the simulation run. These are tied together by a verbal description of the rules. In sum, this generates a kind of "crime novel" to get in conversation with a foreign culture (Geertz, 1973). Getting in conversation means that the reader would be able to understand interpretations from the perspective of the insiders' worldview (Donmoyer, 2001) and thereby be empowered to be able to react adequately (at least virtually). As the examples of twinkling in the sunlight or secretly exchanging signs, stealing sheep, or – as in our example – making sense of a failed assassination indicate, being able to grasp the meaning of the phenomenology of action is essential for comprehending an adequate reaction or comprehending why the participants failed to react adequately. In our case of participatory research, the storyline of the simulations provides an archive of virtual experience for empowering of the stakeholders (Creswell and Miller, 2000; Cho and Trent, 2006). Certainly, we do not directly engage in the field for empowering criminals but rather with the police interacting in the field with the subjects under study. Therefore, we provide an example of how a storyline of the simulation described above will look like. RC stands for reputable criminal, C for ordinary criminal, and WC for white collar criminal, who is responsible for money laundering. Italics in the text indicate paraphrases of open codings (characteristic text passages of the original data) of the empirical evidence basis of the fired rules.

The drama starts with an external event. For unknown reasons C0, who never was very reputable became susceptible. It might be due to an unspecified norm violation, but it may not be so and just some bad talk behind the back. Eventually he stole drugs or they got lost. However, at least RC1 and RC4 decided to react on it and agreed that C0 deserves to be severely threatened. The next day RC1 approached C0 and told him that *he will be killed* if he is not loyal to the group. C0 was really scared as he could not find a reason for this offence. He was convinced that the only way to gain reputation was to demonstrate that he is a real man. So *threw the head of RC1 against a lamp pole and kicked him* further on until he sank down to the ground. RC1 didn't know what was happening to him, that such a freak as C0 was beating him down, RC1 one of the most respectable men of the group. There could only be one answer: He pulled his gun and shot. However, while shooting from the ground the bullet missed the body of C0.[3] So he was an easy target for C0. He had no other choice than pulling out his gun as well and shot RC1 down to death.

However, this gunfight decisively shaped the fate of the gang. When the news circulated in the group hectic activities broke out: WC *bough a bulletproofed car* and C1 though about a *new life on the other side of the world, in Australia*. In panic RC6 wanted to severely beat of the offender. While no clear information could be obtained he presumed that C2 must have been the assassinator. So with brute force he beat the shit out of C2 until he was fit for the hospital. *His head was completely deformed, his eyes blue and swollen*. At the same time, RC0 and C2 agreed (wrongly) that it was C1 who killed RC1. While C2 argued that they should kidnap him, the more rational RC0 convinces him that a more modest approach would be wiser. He went to the house of C1 and told him that *his family would have a problem* if he ever will do something similar again. However, when he came back RC2 was already waiting for him: with a *gun in his hand, he said that in the early morning he should come to the forest* for handing out money.

This brief "crime novel" can be described as a "virtual experience". Tracing the simulation runs back to the open codings of the empirical evidence base enables developing a storyline of a virtual case that provides a coherent picture of a case (Corbin and Strauss, 2008). The narrative developed out of the simulation results, including some novel-like dramaturgic elements, brings the simulation model back to the interpretative research which has been the starting point of the qualitative analysis in the first step of the research process. It enables checking if the cognitive heuristics implemented in the agent rules reveal observable patterns of behaviour that can be meaningfully interpreted.

For this reason, the narrative description suggests to be a story of human ac-tors for exploring the plausibility of the simulated scenarios. The plausibility check consists of an investigation of whether the counterfactual composition of single pieces of empirical evidence remains plausible. This means to check if they tell a story that creates a sense of verisimilitude for the stakeholders, but, as we hope, also to the reader.

4.4   Conclusions

It has long been demonstrated that the generative paradigm of agent-based so-cial simulation is useful for explaining social phenomena. So far agent-based social simulation has not been used in interpretative research following the "un-derstanding" paradigm in social science. By extending the generative paradigm to growing artificial cultures, we demonstrate that it can be a useful tool for interpretive research as well. This chapter described the more technical details of the research process to simulate the subjective world view of participants in the field. Starting from an analysis of qualitative data via the development of a con-ceptual model to the development of a simulated narrative, the research process fosters to get in conversation with alien cultures. In the next two chapters, the example that is used here for illustrating the methodology will be described in full detail to demonstrate how this approach can be utilized.

Acknowledgement

The research leading to these results has received funding from the European Union's Seventh Framework Programme (FP7/2007-2013) under grant agreement n° 315874., GLODERS Project.

Notes

1 To preserve the privacy of data, names have been replaced by notations such as M., V01, etc.
2 It shall be noted that also the other interpretation can be found as illustrated in the following in vivo code: "I paid but I'm alive".
3 Note that the following description slightly deviates from the story developed in the simulation: in the simulation, the agents reason about the aggression. In contrast here, there is immediate shooting, which might be regarded as "ad-hoc" reasoning. Similar events can be found in descriptions of other cases of fights between criminals as, for instance, the Sicilian Cosa Nostra (Arlacchi, 1993).

References

Arlacchi, P. (1993). *Mafia von innen – Das Leben des Don Antonino Calderone*. Frank-furt a.M.: S. Fischer Verlag.
Axelrod, R. (1997). *The Complexity of Cooperation. Agent-Based Models of Competition and Collaboration*. Princeton, NJ: Princeton University Press.

Barreteau, O. et al. (2003) 'Our companion modelling approach', *Journal of Artificial Societies and Social Simulation*, 6(1). http://jasss.soc.surrey.ac.uk/6/2/1.html

Burg, M. B., Peeters, H. and Lovis, W. A. (eds.) (2016) *Uncertainty and Sensitivity Analysis in Archaeological Computational Modeling*. Heidelberg: Springer.

Cho, J. and Trent, A. (2006) 'Validity in qualitative research revisited', *Qualitative Research*, 6(3), pp. 319–340.

Conte, R., Andrighetto, G. and Campennì, M. (2014) *Minding Norms: Mechanisms and Dynamics of Social Order in Agent Societies*. Oxford: Oxford University Press.

Corbin, J. and Strauss, A. (2008). *Basics of Qualitative Research*. 3rd edn. Thousand Oaks: Sage.

Creswell, J. W. and Miller, D. A. (2000) 'Determining validity in qualitative inquiry', *Theory into Practice*, 39(3), pp. 124–130.

Denzin, N. K. (1989) *The Research Act: A Theoretical Introduction to Sociological Methods*. 3rd edn. New Jersey: Prentice Hall.

Dilaver, O. (2015) 'From participants to agents: Grounded simulation as a mixed-method research design', *Journal of Artificial Societies and Social Simulation*, 18(1). http://jasss.soc.surrey.ac.uk/18/1/15.html.

Dilthey, W. (1976) *Wilhelm Dilthey: Selected Writings*. Cambridge: Cambridge University Press.

Donmoyer, R. (2001) 'Paradigm talk reconsidered', in Richardson, V. (ed.) *Handbook of Research on Teaching*. 4th edn. Washington, DC: American Educational Research Association, pp. 174–197.

Edmonds, B. (2015) 'Using qualitative evidence to inform the specification of agent-based models', *Journal of Artificial Societies and Social Simulation*, 18(1). http://jasss.soc.surrey.ac.uk/18/1/18.html

Elster, J. (1989) *Nuts and Bolts for the Social Sciences*. Cambridge: Cambridge University Press.

Epstein, J. (2006) *Generative Social Science. Studies in Agent-Based Computational Modelling*. Princeton, NJ: Princeton University Press.

Epstein, J. and Axtell, R. (1996). *Growing Artificial Societies. Social Science from the Bottom-Up*. Washington, DC: Brookings Institution Press.

Fieldhouse, E., Lessard-Phillips, L. and Edmonds, B. (2016) 'Cascade or echo chamber? A complex agent-based simulation of voter turnout', *Party Politics*, 22(2), pp. 241–256.

Geertz, D. (1973) 'Thick description: Toward an interpretive theory of culture', in *The Interpretation of Cultures: Selected Essays*. New York: Basic Books, pp. 3–30.

Ghorbani, A., Dijkema, G. and Schrauwen, N. (2015) 'Structuring qualitative data for agent-based modelling', *Journal of Artificial Societies and Social Simulation*, 18(1). http://jasss.soc.surrey.ac.uk/18/1/2.html

Hammersley, M. and Atkinson, P. (1995) *Ethnography: Principles in Practice*. 2nd edn. London: Routledge.

Hedström, P. (2005) *Dissecting the Social: On the Principles of Analytical Sociology*. Cambridge: Cambridge University Press.

Hedström, P. and Ylkoski, P. (2010) 'Causal mechanisms in the social sciences', *Annual Review of Sociology*, 36, pp. 49–67.

Kohler, T. and Gumerman, G. (eds.) (2000) *Dynamics in Human and Primate Societies*. Oxford: Oxford University Press.

Le Page, C., Bobo, K. S., Kamgaing, T. O. W., Ngahane, B. F. N. and Waltert, M. (2015) 'Interactive simulations with a stylized scale model to codesign with villagers an agent-based model of bushmeat hunting in the periphery of Korup National Park (Cameroon)', *Journal of Artificial Societies and Social Simulation*, 18(1). http://jasss.soc.surrey.ac.uk/18/1/8.html

Lincoln, Y. S. and Guba, E. G. (1985) *Naturalistic Inquiry*. Beverly Hill, CA: Sage.

Lotzmann, U. and Meyer, R. (2011). A declarative rule-based environment for agent modelling systems. *The Seventh Conference of the European Social Simulation Association, ESSA 2011*. Montpellier, France.

Lotzmann, U. and Wimmer, M. (2013). Evidence traces for multi-agent declarative rule-based policy simulation. *Proceedings of the 17th IEEE/ACM International Symposium on Distributed Simulation and Real Time Applications (DS-RT 2013)* (pp. 115–122). IEEE Computer Society. doi:10.1109/ds-rt.2013.20.

Lotzmann, U. and Neumann, M. (2017). A simulation model of intra-organisational conflict regulation in the crime world, in Elsenbroich, C., Gilbert, N. and Anzola, D. (eds.). *Social Dimensions of Organised Crime: Modelling the Dynamics of Extortion Rackets* (pp. 177–213). New York: Springer.

Manninen, J. and Tuomela, R. (eds.) (1976) *Essays on Explanation and Understanding. Studies in the Foundations of Humanities and Social Sciences*. Dordrecht: Reidel.

Mithen, S. (1994) 'Simulating prehistoric hunter-gatherer societies', in Gilbert, N. and Doran, J. (eds.) *Simulating Societies*. London: UCL Press.

Möllenkamp, S., Lamers, M., Huesmann, C., Rotter, S., Pahl-Wostl, C., Speil, K. and Pohl, W. (2010) 'Informal participatory platforms for adaptive management. Insights into niche-finding, collaborative design and outcomes from a participatory process in the Rhine basin', *Ecology and Society*, 15(4). http://www.ecologyandsociety.org/vol15/iss4/art41/

Nardin, L. G., Székely, Á and Andrighetto, G. (2016). GLODERS-S: A simulator for agent-based models of criminal organisations. *Trends in Organized Crime*, 20(1), pp. 85–99.

Neumann, M. and Lotzmann, U. (2014). Modelling the collapse of a criminal network, in: Squazzoni, F., Baronio, F., Archetti, C. and Castellani, M. (eds.), *28th European Conference on Modelling and Simulation, ECMS 2014* (pp. 765–771). European Council for Modeling and Simulation.

Neumann, M. and Lotzmann, U. (2017). 'Text data and computational qualitative analysis', in Elsenbroich, C., Gilbert, N. and Anzola, D. (eds.), *Social Dimensions of Organised Crime: Modelling the Dynamics of Extortion Rackets* (pp. 155–176). New York: Springer.

Nguyen-Duc, M. and Drogul, A. (2007). Using computational agents to design participatory social simulations. *Journal of Artificial Societies and Social Simulation*, 10(4). https://www.jasss.org/10/4/5.html

North, M. J., Collier, N. T. and Vos, J. R. (2006) 'Experiences creating three implementations of the Repast agent modeling toolkit', *ACM Transactions on Modeling and Computer Simulation*, 16(1), pp. 1–25.

Ponterotto, J. G. (2006) 'Brief note on the origins, evolution, and meaning of the qualitative research concept thick description', *The Qualitative Report*, 11(3), pp. 538–549.

Ryle, G. (1971) *Collected Papers. Volume II Collected Essays, 1929–1968*. London: Hutchinson.

Scherer, S., Wimmer, M., Lotzmann, U., Moss, S. and Pinotti, D. (2015) 'An evidence-based and conceptual model-driven approach for agent-based policy modelling', *Journal of Artificial Societies and Social Simulation*, 18(3). https://www.jasss.org/18/3/14.html.

Scherer, S., Wimmer, M. and Markisic, S. (2013) 'Bridging narrative scenario texts and formal policy modeling through conceptual policy modeling', *AI and Law*, 21, pp. 455–484.

Squazzoni, F., Jager, W. and Edmonds, B. (2014) 'Social simulation in the social science. A brief overview', *Social Science Computer Review*, 32(3), pp. 279–294.

Turner, J. (2006) 'Sociological theory today', in Turner, J. (ed.) *Handbook of Sociological Theory*. New York: Springer, pp. 1–17.

von Wright, G. (1971) *Explanation and Understanding*. London: Cornell University Press.

5 Analysis of the breakdown of a criminal network*

Criminal collapse

Martin Neumann and Ulf Lotzmann

5.1 Introduction

In the previous chapters, we elaborated the methodological foundations for an interpretive account to agent-based modelling, ranging from the epistemological foundations to the technical details and software solutions for integrating understanding and computational modelling. Now this chapter and the following chapter provide an example of how the research process is actually put into practice. While this chapter focusses on the analysis perspective by developing a conceptual model from empirical data, the next chapter will highlight the modelling perspective, showing how a simulation model is developed and analysed. The example is an investigation of how social relations within criminal organizations are regulated. We approach the investigation of the modes of organizational behaviour in the crime field from its reverse angle: the breakdown of a criminal group in an escalation of intra-group violence. Specific problems of criminal organizations are rarely investigated (see Diesner et al., 2005 for an example). However, as criminal organizations operate outside the legal world in which social order is secured by the state monopoly of violence (Sofsky, 1996), they face specific problems. In fact, while scientific research approaches criminals mainly as offenders, they are potential victims as well (van Putten, 2012). In the case of a criminal offence, reliance on the law enforcing agencies of the state such as the police comes along with high costs for criminals. For instance, they might be a subject of a criminal prosecution themselves or need to be protected against their former criminal comrades. This provides a source that criminals themselves are highly vulnerable against criminal offences. Therefore, examining the malfunction of a criminal group sheds light on the conditions for their organizational behaviour. For this reason, we apply an organizational science perspective to the investigation of the intra-organizational norms in the criminal world (Weick, 2007; Gottschalk, 2010).

* This chapter is based on Neumann, M. and Lotzmann, U. (2017) 'Text data and computational qualitative analysis', in Elsenbroich, C., Anzola, D. and Gilbert, N. (eds.). *Social dimensions of organised crime. Modelling the dynamics of extortion racket systems.* Cham: Springer, pp. 155–176.

DOI: 10.4324/9781003393207-5

For instance, in our examination of a case of extortion, it turned out that the very term "extortion" implies a perspective of criminal law on a certain kind of behaviour. However, from an organizational science perspective, the very same activity appears as a run on the bank (Merton, 1968). Certainly, this does not entail any justification of criminal activities but rather has to be perceived as an analytical concept for disentangling criminal norms.

The state of the art of research on the organization of organized crime can be disentangled along with the question of the degree of organizational growth and rationalization of labour (von Lampe, 2015). The starting point for the academic debate has been the Mafia as the paradigm of a professional, hierarchically organized crime syndicate (Paoli, 2003; La Spina, 2005). Whereas Cressey (1969, 1972) developed the thesis that like legal companies criminal organizations also tend to grow and develop an increasingly rational management of labour, Reuter (1983) argued for the contrary thesis that particular conditions of criminal markets favour small and local enterprises. Chang et al. (2005) developed a model to determine organizational size as a variable dependent on environmental conditions. Namely, criminal organizations face a trade-off between efficiency and security (Morselli et al., 2006). While organizational growth, structural differentiation, and a rational organization of the group management might increase returns, organizational growth comes at the cost of increasing danger of being detected (von Lampe, 2015). Small and local groups provide more security against criminal prosecution. Thus, the specific condition of covertness shapes the kind of interactions and relations within and beyond the criminal organizations. It is argued that covertness favours flexible and adaptive networks without hierarchical relations. These might quickly emerge and dissolve for temporarily taking advantage of criminal opportunities (Sparrow, 1991; Klerks, 2002; Krebs, 2002; Morselli, 2009). For instance, in the case of New York's heroin market, Natarajan (2006) found only small groups of entrepreneurs rather than big criminal syndicates. Thus, the emphasis has shifted from studying organizations to processes organizing (Hobbs, 2001). However, current research is focused on a static picture. Predominantly the structure of criminal organizations is perceived as a kind of rational or evolutionary adaptation, may it be to environmental conditions (favouring small networks) or conditions for the efficiency of production (favouring big syndicates). In contrast, here we examine the dynamics of relations within a criminal group. Investigating the dynamics sheds light on the pitfalls in which criminal groups might be trapped. These are not based on deliberate decisions but can be perceived as unintended consequences of actions. Thus, we explore actions and reactions when things go wrong and get out of control under the specific circumstances of criminal organizations. In contrast to the picture of adaptive flexibility of small networks drawn in the literature, the case examined here reveals the negative side effects that organizational growth has on small and flat organizational structures.

5.2   Data basis

The analysis is based on several police investigations in which numerous interrogations are documented. Police interrogations can be described as situations of dialogical conversation. An in-depth analysis of subjective meaning attributed to certain situations brings the empirical analysis very close to the subjective perception of the actors. Certainly, interrogations are artificial situations which might be alien for the respondents who might answer strategically or simply lie. Moreover, the talk is guided by certain interests of the police. In this case, for instance, the police investigations focused on persons related to money laundering and less on drug production. This uncertainty is typical for criminological data (Bley, 2014). On the other hand, police interrogations differ from court files in which respondents can be put under oath. Moreover, police interrogations are confidential. Many of the respondents were witnesses as, for instance, relatives of victims who were themselves interested in elucidation of the cases. This gives their statements certain credibility. For this reason, the data provides a rather good basis for analysing the cognition of a certain situation as "corrupt chaos". The aim is to infer hypothetical, *unobservable* cognitive elements from *observable* actions and statements to analyse cognitive mechanisms that motivate action in very confused and opaque situations.

Empirically, the chapter investigates the collapse of a gang of criminals involved in drug trafficking and laundering the illegal money. Data bases are transcripts of police interrogations of witnesses as well as suspects in a number of cases that were related to each other insofar as a core group of persons was involved in all these cases. This core group consisted of ca. 20 to 30 persons. Some of these persons knew each other already for several decades, partly also by a record of co-offences in a long-time criminal career. In contrast to Mafia type organizations, the group had no hierarchical structure or formal positions such as a capo di famiglia, i.e. the head of a certain sub-unit of the Cosa Nostra operating in a certain district. Whereas Mafia type organizations are professional organizations (La Spina, 2005; Scaglione, 2011; Neumann et al., 2016), the group subject of these police investigations was more of a network of old friends. While certainly some individuals gained more prestige than others, the structure of the group did not consist of positions with managerial authority or right of command. However, at least for a decade, the group operated extremely successfully in the drug market. The groups were formed presumably in the early 1990s and made a lot of money, in particular with ecstasy cooking that had been laundered in highly professional, worldwide financial transactions (Neumann and Sartor, 2016).

However, in the early to mid-2000s, the group collapsed in an escalation of violence. An informal network cannot terminate as a legal company, declaring bankruptcy. So, collapse in this case means that the business relations terminated, either because they killed each other or because of a loss of trust, partly due to the murders and other acts of violence including kidnapping, intimidation, and extortion. Collapse of trust is essential for the breakdown of the group. As already in legal organizations, trust is essential for the efficiency of labour relations (Colquitt and Rodell, 2011; Colquitt et al., 2012). This holds the more in the case of illegal organizations operating outside the state monopoly of violence. In the legal domain, organizations can at least ultimately rely on the state monopoly of violence: as labour relations are contractual relations, norm-enforcement can be delegated to the third party of the court. In criminal organizations, recourse to the court is impossible. Thus, a criminal organization needs to rely on the commitment of the members to the organization. For this reason, trust is essential. For instance, in the case of money laundering, black collar criminals need to hand over the money to their partners and trust that they will get the return of investment back from the trustee. In a covert organization, this cannot be secured by formal contracts. Once trust is corrupted, the business relation breaks apart. In fact, the collapse of the group triggered massive violence, including many assassinations. For instance, three murders happened within one week. In turn, the violence fostered further breakdown of trust. The escalation of violence has been described by involved persons as a "corrupt chaos" governed by a "rule of terror" in which "old friends are killing each other". The notion of a "chaos" indicates that seemingly the "terror" was not governed by an individual such as Nero burning Rome but – from the perspective from inside – by an invisible hand. The involved persons could no longer keep track of the complexity of incidences. This is an emergent phenomenon in which the macro level of the situational complexity generates a perception of the situation as a "corrupt chaos" on the micro of the involved individuals. This motivates the research question of the data analysis: dissecting the mechanisms of the chaos on a level of fine-grained individual interactions.

5.3 Conceptual model

Investigating subjective perceptions calls for an interpretive research methodology. Therefore, in this section, the conceptual model of the data and its empirical trace will be presented, based on the methodology that has been outlined in the previous chapter. This is an example of how a conceptual model using the CCD tool (Scherer et al., 2013, 2015) looks like. Moreover, the CCD tool creates a code template which can be implemented in a simulation model. The model will be presented in the next chapter. On the other hand, traceability to the empirical data is secured by annotations that refer to the open coding performed in the first step of the analysis (Lotzmann and Wimmer, 2013). In sum, a web of condition-action sequences is generated that represents the conceptual model of the data. Developing the conceptual model is an iterative process: first, the individual condition-action sequences need to be consistent with empirical domain knowledge. Second, the overall web of relations needs to provide a meaningful big picture that is sufficient to represent the overall corpus of the data. Therefore, the development of the conceptual model has been a participatory modelling process, i.e. stakeholder knowledge of police experts went into the model. Several developmental stages of the model have been discussed with stakeholders until they perceived it as valid. This is equivalent to the concept of theoretical saturation in a Grounded Theory approach (see Corbin and Strauss, 2008). Finally note that the data basis of interrogations allows including cognitive conditions (such as "fear for life") and actions (such as "member X interprets aggressive action"). This is an important feature to achieving a thick description from a situational phenomenology. For understanding the chaotic terror, it is essential to retrieve the meaning attributed to particular situations, observable at a phenomenological level.

The description concentrates on the relation between "black collar criminals" involved in drug trafficking and "white collar criminals" responsible for money laundering. This means that the production and distribution of drugs, i.e. the source of the illegal money, is not taken into account. The conceptual model is realized in the action diagram of the web of condition-action sequences. Thus, in this section, the mechanisms of the collapse at the micro level of single actions are investigated. In the next section, a theoretical analysis of the conceptual model will discuss the mechanisms on the macro level of the structural properties of the criminal group which can be revealed from the micro-level analysis. First, it has to be noted that in the investigated relations, the following three kinds of actors are involved:

- "Black collar criminals" who gained illegal money in the drug business.
- "White collar criminals" with a good reputation in the legal society in order to be able to invest huge amounts of money in the legal market. They might not have a long record of criminal offences but might be pushed towards criminal behaviour in the course of interactions (Gross, 1978).
- So-called "straw men" who played a decisive role in concealing the source and target of the money flow.

Once the data has been transformed into an action diagram, the following five phases in the process of the collapse can be distinguished in the analysis of the action diagram:

a *Ordinary business* of money laundering: This is the status quo before the collapse took place. Note that production and distribution of drugs is not investigated.
b A *crystallizing kernel of mistrust* disturbing the ordinary business, initiating the collapse.
c If the mistrust cannot be encapsulated, spreading of mistrust through the group generates a *conflict escalation*.
d Conflict escalation finally leads to what has been denoted by a witness as a *Corrupt chaos*.

e This includes a *run on the bank*. This was part of the "corrupt chaos". However, it can be analytically distinguished because the financially oriented relations of conditions and subsequent actions remain separated from the purely existential violence.

In the following, the individual elements of the conceptual model (from the ordinary business to the run on the bank) will be described in detail. First, the individual condition-action sequences of the process of the ordinary business of money laundering are considered. We describe the individual sequences and provide text passages in the police interrogations from which these sequences are derived.

5.3.1 Ordinary business of money laundering

The process of money laundering, described in Fig. 5.1, starts with two conditions: obviously, illegal money must be available. However, black collar criminals invested a huge amount of money in the business of white collar criminals. In the absence of formal contracts which are secured by the possibility that claims can be enforced by legal action, trust is also required in order to trigger a process of money laundering. These two conditions are inferred from statements in the police interrogation, for which the following two citations are exemplary.[1] The level of trust is expressed in the following statement of a witness, in which O1 is a black collar and V01 a white collar criminal,[2] namely the statement that money was available is documented in the second report:

- "O1 and V01 seem to be friends for me".
- "In the period between 1990 and Feb 14, 1992 police investigations had been undertaken. These revealed a criminal organisation concerned with drug trafficking. The report from June 1992 estimated the income and the costs. It is estimated a transaction volume of nearly 300 million".

If these two conditions are fulfilled, a process of money laundering is triggered. In this case, illegal money is given to a trustee with a legal business who invests the money in the legal market. The trustee is the link between the illegal and the legal world. That illegal money has been available is testified by the following statement:

- "... inserted a significant value of black money in the structure of the company of V01".

The money that had been inserted in the company of V01 has been invested in the legal market, as testified in the following statement:

- "At the moment I paid 800 000 in the firm which are now worth several millions through legal trade".

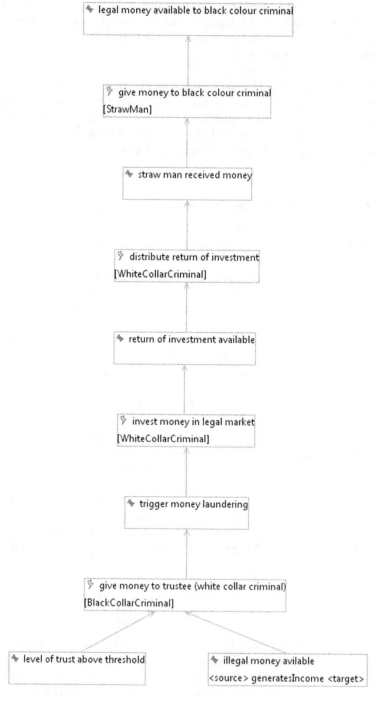

Figure 5.1 Money laundering

The investment of the money triggers the redistribution of the now legal money back to the black collar criminals. However, it turned out that for the concealment of the source and target of the money, third parties had extensively been used. These need to be individuals who are not, in the first instance, visible parts of the criminal group but nevertheless are trusted by group members. We call them straw men.

- "Finally, V01 paid 59 million. The cash money had been invested through a construction in Curacao. Here the brother of V01 played a decisive role".

The brother is but one example. Another one had been the girlfriend of a criminal. However, this example makes clear the two functions of (a) not being visible as part of the group but nevertheless, (b) being highly trusted by group members. Here, the family ties play a decisive role.

5.3.2   A crystallizing kernel of mistrust

This process could have gone on without any specific terminal point. However, factually, at some point in time, a crystallizing kernel of mistrust invaded the group. Obviously, this is a contingency of the investigated data: the interrogations are based on the fact that the group became visible, and factually the group became visible only in and through the process of its collapse. This is a kind of happenstance. In particular, individual events remain contingent. The story of this particular case will be developed in the textual annotations below. These gave rise to the identification of the mechanisms of the decline of the group. However, it has to be noted that it is rather likely that in the course of time some such events happen that trigger follow-up actions. For this reason, the conditions have been specified in the condition-action sequences in a very general way: it is simply stated that some members of the group become disreputable. In the first instance, this is due to the limits of the data. In the interrogation, it cannot be identified unequivocally why and how this happened. In the data only the follow-up steps can be found; i.e. it is a theoretical inference that someone became disreputable. However, first, this is a very general condition which makes it rather likely that at some point of time, it will occur. Second, in a group, some form of conflict resolution is needed. The crucial question is, how the group handles conflicts. This is a critical juncture for the stability of the group.

As justified above, the starting point of the process outlined in Fig. 5.2 is treated as an external event, namely that a member of the group becomes disreputable. This may be due to several reasons: for example, a member may become too greedy. Once this event happens, it calls for a mechanism of conflict resolution. Conflict resolution might trigger an act of aggression against this member. This might be an attempt to sanction this member or motivated by some causes such as, for instance, simply anger or irritation about him or her.

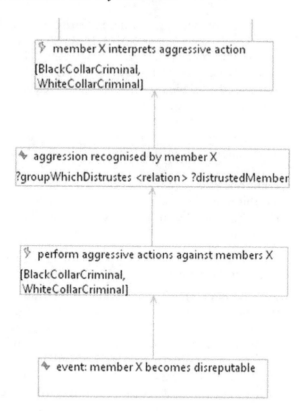

Figure 5.2 Crystallizing kernel of mistrust

However, it may also be the case that mistrust is based on other reasons or that the motivation is based on self-interest or simply remains unclear. In the following, some examples of how an aggression might look like in the context of a criminal group are provided:

- "An attack to the life of M."
- "O1 had V01 in his grip. He shall do as told otherwise his family would have a problem".
- "... O5 came to my house in order to say that at 8 in the evening I should come to the forest. This is standard: intimidate and request for money".

The aggression in these examples is of very different severity. Obviously, murder is a severe aggression. It shall be noted that assassination might be motivated by several reasons, ranging from greediness to death penalty. In fact, M. survived the attack but had been killed some years later because he had been accused of stealing drugs. The latter can be interpreted as the execution of a death penalty. In the other two examples, the objective of the action is not the liquidation of the victim. If effective, the aggression is recognized by the victim. This triggers reasoning on the aggression. In contrast to (successful) murder, the aggression in the two other cases is intended to initiate certain behaviour or behaviour change, respectively. In the second example, O1 "shall do as told", whereas in the third one the objective of the intimidation is a "request for money". Recognizing the aggression triggers a crucial cognitive process: namely, interpreting the possible motivation of the aggressive act (see the last action in Fig. 5.2).

The objective of the abstract condition-action sequences is not to tell the story of a particular case but rather to infer general social mechanisms. For this reason, the reasoning is described in a most general way. Two options had been identified which are characteristic for all cases in the data: to interpret the aggression as norm enforcement or norm violation. Norm enforcement is denoted as the "norm of trust demanded", i.e. as a form of punishment. As the condition of covertness of criminal organizations demands secrecy, it is an advantage not to talk too much. Moreover, norms are not codified. Therefore, this is done typically without informing the victim that he is being punished because of the violation of a certain norm. Norm violation is denoted as "norm of trust violated", i.e. as a violation of the informal code of conduct within the criminal group (see the first branching in Fig. 5.3). Obviously, this broad characterization covers a number of concrete interpretations. For instance, norm violation might be some kind of self-interested action which can be due to an infinite number of intentions.

Depending on the interpretation of the aggression, different behavioural options are triggered. Obviously, the reasoning is not documented in the data. However, what can be found is the reaction to the aggression. First, we discuss the case of interpretation as norm enforcement (on the right side of Fig. 5.3). In this case, the victim may either obey or deliberately decide to cheat. Obedience may restore the trust in the organization, or at least ensure that the code of conduct in the group is respected. This is denoted as the "level of trust might

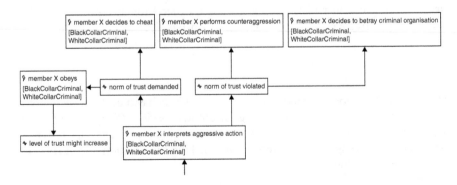

Figure 5.3 Reasoning on aggression

increase". In this case, mistrust may fade away or at least remain encapsulated. Obedience is shown in the example of the reaction to the "request for money":

- "I paid but I'm alive".

5.3.3 *Conflict escalation*

In the case of interpreting aggression as norm violation (on the left side of Fig. 5.3), the victim decides about the reaction. Two action classes had been identified, denoted as counter-aggression and betrayal. This shall be discussed by the first example: the failed assassination. This is an intricate case, demonstrating the pathway to the diverging interpretation, "norm of trust violated". After M. survived the attack on his life, it is plausible that he lost trust in his business partners. The reaction was as follows:

- "M. told the newspapers 'about my role in the network' because he thought that I wanted to kill him to get the money".

This reaction is instructive: it allows reconstructing how he interpreted the aggression. M. interpreted the attack on his life not as a penalty for deviant behaviour from his side (i.e. death penalty as in his later assassination for being accused of stealing drugs). Instead, he concluded that the cause of the attack was based on self-interest (the other criminal "wanted his money"). Thus, he interpreted the attack as norm deviation rather than enforcement. Next, he attributed the aggression to an individual person and started a counter-reaction against this particular person by betraying "his role in the network". This is an example of betrayal. An example of counter-aggression will be provided when the escalation of the conflicts to a "corrupt chaos" is discussed. First, it shall be noted that this reaction caused another member of the group to become a victim of an act of aggression. While it remains unknown who was responsible for the assassination, it was not this individual. However, the betrayal had severe consequences for this individual. Thus, a new member of the group faced an act of aggression which further caused the need for interpretation. This induces a positive feedback loop as outlined in Fig. 5.4.

5.3.4 *A corrupt chaos*

Positive feedback loops generate unstable systemic behaviour. Thus, they are a well-known cause for generating strange systemic behaviour (Senge, 1990). This systemic property caused spreading of mistrust throughout the group. It generated a cycle of revenge and counter-revenge, making the situation uncontrollable, as documented below:

- "There is a rule of terror in the town".

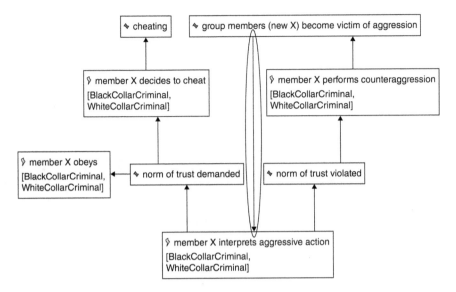

Figure 5.4 Positive feedback loop indicated by the circle

The feedback cycle generates a complexity that, from the perspective of the people involved in the situation, could not be attributed to a particular individual anymore as indicated in the following statement:

- "There is a corrupt chaos behind it".

In the following, the condition-action sequences of this segment of the process of disintegration of the group are displayed in which the trust required for the covert activities breaks down. Not the overall diagram will be substantiated by textual annotations from the data. Instead, only two elements, denoted as fear for life and counter-aggression, will be highlighted in Fig. 5.5.

Fear for life is proven by the following testimony of a witness:

- "V01 was in great fear of O1. When he had an appointment with O1, he was wearing a bulletproof jacket".

However, being thrown into a situation of existential threat is likely to initiate attempts of counter-aggression. This is demonstrated in the following two examples:

- "He was at a point in which he was in a totally despaired situation. HLJ had several times tried to counteract. He had a plan to approach O1 with a weapon. However, in the last moment he didn't dare. At a different time he had two pistols with him. He planned to shoot O1 to death and to pass

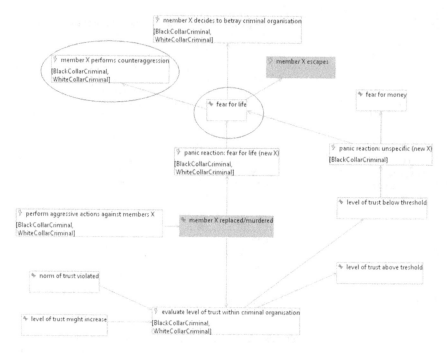

Figure 5.5 Corrupt chaos

the other weapon in his hand in order that it appeared as if he had shot in self-defense".

• "Presumably V01 asked the [Motorcycling gang] to make an operation against O1 in return for a huge amount of money".

5.3.5   *Run on the bank*

Existential threats are likely to induce unpredictable behaviour. However, in the ordinary business of money laundering, a huge amount of illegal money had been invested in the legal market through the white collar criminals. In a criminal organization, investment could not be ensured by legal contracts. The black collar criminals needed to trust that they will get the return of investment back from the white collar criminals. In the case of the breakdown of trust, a well-known mechanism from legal financial markets becomes effective: fear for money provides an incentive to get as much money of the investment back as soon as possible. Moreover, if it becomes visible that one member attempts to get the money out, the classical mechanism of a self-fulfilling prophecy (Merton, 1968) initiates a "run on the bank". It is known from the legal world that this has a destructive effect on the market. In Fig. 5.6, an overview of the process in the case of a criminal organization is provided.

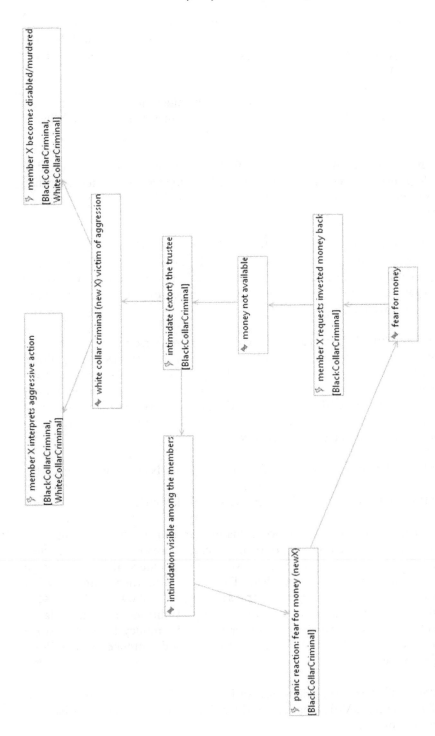

Figure 5.6 Run on the bank

The overall process shown in Fig. 5.6 will now be documented, start-ing with the bottom element of Fig. 5.6. As approved by the following testimony, fear for money initiated attempts to get money out of the investment:

- "Starting from Oct. XXXX[3] S.K. came in the office. She told the employees that she needed to talk to me because her former man (who died) had 7 million active debts".

This is the beginning of the process. However, once money is invested in the legal market such as constructions, it is no longer immediately available. This is indicated by the condition "money not available" which is testified by several witnesses:

- "At a certain point he had problems with his liquidity".
- "There is a considerable backlog demand in the back-payment. The reason is twofold: first, it's becoming difficult to gain new funding because of the negative reports in the media and second much of our liquidity has been lost in payments to O1".

Since financial claims cannot be enforced by recourse to the court in the case of an illegal covert organization, a run on the bank has the additional effect that the use of violence becomes likely to force the passing over of the money. An attempt to get the money back, nevertheless, might trigger intimi-dation of the trustee (the white collar criminal) who now becomes a victim of aggression of his business partners. This results in extortion of the trustee to enforce the claim as testified in two examples below:

- "In the last year he was strongly under pressure because he had been ex-torted. That's what he said to me".
- "If I don't pay, her Yugoslav friend O6 would kill me".

It is unlikely that intimidation remains secret in the closed community of a small group. Rather, rumours might easily spread in the group. Once attempts to get money out of the investment become visible, a new stage of the run on the bank is reached. The business partner might now get "in fear for money" as well and the same loop, as shown in Fig. 5.4, is initiated, now by a new member of the gang. Additional monetary claims generate a cycle of extortion in order to get the money back. A positive feedback cycle is closed. An example is the second sentence in the follow-ing example:

- "Soon after his death the widow of K had an affair with O1. She extorted 7 million from V01. Contrary to the claim of M. his entitlements had not been captured by this deal".

Thus, intimidation stimulates further intimidation, making the white collar criminal a victim of aggression of his business partners and turning a formerly symbiotic into a parasitic relationship (see Transcrime Joint Research Center on Transnational Crime, 2008). An example of how payment had been enforced is provided below:

- "V01 was ordered to the office of his lawyer. However, when he entered the office the lawyer was not there. Instead O1 and seemingly 3 Yugoslavs were there. These ordered him to go on his knees and hold a machine gun in his stomach".

5.4   Conclusion: Structural insights of the conceptual model

The thick description on the micro level of the *process* of the escalation of violence provides insights into the macro level of the *structural* properties of the group that reveal reasons which triggered the process that finally generated a situation perceived as a "corrupt chaos". This can be described as revealing certain elements which are crucial for a specific criminal culture. In abstract terms, the conceptual model describes a cascading effect: mistrust generated violence which in turn enforced mistrust in the overall group. That such a cascading effect was possible can be ascribed to the organizational structure of the group. Since the group could not rely on formal procedures of conflict regulation, no mechanisms existed to encapsulate the mistrust. This was due to some characteristic features of the group structure which will be described in more detail below.

- While a horizontal differentiation between the tasks of white and black collar criminals existed, on the vertical axis the group had a flat structure. Some informal hubs existed which characterize people involved in many of the actions which had been the subject of police investigations. However, while the hubs might have had a certain prestige, all members were equal insofar as no individual had a right of command.
- As a consequence of the flat structure of the group, trust was not secured by formal authority but simply based on interpersonal relations. Some individuals knew each other for quite a long time, whereas others, such as straw men, had been involved in the activities through a referee. An example is the brother of V01.
- This entails that the norms of conduct remained only implicit.

However, once an initial element of mistrust was intruded upon, the crisis was characterized by a highly unstructured situation and individuals could not rely on formal rules of crisis management. They had to improvise ad hoc to react to unanticipated situations such as an attempt of an assassination or reading their names in the newspapers, or even being betrayed by a criminal comrade. The reaction had to rely on interpretations of the situation. Since the interpretation could not be guided by a formal code of conduct, it remained fallible. Factually, the conflict escalation was characterized by misperceptions and diverging interpretations of the situation. The likelihood of such misunderstandings can be traced back to the organizational structure, characterized by a lack of authority which could reduce contingency by providing an unequivocal definition of a situation, simply by its normative power. Thus, in consequence of the organizational structure, the differentiation of punishment and revenge remained blurred. In behavioural terms, both actions can be described as an act of aggression. However, both terms constitute social concepts with essential differences with regard to potential follow-up actions: whereas in the case of punishment the aggression might stop once the punishment has been applied, revenge might lead to an endless circle. Since in behavioural terms both punishment and revenge are an act of aggression, interpretation is needed to decide about how to react once an individual member of the organization becomes a victim of an aggression. Indeed, the data hints at both interpretations. This is dependent on the subjective perception of the situation.

This chapter has presented an example of a conceptual model and the insights that can be gained from such an interpretive analysis procedure. In the next chapter, the simulation model that has been derived from this conceptual model will be presented. Moreover, it will be shown how the feature of traceability shapes the simulated scenarios, enabling an interpretive analysis of simulation results.

Notes

1 These are open codings derived with MaxQDA which are then inserted as annotations in the CCD framework.
2 For reasons of protection of private data, names are anonymous and no reference to the source in the police interrogations is provided.
3 To preserve anonymity the date has been replaced by XXXX.

References

Bley, R. (2014) *Rockerkriminalität. Erste empirische Befunde. Frankfurt/M.* Verlag für Polizeiwissenschaft.

Chang, J. J., Lu, H. C. and Chen, M. (2005) 'Organized crime or individual crime? Endogenous size of a criminal organization and the optimal law enforcement', *Economic Inquiry*, 43(3), pp. 661–675.

Colquitt, J., LePine, J., Piccolo, R. and Zapata, C. (2012) 'Explaining the justice – Performance relationship: Trust as exchange deepener or trust as uncertainty reducer?', *Journal of Applied Psychology*, 97(1), pp. 1–15.

Colquitt, J. and Rodell, J. (2011) 'Justice, trust, and trustworthiness: A longitudinal analysis integrating three theoretical perspectives', *Academy of Management Journal*, 54(6), pp. 1183–1206.

Corbin, J. and Strauss, A. (2008). *Basics of Qualitative Research*. 3rd edn. Thousand Oaks: Sage.

Cressey, D. R. (1969) *Theft of the Nation: The Structure and Operations of Organized Crime in America*. New York: Harper & Row.

Cressey, D. R. (1972) *Criminal Organization: Its Elementary Forms*. New York: Harper & Row.

Diesner, J., Frantz, T. and Carley, K. (2005) 'Communication Networks from the Enron Email Corpus. It's always about the people. Enron is no different', *Journal of Computational and Mathematical Organization Theory*, 11(3), pp. 201–228.

Gottschalk, P. (2010) 'Criminal entrepreneurial behavior', *Journal of International Business and Entrepreneurship Development*, 5(1), pp. 63–76.

Gross, E. (1978) 'Organizational crime: A theoretical perspective', *Studies in Symbolic Interaction*, 1, pp. 55–85.

Hobbs, D. (2001) 'The firm: Organizational logic and criminal culture on a shifting terrain', *British Journal of Criminology*, 41(4), pp. 549–560.

Klerks, P. (2002) 'The network paradigm applied to criminal organizations', *Connections*, 24(3), pp. 53–65.

Krebs, V. (2002) 'Mapping networks of terrorist cells', *Connections*, 24(3), pp. 43–52.

La Spina, A. (2005) *Mafia, legalità debole e sviluppo del Mezzogiorno*. Bologna: Il Mulino.

Lampe, K. (2015) 'Big business: Scale of operation, organizational size, and the level of integration into the legal economy as key parameters for understanding the development of illegal enterprises', *Trends in Organized Crime*, 18(4), pp. 289–310.

Lotzmann, U. and Wimmer, M. (2013) Traceability in evidence-based policy simulation. *Proceedings of the 27th European Conference on Modelling and Simulation, ECMS 2013* (pp. 696–702). Dudweiler: Digitaldruck Pirrot GmbH.

Merton, R. (1968) *Social Theory and Social Structure*. New York: Free Press.

Morselli, C. (2009) *Inside Criminal Networks*. New York: Springer.

Morselli, C., Giguere, C. and Petit, K. (2006) 'The efficiency/security trade-off in criminal networks', *Social Networks*, 29(1), pp. 143–153.

Natarajan, M. (2006) 'Understanding the structure of a large heroin trafficking network: A quantitative analysis of qualitative data', *Journal of Quantitative Criminology*, 22(2), pp. 171–192.

Neumann, M., Frazzica, G. and Punzo, V. (2016) 'Mechanisms of the embedding of extortion racket systems. The case of Cosa Nostra', in Stachowiak, A. and Mangia, G. (eds.). *Dark Side of Organization and Social Irresponsibility: Tool and Theoretical Insights* (pp. 259–286). Charlotte: Information Age Publishing.

Neumann, M. and Sartor, N. (2016) 'A semantic network analysis of laundering drug money', *Journal of Tax Administration*, 2(1), pp. 73–94.

Paoli, L. (2003) *Mafia Brotherhoods. Organized Crime, Italian Style*. Oxford: Oxford University Press.

Putten, C. van (2012) The process of extortion: Problems and qualifications. *Conference on Extortion Racket Systems* (pp. 7–11). University of Vienna, Vienna.

Reuter, P. (1983) *Disorganized Crime: The Economics of the Visible Hand*. Cambridge, MA: MIT Press.

Scaglione, A. (2011) *Reti Mafiose. Cosa Nostra e Camorra: organizzazioni criminali a confronto*. Milano: FrancoAngeli.

Scherer, S., Wimmer, M., Lotzmann, U., Moss, S. and Pinotti, D. (2015) 'An evidence-based and conceptual model-driven approach for agent-based policy modelling', *Journal of Artificial Societies and Social Simulation*, 18(3). https://www.jasss.org/18/3/14.html

Scherer, S., Wimmer, M. and Markisic, S. (2013) 'Bridging narrative scenario texts and formal policy modelling through conceptual policy modelling', *Artificial Intelligence and Law*, 21(4), pp. 455–484.

Senge, P. (1990) *The Fifth Discipline. The Art and Practice of Organizational Learning*. New York: Dubeday Currency.

Sofsky, W. (1996) *Traktat über Gewalt. Frankfurt/M.* Fischer.

Sparrow, M. (1991) 'The application of network analysis to criminal intelligence: An assessment of the prospects', *Social Networks*, 13(3), pp. 251–274.

Transcrime Joint Research Center on Transnational Crime (2008) *Study on extortion racketeering. The need for an instrument to combat activities of organized crime. Final report*. University degli studi di Trento and Universita Cattolica del Sacro Cuore di Milano.

Weick, K. (2007) *Der Prozess Des Organisierens*. Frankfurt a. M: Suhrkamp.

6 A simulation model of intra-organizational conflict regulation in the crime world*

Ulf Lotzmann and Martin Neumann

6.1 Simulation model description

The implementation of the simulation model follows closely the modelling process developed in the EU project OCOPOMO[1] and uses the toolbox provided by this project. The conceptual model was developed with the CCD Tool – the core component of the OCOPOMO Toolbox – which also provides a transformation tool called CCD2DRAMS that allows the semi-automatic transformation into a basic simulation model. The applied modelling process is presented in Lotzmann et al. (2015). The target platform of this transformation tool is the popular simulation framework Repast (North et al., 2006), with the declarative rule engine DRAMS (Lotzmann and Meyer, 2011) as an extension for specifying the agent behaviour. Primarily the use of DRAMS shapes the implementation style in a particular direction: the entire agent behaviour is specified by declarative rules, which operate on the knowledge stored as facts in so-called fact bases. As DRAMS is designed as a distributed rule engine, each agent is equipped with its own fact base and own rules, while for "world knowledge" and communication purposes a global fact base is provided. Even global rules are allowed to implement activities that cannot be located to concrete agents. Each rule consists of a condition part, the so-called left-hand side (LHS), and an action part, the right-hand side (RHS). The conditions in the LHS are specified using a set of clauses, e.g. for performing fact-based queries, binding variables, comparing variables and constants, doing mathematical calculations, and so on. The RHS consists of clauses that allow for modifications of fact bases (asserting new facts, retracting existing facts) as well as clauses for writing simulation outcomes in different ways. The basic mechanism of the rule engine is then to evaluate the LHS of all rules for which the facts are available and other matching conditions are fulfilled, and then fire the rule by executing the RHS, setting the condition for new rules to fire, and generating the simulation log.

---

* This chapter is based on Lotzmann, U. and Neumann, M. (2017) 'A simulation model of intra-organizational conflict regulation in the crime World', in Elsenbroich, C., Anzola, D. and Gilbert, N. (eds.). *Social Dimensions of Organised Crime. Modelling the Dyamics of Extortion Rackets.* Cham: Springer, pp. 177–213.

DOI: 10.4324/9781003393207-6

The actual implementation of the simulation model follows closely the conceptual model, not at least due to the code generation facility provided by the toolbox. All the actions modelled in the CCD action diagram are also present as DRAMS rules in the simulation model. However, to achieve a consistent implementation, a number of aspects had to be added to the model which are not described in the evidence base, instead relying on cognitive heuristics. On the other hand, some details included in the conceptual model had to be left out to keep the complexity of the simulation model manageable, but also due to decisions to concentrate the focus on some crucial aspects of interest for the stakeholders. These implementation decisions were in most instances discussed with the data analysis expert and partly also with domain experts.

Another reason to ground the simulation model on DRAMS is the opportunity to benefit from the traceability functionality built in the OCOPOMO toolbox (Lotzmann and Wimmer, 2013). Herewith it becomes possible to trace simulation results back to the phrases from the evidence base annotated to elements of the conceptual model. That is, this functionality opens a way to efficiently perform qualitative analysis of simulation results by means of unveiling the relations between dynamics in simulation runs and events in the real criminal network described in the evidence base.

The following section gives an overview of the simulation model both in terms of static and dynamic aspects. The former includes the agents and related attributes from which the model is comprised and the latter the control flow in the different parts of the model. In the subsequent sections, this control flow is further detailed to give quite deep insights into concrete design decisions to show how the evidence is reflected in the implementation.

6.1.1 Simulation model overview

In the simulation model, agents are included for the CCD actor types Black Collar Criminal, White Collar Criminal, and Police. While for the two types of criminals' arbitrary numbers of instances can be set for simulation runs, the Police is represented as an institutional agent; i.e. a single agent instance covers the activities of this actor. In a typical simulation run, there exists a single White Collar Criminal, who is responsible for money laundering and is typically also part of the legal world, but might become involved in aggressive practices of the Black Collar Criminals. These are the actual representatives of the illegal world of the criminal network. There are two types of Black Collars distinguished, one called the Reputable Criminal, which is initially in the so-called rational mental frame, while the other "normal" Criminal only acts in the emotional mental frame. In the course of the simulation also the Reputable Criminal might switch to the emotional frame, e.g. due to violent events. This distinction between the two types of mental frame is illustrated below.

The model is implemented in a tick-based way where the course of time is represented by discrete ticks, but no defined time period between ticks is specified. Actions or reactions involving multi-staged decision process are typically spread across several ticks, as are the consequences of actions and police investigations, to give a few examples.

This temporal relationship is one of the information given in the activity diagram in Fig. 6.1, which furthermore shows the control flow between the important behavioural elements (represented by activities) of the entire model, structured in different parts (grey background boxes). Some of the edges are labelled to improve readability. Temporal relations as mentioned above are put in square brackets, and phrases in italics give further details on conditions if the subsequent activities do not allow to infer this information. The most important edge label is printed in bold font: the (type of) agent who is the executor of the following activity. Edges with no label indicate the transition to the next activity within the same tick and as part of the behaviour of the same agent. The diagram can be read as follows.

The dynamics start with an initial normative event at the first tick regarding a random criminal. This normative event is observed by a fellow criminal at

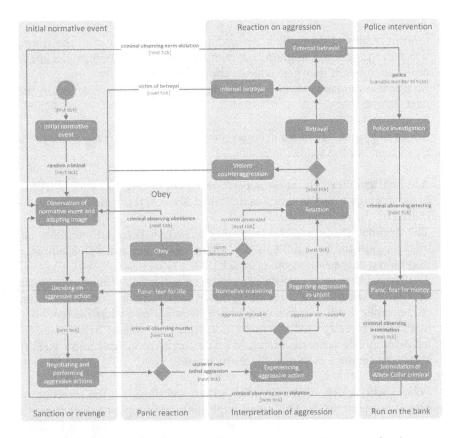

Figure 6.1 Overview activity diagram of the simulation model (see text for the meaning of edge label styles)

the next tick, who might adapt the image of this criminal. In case of a norm violation event, the image is decreased, which triggers a decision process on whether and how to perform aggressive actions against the deviating criminal. In the next tick, the possibly many criminals who decided to sanction the norm violation "negotiate", and finally one of them performs a single aggression, whose consequence manifests in the next tick:

- Either the aggression is lethal, which might cause panic and "fear for life" among other members of the criminal network, or
- the victim of the aggression experiences the aggression and starts with an interpretation process.

This interpretation begins with the distinction of whether the aggressor is reputable or not. In the latter case, the aggression is regarded as unjust which triggers an obligatory reaction in the next tick. If the aggressor is judged to be reputable, then a normative process is performed that leads to the conclusion that either

- a norm is indeed demanded, persuading the criminal to obey the norm, which in the next tick might fellow criminals motivate to increase the image of this member, if they get to know about the obedience, or
- no norm is demanded which again triggers an aggressive reaction in the next tick.

About the actual reaction a decision process is conducted (taking one more tick), with one of the following results:

- A violent counter aggression is performed, employing the same activities as for normative sanctioning (as described above), this time of course executed by the reacting agent.
- The criminal who issued the original aggression is betrayed internally, i.e. involving just the two criminals. The victim of this betrayal will decide on a responding aggression in the next tick.
- An external betrayal is performed, which can either be to inform the Police or to go to the media and revealing the criminal network (or its members) to the public. Both actions trigger police investigations, while the latter one in addition is recognized as a norm violation, which might be observed by fellow criminals in the next tick and might furthermore lead to the already known consequences of new aggressive actions.

Police investigation ultimately leads to interventions, i.e. the arresting of members of the network. This arrest might also be observed by other members and in the next tick cause a panic about the potential loss of invested money. This fear usually triggers intimidation of the White Collar Criminal, which might also be observed by other criminals, starting (with a time delay of one tick) a vicious cycle of cascading acts of extortion towards the White Collar in the form of a "run on the bank". The refusal of repayment of invested money by the White Collar is at the same time regarded as a norm violation, observable by further criminals (again with a delay of one tick).

6.1.2 *Decision processes*

The functional blocks shown in Fig. 6.1 are described in more detail in the following subsections, complementing the very brief walk through the model. Several concepts partly introduced already are repeatedly used throughout the chapter. These are as follows:

- Rational and emotional mental frame. As mentioned above, these different "modes of operation" of criminals influence their behaviour. In the emotional frame, the criminal is less able to foresee the consequences of the performed actions; hence, the probability of severe aggressions and acts of strong violence is higher as for the rationally acting criminal.
- Image and reputation of criminals. Both are properties expressing the standing of a criminal, the rank in the hierarchy in a way. Reputation is initially set for each criminal agent in the initialization of a simulation run, is known to all members of the criminal network, and does not change in the course of time. In contrast, the image is information private to each criminal agent. That is, each criminal has his own view on the image of each fellow criminal. The image values do change during simulation runs.
- Levels of image and reputation. These are ordinal scaled attributes: very high, high, modest low, and very low.
- Levels of severity of aggressive actions. The severity of an aggressive action is measured by the ordinal scaled attribute "strength": low, modest, and high.

6.1.2.1 *Initial normative event*

To create the initial event that a member of the criminal network suddenly becomes disreputable – as discussed in the previous chapter – a global rule throwing an external event is provided. This rule picks randomly one of the members and issues a normative event about an alleged violation of the norm of trust by this member. This event is triggered just once, at tick 1.0.

6.1.2.2 *Sanction or revenge*

This functional block basically implements the CCD action "perform aggressive actions against member X" (Fig. 6.2) and is an example where the implementation that formalizes this action is much more convoluted than the action might indicate. The reason for this discrepancy in granularity is the fact that

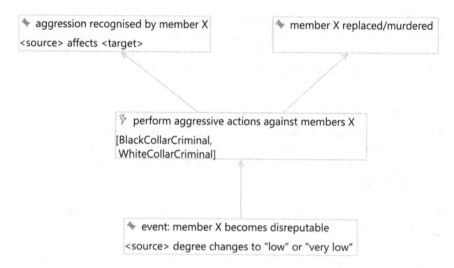

Figure 6.2 CCD action "perform aggressive actions against member X"

for this action not much evidence is available – the internal decision processes of criminals that lead to aggressive actions have to be regarded as a black box. Therefore, the mechanisms have to be constructed in some plausible and – where possible – well-informed way, with the aim to reproduce the observed results of these decisions by the simulations.

In Fig. 6.3 the decision tree formalizing this action is shown. The initial condition – a criminal "X" violates a norm – can in principle be observed by each fellow criminal and might lead to a reaction. This perception involves both the observation of the event and also the "willingness" to care about the event and is modelled as a stochastic process.

As annotated in (A1), the White Collar Criminal perceives this event with a very low probability of 0.05 since he typically keeps out of the thuggish business of the Black Collar Criminals, while for the Black Collar Criminal the probability is dependent on the image of the criminal respective to the event: with a very high image, the probability is 0.1, with high image 0.2, and otherwise 0.3. The rationale behind this differentiation is that a norm deviation of a criminal with a higher image seems less likely to be an offending act against fellow criminals or a threat to the entire network.

The first step of the process that is triggered on successful perception is a change in the image of the criminal. If the normative action was a norm violation, then the image strongly decreases ("two levels"), and in the case of norm obedience (not shown in the decision tree) the image increases by one "level".

The new image of the criminal related to the normative event then triggers the next step of the decision process, where the behaviour differs if the criminal is in the rational or emotional mental frame.

In both cases, an aggression is planned only if the new image of the criminal related to the normative event is low or even very low, but in the case of the

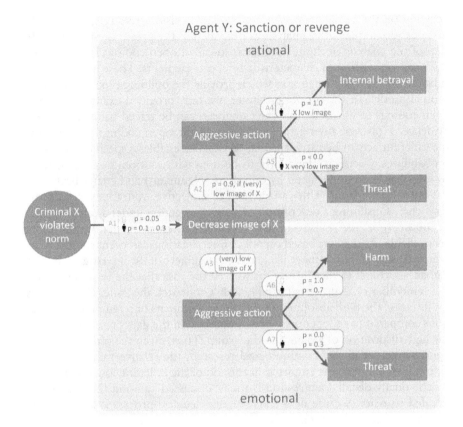

Figure 6.3 Decision tree for sanction or revenge

rational frame the planning is followed only with a probability of 0.9 (A2), whereas an emotionally acting criminal would always punish because he might not be able to foresee the consequences of his aggressive actions (A3).

If once the plan is conceived, then again the category of criminal (Black or White Collar) and the mental frame determine the type of reactions, but in some cases also the image of the criminal to be punished (decisions A4 and A5 of Black Collar Criminal).

A rational White Collar Criminal will always (A4) perform the – compared to the other options – mild punishment of (internal) betrayal, while in the emotional frame he will always answer with violence (A6). A rational Black Collar Criminal considers the option of betrayal only if the target of the aggression has still a low image (A4); in the case of a very low image (A5), the only appropriate action is considered to be a threat. An emotionally acting Black Collar Criminal tends more towards a violent reaction (probability of 0.7; A6) than a threatening action (probability of 0.3; A7). The cognitive heuristics modelled in these decisions are suggested by information from the evidence base; this connection to evidence becomes more concrete when deciding on the actual aggressive action. The decision trees refer back to the first phase of a qualitative analysis as described in the previous chapter. In the step of the analysis of the textual data, so-called open codings had been created, i.e. annotations of characteristic brief text-elements. These had then been subsumed to broader categories which provide the building blocks of the conceptual model. In the previous chapter, we only provided examples of these open codings to illustrate how the categories can be traced back to empirical evidence. However, the relative frequency of the open codings subsumed to the different acts of betrayal, threats, or violence enables a specification of the probabilities. Certainly, these have to be used with caution: first, the categorization has been undertaken by one of us (Neumann) and cross-checked by the other (Lotzmann). Thus, an element of subjective arbitrariness comes into play when subsuming a description of a concrete action under a category such as "outburst of rage", etc. Second, the relative frequencies in data might not be very reliable. As they are based on police interrogations, an event such as an attempted assassination is more likely to be the subject of the interrogation than, e.g. an "outburst of rage". It might well be the case that the respondents did not remember or that the talk simply didn't approach the issue. Nevertheless, for instance, the high absolute number of death threats or attempted assassinations compared to other courses of action found in the data provides a hint for the high disposition of violence in the group. Thus, given the problem of dark figures inherent in any criminological research, the relative frequencies provide at least a hint to the empirical likelihood of the different courses of action.

The finally decided aggression is then "discussed" among the agents that decided to react. So, the final result of this decision process is an individual aggression. However, not all criminals who decided to react perform their aggression individually, but rather a single aggression is perpetrated against the criminal X. After some kind of "negotiation" among the potential aggressors, one aggressor and the related aggression are determined. This two-staged process is not associated with any agent, but is part of the "global" environment. In the first stage, the criminal with the highest image is chosen. In the second stage, the aggression with the highest severity is selected, involving a stochastic process if more than one candidate fulfils these criteria.

The subsequent (implicit) execution of the aggression is immediately evaluated in terms of impact for the victim (by another global rule). For acts of violence, a certain (quite low) probability for lethal consequences is considered (0.2 for murder attempt, 0.1 for beating up). All other possible types of aggression are not assumed to be lethal, anyway.

6.1.2.3   Panic reaction

If the aggression turned out to be lethal, the CCD action for "fear for life" panic in Fig. 6.4 comes into play. This is a simplification of the original action diagram from the previous chapter, where also a more general panic might lead to fear for life if the overall trust in the criminal network has been destroyed.

Figure 6.4 CCD action "panic reaction: fear for life (new X)"

This simplified implementation, however, covers the aspect of loss of trust in the network quite well, based on the loss of the image of individual fellow criminals.

Panic is a situation where rational deliberations do no longer play a role in the behaviour of the individual criminal. It plays a central role in terms of escalating aggression and violence among the network members.

However, the implementation as shown in Fig. 6.5 does not need to be particularly complicated. As soon as a murder of a fellow criminal is observed, the "fear for life" panic state is established with a probability of 0.5 (B1). The criminal "switches" into the emotional frame and becomes active in some way in order to defend himself. Here, he just picks randomly one of his fellow criminals (B2) – which can be interpreted as the one guilty of the murder as perceived by the criminal in panic – and just strongly decreases the related image.

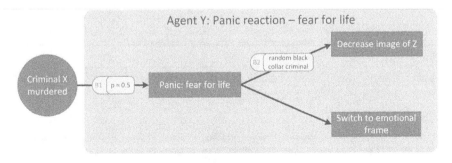

Figure 6.5 Decision tree for the panic reaction: fear for life

This decrease in the image might then trigger further actions, as shown in Fig. 6.3. Hence, the spiral of violence escalates.

6.1.2.4   *Interpretation of aggression*

If the aggression was not lethal, the victim has to interpret the reasons for being attacked.

This is modelled in the part of the CCD action diagram displayed in Fig. 6.6. In addition to the condition focussed here – the aggression motivated by an alleged norm deviation "recognised by member X" – there are two other circumstances when a criminal becomes a victim of an aggression: either as a result of a counter aggression or – as a special case – the intimidation of the White Collar Criminal. Both cases are not directly linked to a normative event and become relevant at later stages in the dynamics. This interpretation process remains the same for all cases.

In the implementation, it is assumed that the victim always perceives the aggression against him. In the following, the implementation of the quite complicated reasoning process is spread out in more detail.

This interpretation process, again, consists of several sub-processes, as shown in Fig. 6.7. The first stage covers the perception of the aggression, followed by a first evaluation of the appearance of the attacker – deduced from the attacker's reputation.

Dependent on this reputation information, the interpretation is fundamentally different. For the case of a reputable attacker (C1), the second stage is reasoning about whether the attacked criminal might have violated a norm in the recent past which would have led to a sanction of another fellow criminal. This interpretation as a possible sanction is as a "normative process" which is at the heart of this branch of behaviour. The basic idea of this normative reasoning is quite simple: It is evaluated whether own aggressive actions performed in the past stand in some kind of temporal relationship with a normative event assigned to this criminal. To conduct this evaluation, each criminal can access a global event board where all aggressions performed by each criminal are recorded. Also, the normative events are logged

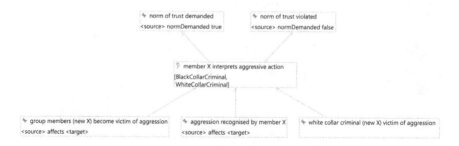

Figure 6.6 CCD action "member X interprets aggressive action"

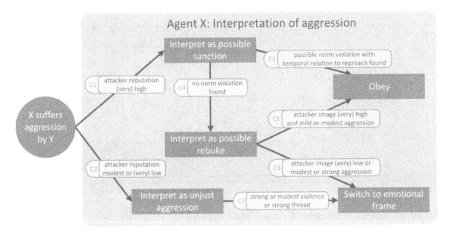

Figure 6.7 Decision graph for interpretation of aggression

in a similar way so that temporal relations between these types of events can easily be derived. The normative process is considered successful if aggressions are found which at most 16 ticks later led to normative events (C3). If such relations exist, the criminal regards a norm demanded and typically reacts with an obey.

Even if the normative process failed (C4), the aggression might still be regarded as a justified sanction: if either the attacker has a high or very high image, or the aggression was mild or modest (C5), then it is assumed that a norm is demanded as well. This cognitive heuristic has been included in the model to cover the possible aptitude of criminals with a high image (and high reputation) to mitigate conflicts, either by mediating or by just exercising authority.

In contrast, if either the attacker's image is modest or low (C2), or the aggression was of high severity ("strong aggression"; C6), then the aggression is perceived as arbitrary, which means that no norm can be demanded. As a victim of such a kind of aggression, the change in the emotional mental frame appears to be indicated. The same holds for the case of a non-reputable attacker: the aggression is interpreted as unjust. As a result the mental frame might change to an emotional state (due to fear or rage), namely in case of strong or modest violence or strong threat (C7). Entering the emotional frame triggers a reaction, as described in the next but one subsection.

A special role plays the internal betrayal, on which the affected criminal always reacts with decreasing of image of the betraying criminal (Fig. 6.8). A betrayal with low or modest severity initiates a decrease of image by one level (D1), while highly severe betrayal causes a drop by two levels (D2). Without bothering with normative reasoning, a responding action might immediately be triggered according to Fig. 6.3.

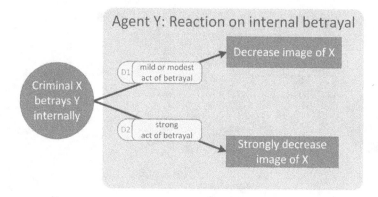

Figure 6.8 Decision tree for the reaction to internal betrayal

6.1.2.5 *Obey*

The action diagram fragment shown in Fig. 6.9 covers the criminal's reaction if the normative reasoning resulted in the insight that the experienced aggression is likely to be justified, be it as a sanction for an own actual norm violation or just due to the high image of the aggressor. The only possible action implemented here is to obey to the aggression to recover the trust among the criminals.

The respective implementation in the simulation model foresees the following two possibilities for this obeying behaviour, one for each of the two circumstances to obey as mentioned above:

- A rule "member X obeys", if the normative process classified the aggression as a sanction.
- A rule "member X obeys due to high image of aggressor".

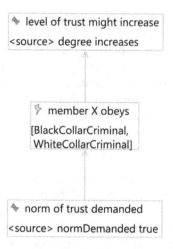

Figure 6.9 CCD action "member X obeys"

The result in both cases is the same: a normative event carrying the message that the criminal is willing to obey to the norm is send to the environment, i.e. made known to the other members of the criminal network, who might react by increasing the image of the obeying member.

6.1.2.6 *Reaction on aggression*

The opposite result of the normative reasoning is the awareness that the aggression cannot be a justified sanction, or the aggressor has such a low image that he is ineligible to be a sanctioning agent (i.e. aggression by a non-reputable attacker). This specific instance only leaves margin for two types of reaction, either betrayal or violent aggression.

The pre-selection between betrayal and violence is implicitly modelled in the different actions branching from the condition "norm of trust violated". One of the two options to respond to unjust aggression is to perform counter aggression, which in this context means some kind of violent act. The second option is to betray the criminal network. There are basically two possible categories of betrayal: the quite harmless internal betrayal and the serious and (for the criminal network and the individual) existence-threatening external betrayal. If the choice in the pre-selection is internal betrayal, then a "nasty" action is performed which is invisible for others. The consequence for the attacker to be expected (as mentioned in the last but one subsection) is to become disreputable in a similar way as it is the case with the initial normative event, provoking respective aggressive actions. The two options for external betrayal are either the criminal provides a hint (or a criminal complaint) directly to the Police, or details of the criminal network or associated activities are revealed to the public (and, hence, also to the Police) by informing newspapers or other media.

6.1.2.7 *Police intervention*

The third actor besides the Black and White Collar Criminals included in the simulation model is the Police as an institutional agent. The only action modelled in the CCD action diagram is the start of an investigation because of a criminal complaint or media reports, which finally results in a juridical decision, i.e. the arrestment of a criminal (Fig. 6.10).

The implementation of this action involves a few more aspects. Both mentioned pre-conditions trigger Police activities. The first step is the generation of a report, which contains information about the reason for and the subject of an investigation to initiate, as well as the source of information. The reason can be either a media report or a criminal complaint, and the subject is the criminal network. If the subject is unknown to the Police so far, then a new investigation is initiated, and the investigation progress starts with 0 per cent. If the subject is known already, then the progress advances (with an additive calculation) by 50 per cent. In any case, the progress of the investigation changes

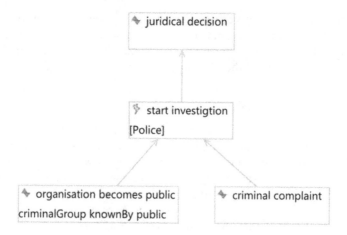

Figure 6.10 CCD action "start investigation" by Police

randomly with every tick: it (expectedly) increases by up to 40 per cent but might also decrease by up to 10 per cent. This negative progress expresses a possible "dead end" in which an investigation branch might enter.

If finally 100 per cent progress is reached, members of the criminal network are known to the Police so that measures can be decided and finally taken by arresting a randomly selected criminal. An arrested criminal no longer takes part in any business of the criminal network.

6.1.2.8   *Run on the bank*

Starting point for the effect of a "run on the bank" is another kind of panic, the fear to lose invested money. This is modelled in the CCD as shown in Fig. 6.11. Three possible pre-conditions for this panic are envisaged: the arresting of a member of the network due to a police intervention, the knowledge about intimidating activities against the White Collar Criminal, and the conjuncture that the network became public. In the implementation, a slight variation is realized as the latter of these three conditions is not considered. This simplification is justifiable because the uncovered network triggers police investigations that ultimately lead to arresting of criminals, which then cause panic reactions anyway.

The panic might cause intimidation of the White Collar Criminal – in this context called the "trustee". This is a two-stage process, where a (Black Collar) Criminal in panic to lose the invested money starts an approach to get the money back. If the White Collar is unable to return the money, the actual intimidation – often in the shape of an extortion attempt – takes place. This extortion results, on the one hand, in aggressive actions against the trustee, but, on the other hand, might be observed or become known by other members of the criminal network. The latter leads to an escalating number of approaches to get hold of invested capital.

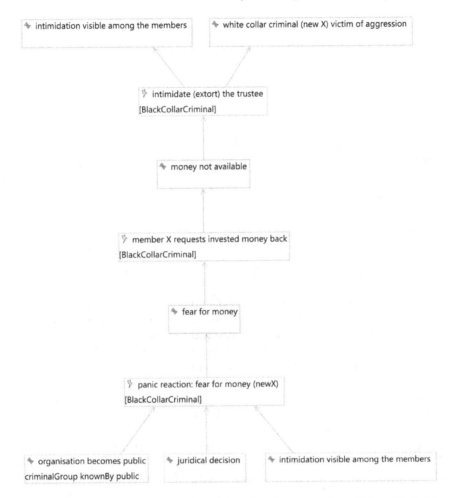

Figure 6.11 CCD actions for "panic reaction: fear for money (new X)" and intimidation of White Collar Criminal

The entering of the panic mode is implemented as drawn by the decision tree in Fig. 6.12. The request to get the money back from the White Collar Criminal as a result of the panic sets in with a probability of 0.6 (G1) if one of the following conditions holds:

- The state of a fellow criminal changes to "arrested".
- An aggression against the White Collar Criminal is observed.
- The image of the White Collar Criminal decreases to a modest or worse level. This case is not explicitly modelled in the CCD but becomes important for the dynamics when the White Collar is involved in a conflict, and the opposite party of the conflict at some time responds with requesting the invested money back.

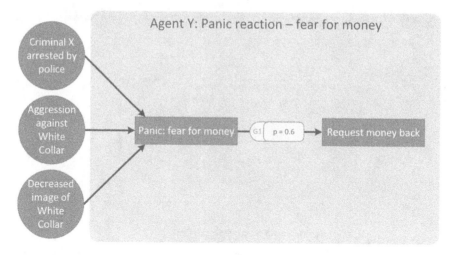

Figure 6.12 Decision tree for the panic reaction: fear for money

The mechanism with which the intimidation is implemented is deterministic. The approached White Collar Criminal processes this request by trying to fulfil as many as possible of the requests appearing at the same tick. A capital stock of 20 million units is available initially, which is refilled by another 20 million units each tick after some amount was requested and paid back. The decision to pay or not to pay is communicated to the requesting criminal. For Black Collar Criminals who got their money back, the crisis is resolved for the moment, and no reaction is to be expected. In the other case, the refusal to return the money is interpreted as a norm violation. Hence, a request for a normative event containing the message that the norm of trust is violated by the White Collar Criminal is issued. This normative event triggers the mechanism of revenge or sanctioning again, as described at the beginning of the chapter.

6.2   Conclusions on the simulation model description

The previous sections are intended to present the simulation model in a way to enable interested readers to comprehend the formalizations done on the base of the conceptual model as well as the simulation experiments elaborated in the following sections. However, all the technical details that are inevitable for executable software systems can obviously not be presented in the frame of a book chapter. These are aspects like the configuration of parameter settings, the control of simulation runs, and the generating and visualization of simulation outcomes. In the following, a few remarks are given on each of these aspects.

Simulation parameters are implemented in the following three different ways:

- Parameters interesting for experimentation and typically without relation to the evidence base can be put on the Repast user interface. This is done for the number and relation of reputable and normal Black Collar Criminals.

- Parameters that have a close relation to the evidence base are typically modelled in the conceptual model and annotated with phrases from the evidence. Hence, these parameters have to be changed in the CCD, and the following code transformation updates the parameters in the simulation model. For example, the types and probabilities of the aggressive actions are modelled in this way.
- All other parameters are coded in the rules, in most cases as probabilities, with comments in the source code.

To run a simulation, the procedure typical for RepastJ 3.1 simulation models has to be followed. Since DRAMS is just a software framework used from within the Repast/Java code, it is basically transparent to the user.

During simulation runs, outputs are generated which are presented and stored in different ways. The DRAMS rules produce text statements, written to a console window and stored in a log file. Per run there is also a sequence diagram generated and stored in an UMLet[2] file, showing all the interactions that appeared in the run. Finally, a graphical visualization of the agents with animations of the events happening in each tick is presented while running a simulation. All these different representations are base for the results presented in the following section.

6.3   Simulation results

6.3.1   *Narrative of the scenarios: A virtual context for possible courses of action*

Simulation models typically generate an output such as times series or histograms. Here the output is different: a simulation run generates a story which describes a scenario. In the following, some of these scenarios generated by model runs will be described. The objective of the scenarios is to explore the fact that the development of the behavioural rules of the agents is based on a qualitative analysis of textual data. The rules that are fired during the simulation runs can be traced back to annotations in the original textual documents. Examples of these "open codings" have been shown in the previous chapter describing the analysis of the textual data. In the description of the scenarios, the rules are now traced back to the original annotations in order to develop a narrative of the simulation runs, i.e. the scenarios are a kind of *collage* of the empirical basis of the agent rules. Thus, the reader will find text-elements that had already been used to illustrate the conceptual model. However, a different composition of single pieces of evidence (generated by the execution of the program code) generates different stories. Firing of certain rules makes certain follow-up actions more likely whereas others are excluded. By exploring the behavioural space of the model, the scenarios attempt to explore counterfactual situations of a complex configuration in which many decisions are involved that make different outcomes likely. This can be described as a "virtual experience". For this reason, the scenarios develop a storyline of a virtual case (see Corbin and Strauss, 2008 for the notion of a storyline that provides a coherent picture of a case. They treat the storyline as the theoretical insight of a qualitative analysis). In sum, the scenarios close the cycle of qualitative simulation, beginning with a qualitative analysis of the data as a basis for the development of a simulation model and ending with analysing simulation results by means of an interpretative methodology in the development of a narrative of the simulation results.

For this reason, the description suggests being a story of human actors for exploring the plausibility of the simulated scenarios. The plausibility check consists of an investigation of whether the counterfactual composition of single pieces of empirical evidence remains plausible, i.e. if they tell a story. Nevertheless, the reader should be aware that the story is about software entities which execute rules programmed in the code. Italics in the text indicate that the description paraphrases annotations of the empirical text basis of the fired rules. The scenarios explore the path dependency of the simulation runs generated by probabilistic decision rules. The only variation of the parameters is the number of so-called "reputable" and "ordinary" criminals (see description of the model). RC stands for Reputable Criminal, C for ordinary criminal, and WC for White Collar Criminal, who is responsible for money laundering. The scenarios presented here do not represent the full behaviour space of the model but only those that are of interest for examining modes of conflict resolution and outbreak of violence in a group with properties comparable to the empirical case, namely a group with no managerial authority assigned to certain positions such as a "boss" or "godfather" in a professional, Mafia type organization. Nevertheless, individuals differ in their reputation. We show cases that are representative of certain typical classes of the course of simulation runs. First, a scenario is presented that resembles central features of the data. Second, this is contrasted by a simple example of how escalation of violence could have been avoided. The third scenario represents a case in which the group managed to overcome a severe escalation of violence. Finally, the fourth scenario shows a case of successful police intervention.

6.3.1.1   *Scenario: Eroding of a criminal group by increasing violence*

The scenario consists of 7 RC, 3 C, and 1 WC.

6.3.1.1.1   TICK 2 – TICK 15: INITIAL VIOLENCE

The drama starts with an external event. For unknown reasons C0, who never was very reputable, became susceptible. It might be due to an unspecified norm violation, but it may not be so and just some bad talk behind the back. Eventually, he stole drugs, or they got lost. However, at least RC1 and RC4 decided to react on it and agreed that C0 deserves to be severely threatened. The next day RC1 approached C0 and told him that *he will be killed* if he is not loyal to the group. C0 was really scared as he could not find a reason for this offence. He was convinced that the only way to gain reputation was to demonstrate that he is a real man. So *threw the head of RC1 against a lamp pole and kicked him* further on more when he sank down to the ground. RC1 didn't know what was happening to him, that such a freak as C0 was beating him down, and RC1 one of the most respectable men of the group. There could only be one answer: he pulled his gun and shot. However, while shooting from the ground, the bullet missed the body of C0. So, he was an easy target for CO. He had no other choice than pulling out his gun as well and shooting RC1 down to death.

6.3.1.1.2   TICK 16 – TICK 17: SPREADING OF MISTRUST

However, this gunfight decisively shaped the fate of the gang. When the news circulated in the group, hectic activities broke out: WC *bough a bulletproofed car* and C1 though about a *new life on the other side of the world, in Australia.* In panic, RC6 wanted to severely beat the offender. While no clear information could be obtained, he presumed that C2 must have been the assassinator. So, with brute force RC6 beat the shit out of C2 until he was fit for the hospital. *His head was completely deformed, his eyes blue and swollen.* At the same time, RC1 and C2 agreed (wrongly) that it was C1 who killed RC1. While C2 argued that they should kidnap him, the more rational RC0 convinces him that a more modest approach would be wiser. He went to the house of C1 and told him that *his family would have a problem* if he ever will do something similar again. However, when he came back, RC2 was already waiting for him: with *a gun in his hand, he said that in the early morning he should come to the forest* for handing out money.

6.3.1.1.3   TICK 18 – TICK 35: INCREASING PANIC

But now all the victims are scared: RC0 and C1 and C2 thought about the aggression but find no norm demanded by their offenders. RC0 was fed up with being attacked by his *old friend* RC2 and invoked the general public as audience to articulate his disappointment: *in an interview with a major newspaper, he betrayed his role in the network.* However, also C1 learnt quickly. When he read the interview, he *contacted the newspaper and told them about the role of RC0.* Meanwhile, C2 planned his revenge: He *contacted a contract killer* to murder RC6, but the alleged professional turned out to be an amateur: the assassination was a failure. However, at least RC6 could not identify C2 as the purchaser of the killer and was unable to counteract. At the same time, RC2 was wondering why his old friend RC0 betrayed him in the news and thought that he deserves a severe beating. On the next occasion, he slammed his face. Now *remarkable tensions in the relation between RC0 and RC2 broke out. RC2 was really in fear.*

Secretly *he wrote an anonymous letter to the police* and the Police started an investigation of the case. However, it took a while until they were able to collect sufficient evidence for action. For quite a long time nothing seemed to happen. The group went back to its usual business, and it seemed that peaceful relation had been restored.

6.3.1.1.4   TICK 36 – TICK 41: BEGINNING OF EXTORTION

But the silence was only an illusion. Unexpected by the criminals one day the Police arrested RC4. This put the final nail in the coffin: in retrospective one can say that in this moment *a corrupt chaos* broke out. As they realized that their secret had been disclosed, all criminals were in fear for their money. In panic RC2, C1, C2, and RC5 attempted to get their money back. However, after WC paid back RC5, *he had serious problems with his liquidity* and was not able to fulfil the demands of the others. They debated what to do and decided that RC2 was best suited to enforce their claim: he went to the office of WC and *told him that he should repay his debt, because otherwise he will be killed.* However, rumours spread in the group that WC is about to be killed. This had a serious side effect. Now the others got in panic and started *extorting WC.* Indeed, WC obeyed. *He arranged a deal in an offshore financial centre to get a credit* and paid most of the demands. *He paid but at least he survived.* Nevertheless, RC3 and C2 came away empty-handed and enforced their claims. *WC was now in a completely despaired situation and tried to counteract. He hired an outlaw gang for murdering RC3* because he knew that *in the gang many hated RC3.* However, the gang did a bad job and he survived. Nevertheless, RC3 was shocked as he thought that his standing in the group would make him untouchable. As WC realized that the assassination failed, he obeyed the demand for money. Nevertheless, RC3 retaliated, but also his attempted assassination remained unsuccessful. This caused RC6, RC2, RC0, C1, and C2 to try to get their money back as long as WC is still living. Indeed, WC made a deal with C1 and RC2 by *selling them a building far below the true value.* When C2 and RC0 heard that, they got outraged and decided for a plan made by RCO: He arranged an appointment between WC and his lawyer. *However, when WC entered the office, RC0 waiting for him instead of the lawyer, accompanied by two seemingly Russian guys. One of them ordered him on his knees and pressed a machine gun at his head. … Then they forced him to sign a contract that he is no longer the owner of his investment company ….* WC was in great fear for his life. *From that moment on, when he made appointments with RC0, he was wearing a bulletproof jacket.* And still the extortion of WC went on for longer. RC2 ordered him to *come in the night to the forest near the town and still wanted more money. WC was so much in stress that he looked like years older.* He wondered why RC2 threatened him because usually RC2 was a reliable guy and he paid him already.

6.3.1.1.5 TICK 41 – TICK 73: RAMPAGE OF WC

It was a vicious cycle: the more he got extorted, the more urgently did all others demand their money back. It was like a run on the bank. After rumours arose of RC2's threatening WC, also RC0, C1, RC3, and RC5 made claims. WC *borrowed some money from a friend* for RC5 but refused the claims of the others. Now *he was like a hunted cat.... Isolated from the rest of the group,* he *became completely hysteric.*

WC wondered if he should kidnap RC6 but then he made a different plan. *He called to meet RC2 at the construction site for a discussion. However, in fact he came with two weapons. With one weapon he wanted to shoot down RC2 and put the other weapon in the hand of RC2 to claim that he shot only in self-defence.* When RC2 saw him with the gun, he *pulled out a machine gun and tried to hold it in his stomach,* but WC was faster and shot him to death. Still outraged, he wanted to go on and kill also C2 but this time he failed. But still his feelings of vengeance were not satisfied. He arranged *an interview in a newspaper* in which made severe accusations against RC5. RC5 was shocked because he thought that WC was a trustworthy guy. Still, WC had to handle extortion. Several plans for squeezing him out had been made. C2 and RC3 now completely lost any trust in WC. While being in fear for his life, their fear for money was even stronger and they requested money back. Indeed, WC found a way to give money to RC3 but refused the claims of C2. Instead, he *told the newspaper also the crimes* of C2. Now all were in panic, and the fate of the group was governed by a *rule of terror.* It was RC3 who finally *killed WC in the middle of the street* in front of his office. After the assassination, the Police captured C0, and several haphazard plans had been made. Still, many wanted revenge for the WC's rampage and tried to find a way to get their money. For instance, RC3 did not give up a plan for kidnapping. But after a while the group faded away. Only RC2 remained silent. Eventually he still enjoys the fruits of his criminal activities somewhere in the South Seas.

Decisive critical junctures

1) Initial gunfight: that the bilateral conflict escalated into murder causing an outbreak of panic in the overall network and therefore diffusion of the conflict in the group.
2) Wrong assignment of perpetration of offence caused spreading of violence in the group.
3) Arresting of RC4 leading to fear for money: this started the cycle of extortion whereas initially WC was not involved in the conflict.
4) Rampage of WC: turned the panic from fear for money to fear for life.
5) Killing of WC blocked restoration of the group.

6.3.1.2 Scenario: A small irritation

The scenario consists of 3 RC, 7 C, and 1 WC.

At the beginning of this story, RC5 began to mistrust WC. Eventually, WC embezzled his money as RC5 *had invested a significant amount of black money in WC's company structure.* However, it remains ambiguous what exactly happened. Anyway, RC5 wanted his money back. *They had a meeting at the office of their lawyer to appraise the value* and WC obeyed the request. So, trust was restored, and the groups continued their criminal activities.

Decisive critical junctures

1) Initial loss of trust against WC (and not another criminal) provided the chance for conflict resolution (by paying) and to avoid escalation of the conflict.
2) WC obeyed the request for money

6.3.1.3   Scenario: The group overcomes severe escalation of violence

The scenario consists of 7 RC, 3 C, and 1 WC.

At the beginning of the story, C1 had been accused by RC1, RC2, and RC5 of having violated their trust. It remained unclear what exactly happened. However, they agreed that C1 should be under observation and RC5 *installed concealed microphones and even a camera in his apartment.* But C1 realized that they mistrusted him and *was in fear of being monitored.* He had a strong ego and even though he knew that RC5 was a respectable man, he could not endure such an affront. Without hesitation, he *shot RC5 to death in the middle of a busy avenue.*

This sudden excessive violence completely out of proportion was a shock. RC0 and C2 got into panic. RC0 *bought a bulletproof car.* C2 attempted retaliation for the murder of *his long-time ally.* He was convinced that such an exorbitant murder, much like an execution could only be mandated by RC1, the *arch-enemy* of C1. He knew that RC1 would come to a big party at the next weekend. There he waited for him with some of his comrades. What followed was *like a Mafia movie: they approached him and slammed his head when he wanted to enter the party room. In panic RC1 run out of the building. One of the guys threw him against a street lamp but he could escape in the dunes directly behind the building. There he wanted to hide but the goons were behind him. He ran to the street and jumped into a taxi. The taxi driver brought him in a hospital.* In fact, C2's suspicion was simply wrong. So RC1 had no idea what was happening to him, but he swore that

C2 will be sorry for his offence. However, his revenge was more sophisticated. He knew that C2 was responsible for a major drug transport, and he stole a considerable amount of the commodity. Nevertheless, as C2 realized that he was betrayed, he suspected that RC1 was behind it. As he was more of a goon, he decided to ultimately solve the problem by shooting him to death. *He called to meet RC1 at the construction site for a discussion. However, in fact he came with two weapons. With one weapon he wanted to shoot him down and put the other weapon in his hand to claim that he shot only in self-defense.* However, RC1 anticipated that the meeting would be a trap. Instead of coming to the meeting, *he gave an interview with a major newspaper in which he provided detailed insights into C2's criminal activities.* So, the conflict between C2 and RC2 finally resulted in a disclosure of the secrecy of the group. In fact, the Police started a criminal investigation.

6.3.1.3.3   TICK 20 – TICK 27: WC BECOMES INVOLVED

As secrecy is obviously essential for undisturbed drug dealing, RC3 wanted to give him a lesson and *started an affair with his girlfriend.* Indeed, RC1 felt cuckolded and was wondering why RC3 betrayed him. At the same time, C2 got outraged when reading the news and repaid in the same coin. He contacted the *newspaper and told them about RC1's role in the group.* Immediately when he read it, RC1 went to the home of C2 and *hold a pistol against his head,* shouting *"now you will die!"* Also, C0 was fed up. He wanted to kill C2, but something cropped up: the police investigation resulted in arresting R6. As it now became clear that the Police were pursuing them, all were in fear to lose their investment and tried to get it back as soon as possible. Now WC was in trouble. RC0, C1, C0, and RC4 *came to his house and ordered that he should come at 10 in the wood near the town. There they asked for money.* In fact, *threatening and intimidation* worked: WC paid as much as he could. *I paid but I'm alive* as he later said. However, it took not long until he got *problems with his liquidity,* and he was unable to pay RC0 and RC4.

6.3.1.3.4   TICK 28 – TICK 37: POLICE INTERFERE IN ONGOING VIOLENCE

The bank refused the monetary transfer because of the negative account balance. RC0 made a phone call to WC. He was really angry. In their favourite club, C0, C1, and RC3 saw how he ran out of the café *with lather in his mouth and kicked a bike against a tree.* This made them wonder how save the rest of their money was. They took their *standard approach: threatening and then asking for the money.* However, now WC was curious. What the hell did they want furthermore? He said to them that he *does not know how to pay anymore because his bank account was completely empty.* Not much later *the police received an anonymous letter.* One may wonder who wrote the letter …

At the same time conflict between RC1 and C2 that occupied the group for a long time already was still not resolved. RC1 *hired an outlaw motorcycling gang to assassinate* C2. However, they did not do a very professional job. C2 survived the attack and *told the newspaper* that he already contacted previously about the attempt. Meanwhile, the individual reactions to the crisis created more and more a *corrupt chaos.* While C0 started making plans to kill WC because he thought that *WC wanted to keep for himself their investment,* WC wanted to take on initiative himself. *He was at a point where he was totally despaired.* He got a gun and had a plan to shoot down RC0. *He made an appointment with RC0 at the construction site for a discussion. However, in fact he came with two weapons.* However, at the last moment he didn't dare because *he was afraid of fingerprints on the gun.* Yet as RC0 saw WC approaching him with a weapon, he was so much in fear for his life that he did not counteract. However, as rumours spread telling this story, RC1, C0, RC2, and RC3 lost trust in WC and demanded their investment back. RC1 told WC that *his family will die if he does not pay.* In fact, WC sold an apartment to C0 but *for a price that was much too low.* However, he did not serve the other demands. They were not amused. However, before they could do anything, C0 got arrested.

6.3.1.3.5   TICK 37 – TICK 55: SEVERE EXTORTION OF WC

In panic all business partners wanted to extort WC the more now. RC1 arranged an appointment between WC and his lawyer. *However, when WC entered the office, RC0 waiting for him instead of the lawyer, accompanied by two seemingly Russian guys. One of them ordered him on his knees and pressed a machine gun at his head* to enforce their claims. Furthermore, on his way home RC4 laid and waited for WC. He fired a gun to shoot him down, but the bullet missed the target. As this news spread, also RC2 threatened him to death, and RC3 and C1 took their *standard program: threatening and then asking for the money.* RC3, RC1, and RC0 shared their job and every day when WC came home from work, one of them *was already waiting for him at the front of the door of his house.* WC *was like a hunted cat* and in great *fear of his daughter.* However, he had no liquid money. He made deals with C1 RC1 and RC2: *he signed certificated that transferred the ownership of his investment company* to them and *RC1 became its new director.* In consequence, the rest of the gang became even more nervous and intensified the pressure on WC. For quite some time the whole group was completely occupied with intimidating and extorting WC. For instance, he was *kidnapped three times* and held in arrest for several hours, *several times he was threatened to death,* and more than once he was beaten until *his head was completely deformed, his eyes blue and swollen.* He was lucky that he survived all the attacks. He undertook several tricks to get money such as *letting apartments owned by his company for half of the price* and *tried to get a mortgage from the offshore market.* He even *asked a friend for money* but could not fulfil all requests. Friends said that *he looked years older.*

6.3.1.3.6   TICK 56 – 60: WC STRIKES BACK

While WC accepted that the demands were justified, finally intimidation was too much. He *secretly contacted the police. ... He was shocked when he was told by the police that they knew that he was on a death list*. However, presumably his reaction was not like the Police expected. Outraged he *contacted an outlaw gang and gave them the rest of the money he had to kill his enemies*. As many of them *hated some members of the gang* for a long time, they undertook a massacre. On their bikes, they drove to the favourite club of the gang and with heavy machine guns they fired haphazardly in the pub until the room was full of blood and impact holes. It lasted only a minute until they drove away at full speed and left back the dead bodies of RC1, RC3, and RC4. This was a shock. Never has such brute violence been observed before and all survivors wondered what happened. However, WC smartly erased any traces of him: He remained in *contact with the police for several times* and *gave a public interview* in which he completely laid open the criminal operations of the group. However, at the same time, he agreed to a financial deal with RC0 in which he *bought fictitious rights right for a major infrastructure construction*. He got a bank loan for that deal. To pretend a prestigious business, *the meeting was held at a lake in Switzerland and WC came with his own private jet*. However, the *whole project was just fictitious*. Thereby WC succeeded to preserve his appearance both to the Police and the criminal group. But then C2 got arrested by the Police and in panic RC0 and RC2 requested their investment back. So his plan failed.

6.3.1.3.7   TICK 61 – TICK 71: RESTORING THE BUSINESS

RC0 undertook another attempt to kill WC and the spiral of intimidation and extortion seemed to start again. WC was afraid that his plan will be disclosed and obeyed the request. He paid at least to C1 but could not pay RC2, who asserted that *he will kill him if he doesn't pay*. In spite of WC's partial cooperation, RC0 *launched intimidating pictures of WC to the media*. However, before anybody could undertake any further action, the Police intervened and arrested RC0. Now worry about the money was more urgent than personal animosities. After RC2 *placed a machine gun in front of his stomach*, WC paid RC2. *The deal was financed by redeeming mortgages on a construction in Curacao* and all agreed that debts have been settled. Nothing happened anymore. Even though many had been killed and arrested, the Police could not break up the network. Step by step the remaining members of the group restored trust and build up their business model again. Eventually, they still sell drugs to street hawkers until today.

Decisive critical junctures

1) Wrong assignment of perpetration of offence caused spreading of violence in the group
2) Police intervention leads to the involvement of WC in the conflict

3) Double-faced counter-reaction of WC could have restored trust (if no further Police interventions would have happened)
4) WC's final acceptance of requests enabled (possibility of) restoration of trust

6.3.1.4 Scenario: Successful Police operations

The scenario consists of 3 RC, 7 C, and 1 WC.

6.3.1.4.1 TICK 2 – TICK 3: BRUTE FORCE

The beginning of the story remains unknown. C4, who never was very reputable, became susceptible to C3 and C6. It might be due to an unspecified norm violation, but it may not be so and just some bad talk behind the back. It must have been a severe offence since C3 and C6 agreed that a severe reaction was in need. While C3 argued for threatening him to death, C6 was convinced that a death penalty would also be a sign to the overall group. He *hired an outlaw gang* for assassinating C4, and *they shot him to death.*

6.3.1.4.2 TICK 4 – TICK 9: SPREADING OF VIOLENCE AND MISTRUST

However, the reaction of the group was different than C6 expected. For instance, RC1 *bought a bullet-proofed car* in panic. However, as it remained unclear who mandated the assassination, the reaction remained ambiguous too: C1 who *was for more than 15 years a friend of* C4 presumed that RC2 was guilty and beat the shit out of him until he was fit for the hospital. *His head was completely deformed, his eyes blue and swollen.* On the other hand, C3 suspected that RC0 mandated the assassination. As revenge, *he planned to approach him with a weapon but at the last moment he didn't dare.* Now C2 and RC0 were scared as they *didn't know what was happening to them. A witness testified that RC0 said that C3 must be crazy.* While for some time they remained silent, RC0 was so frightened that he *wrote an anonymous letter to the police*, nevertheless. Also, C2 planned revenge. On the next occasion, he paid C1 back in kind: he wanted to kill him, but *the attack was betrayed* and C1 was *able to escape to Italy.*

6.3.1.4.3 TICK 10 – TICK 17: POLICE START INTERVENING

For quite some time it seemed that peaceful relation had been restored and the group went back to its ordinary business. They thought *things were going well and finalized some quite successful projects.* But they didn't know that the Police were after them and still C1 wanted revenge. Feeling safe abroad, *he gave an interview with a major newspaper and betrayed the role of C2 in the criminal group.* Finally, the Police arrested C3. As it seemed to be obvious that the arrest of C3 was the fault of C1, C0 *became completely hysterical.* However, it was RC1 who was able to scent out C1's hideout and he shot him to death. Nevertheless, as the Police operation made clear to the group that their criminal activities had been detected, all were in fear for their monetary investments and attempted to get their money back as soon as possible. Indeed, WC was able to *pay several millions to RC0* but soon *he got problems with his liquidity.* The others were not satisfied and intimidated him. After some discussion about what would be the best strategy, RC1 went to WC and told him that *he will be killed if he does not pay.* Yet, at the same time the news of the killing of C1 shocked the group: but since nobody knew the assassinator, the reaction was no more than a shot in the dark. C5 and C6 approached RC2 with a weapon, but at the last moment he was able to run for cover and draw his gun himself. It ended up in a gunfight that all survived.

6.3.1.4.4 TICK 18 – TICK 38: POLICE CRACK THE GROUP

Police investigations revealed that *a huge amount of black money had been transferred to the company of WC.* The Police were able to collect enough evidence to arrest him. Therefore, the group kept silent for quite some time. However, the gunfight still occupied the participants. C5 didn't quit his plans for killing RC2. *He paid a huge sum to an outlaw gang in order that they should kill him* but also these guys didn't succeed. C6, on the other hand, *had several talks with the police.* So, nothing seemed to happen for a while but *the alliance was deeply shattered.* RC2 took revenge and *launched some compromising pictures of C5 to the media.* However, C2 noticed it. Going to the public was a severe violation of trust. Therefore, C2 arranged an appointment between RC2 and his lawyer. *However, when he entered the office, C2 was waiting for him instead of the lawyer, accompanied by two seemingly Russian guys. One of them ordered him on to his knees and pressed a machine gun at his head* in order that he should never do this again. However, it was impossible to restore trust in the group. However, soon after his attack, C2 was arrested by the Police and both C5 and RC5 were too scared by their experience of being threatened to life. Independent of each other they decided to secretly quit the group and thought that their only chance to survive would be to *secretly contact the police.* In fact, their collaboration enabled the arresting of R0 and broke the criminal activities of the group.

Decisive critical junctures

1) Misleading interpretation of sanction (death penalty) generates outbreak of chaotic violence.
2) Police intervention leads to the involvement of WC in the conflict.
3) Arresting of WC terminated extortion and the business model of the group.
4) The fact that many contacted the Police (i.e. secretly changed sides) cracked the group.

6.4   Conclusion: Central Mechanisms

While the purpose of this book is to outline the methodology of interpretive agent-based simulation, this and the previous chapter attempted to provide an example of how this methodology has been used in practice. For this purpose, the case of investigating criminal culture has been consulted. Even though this case has only an illustrative purpose, it might hopefully become transparent what kind of insights can be gained from this approach. The purpose of this chapter was specifically to provide details of how a simulation model is derived from the conceptual model, using the example of simulating conflict resolution and conflict escalation in a criminal network. The attempt of the modelling process is to preserve the meaningfulness of socio-cognitive coupling by focusing specifically on the process of agents' interpreting actions of other agents: namely the interpretation of aggression. The rules implemented in the model aim to preserve the thick description of the interpretive, ethnographic data analysis. As the analysis is an interpretation of the narratives found in the police interrogations, the model is an interpretation of interpretations. Following Geertz, this could be denoted as a "thick conditional" as argued in Chapter 3. The second part of this chapter demonstrated how the concept of traceability shapes the analysis of simulation results. In contrast to traditional simulation approaches in which results are typically displayed as time series, the traceability to the ethnographic evidence base of the rules fired during a simulation run enables the development of narrative scenarios. Narratives provide storylines to "produce for the readers the feeling that they have experienced, or could experience, the events being described in a study" (Creswell and Miller, 2000: 129) which fosters a conversation across cultures (see Chapter 4). Thus, also the outputs of simulations are open for interpretation. In the next chapter, we will show in closer detail the methodological approach of how to interpret counterfactual scenarios. Such a qualitative interpretation of simulation results enables an examination of their meaningfulness. We "understand" the agents' actions. At the same time, "understanding" the agents entails deciphering how they enact a specific culture.

Notes

1 http://www.ocopomo.eu/
2 http://www.umlet.com/

References

Corbin, J. and Strauss, A. (2008). *Basics of Qualitative Research*. 3rd ed. Thousand Oaks: Sage.
Creswell, J. W. and Miller, D. A. (2000) 'Determining validity in qualitative inquiry', *Theory into Practice*, 39(3), pp. 124–130.

Lotzmann, U. and Meyer, R. (2011). A declarative rule-based environment for agent modelling systems. In *The Seventh Conference of the European Social Simulation Association, ESSA 2011*, Montpellier, France.

Lotzmann, U., Neumann, M. and Möhring, M. (2015). From text to agents – process of developing evidence-based simulation models. In Mladenov, V. M. et al. (eds.). *29th European Conference on Modelling and Simulation, ECMS 2015* (pp. 71–77). European Council for Modelling and Simulation (ECMS).

Lotzmann, U. and Wimmer, M. A. (2013). Evidence traces for multiagent declarative rule-based policy simulation. In *Proceedings of the 17th IEEE/ACM International Symposium on Distributed Simulation and Real Time Applications (DS-RT 2013)*, pp. 115–122. IEEE Computer Society.

North, M. J., Collier, N. T. and Vos, J. R. (2006) 'Experiences creating three implementations of the repast agent modeling toolkit', *ACM Transactions on Modeling Computer Simulation*, 16(1), pp. 1–25.

7 Hermeneutics of social simulations*

On the interpretation of digitally generated narratives

Sascha Dickel and Martin Neumann

7.1 Social simulations and their need for interpretation

So far, we have seen how a thick description can be preserved in the formulation of the rules of an agent-based model. As simulations allow us to think about what-if questions, we paraphrased this process as the departure from a thick description to a thick conditional. Moreover, we showed how simulation results can be formulated as narrative scenarios by tracing the rules fired during a simulation to the empirical evidence base, thereby preserving the thick description in these simulated narratives. Before the next two chapters will turn to inter- and transdisciplinary reflections about this research process, we will now dive into the details of the final step of this process: the examination of the meaningfulness of the narrative scenarios.

Simulation models allow for an investigation of "what if?" questions and thus to conduct social experiments in-silicio to assess their potential consequences before intervening in the real world. Such ex-ante scenarios of potential developments thus allow to identify configurations of conditions that make desirable developments more likely, as well as early warning signals for less desirable developments. The computer is thus used as a "virtual laboratory" (Boero and Squazzoni, 2010). While the idea of a virtual laboratory is well known in agent-based research, in this chapter we want to address a problem that has hardly been addressed in the field of simulation research, namely the *interpretation* of social simulations. In doing so, we want to make an explorative contribution to the basic research of social science methods by investigating especially whether and to what extent the problem of algorithmic selectivity can be mitigated by complementary methods of hermeneutics. For not only what one "puts into" a model in terms of assumptions is dependent on existing sociological knowledge, but also what one "reads out" of simulation results is shaped by the researchers' prior understandings. Like any empirical data, computer-based scenarios are subject to interpretation.

* This chapter is based on Dickel, S. and Neumann, M. (2021). Hermeneutik sozialer Simulation. Zur Interpretation digital erzeugter Narrative. *Sozialer Sinn* 22(2): 353–387.

DOI: 10.4324/9781003393207-7

They do not understand themselves but have to be interpreted. This interpretation work differs from the scientific-technical work that has to be done to create and run a simulation. This is because it is no longer a matter of defining parameters, designing algorithms, or correctly applying software interfaces, but of *reading* the model.

For the purpose of reading the narrative scenarios, we explore the possibility of combining two methodological worlds that at first sight seem far apart. Namely, we propose to use the procedure of hermeneutic sequence analysis to interpret agent-based modelling. In doing so, we simultaneously build a bridge between digital methods in sociology (Maasen and Passoth, 2020), which uses novel computer-based procedures to understand social order(s), and an established interpretive technique in qualitative social research. The chapter thus makes a genuine social science contribution to digital hermeneutics (Capurro, 2010), i.e. to the recently articulated effort to relate hermeneutic procedures and digital methods to each other.

The specific simulation model we use as an example is again the escalation of violence within criminal networks which has been described in the previous chapters. Thus, throughout the book we undertake a fourfold translation:

- First, the interrogation protocols formed the source of a so-called consistent conceptual description (CCD, cf. Scherer et al., 2013, 2015) as it has been described in Chapters 3 and 4.
- The consistent conceptual description was in turn the basis for the development of a simulation model based on it as it has been described in Chapters 3 and 5.
- The third translation, and this is already a methodological innovation of the simulation model used as an example here, was a transfer of the simulation processes into a narrative, i.e. the simulation was transferred into an empirically based narrative in a first interpretative step as described in Chapters 3 and 5.
- Finally, the fourth translation is a hermeneutic interpretation of these narratives.

This interpretation, i.e. the last translation step, will be presented in this chapter. We are thus entering new scientific territory, because to our knowledge it is the first attempt to combine hermeneutic sequence analysis and agent-based modelling. This also results in the explicitly exploratory character of the chapter. In the following, we first present our methodological considerations for the interpretation of computer-modelled scenarios and justify our choice of the method of hermeneutic sequence analysis. The fruitfulness of the chosen method will be illustrated by a sequence analysis of two contrasting scenarios resulting from the simulation model of interrogation of actors in a criminal network outlined in the previous chapters. In doing so, we will also discuss the context of the simulation and its genesis. This chapter concludes with reflections on the added value of hermeneutic sequence analysis for agent-based modelling and its potential contribution to methodologically controlled algorithm criticism.

7.2   On the hermeneutic interpretation of scenarios: Methodological considerations

Typically, simulations generate quantitative data, such as time series, which can then be analysed statistically. But for this data of a simulation to become the subject of further scientific debate and/or practice-oriented consulting, it must be verbalized (cf. Scherer et al., 2013). It thus becomes a text. And such a text can be read in very different ways. This does not distinguish the verbalized form of a social simulation from other texts that qualitative researchers have to deal with in their everyday research, be it interview transcripts or documents. The requirements for researchers who have to interpret a linguistic scenario correspond to the requirements that all researchers have to deal with who are confronted with protocols of social reality (Oevermann, 2002). From the perspective of reconstructive social research, agent-based modelling is thus an innovative and promising *data collection* method, which, however, would have to be supplemented by substantive *evaluation* methods, i.e. procedures of data interpretation, which focus on the methodologically controlled interpretation of texts.

This is especially true because in agent-based simulation as a social science research method, the algorithmically determined behaviour of the agents is interpreted as social action. This is a special case of attributing agency to technology (Schulz-Schaeffer, 2008). The agents of the simulation are not understood as agents in social reality, but as agents in a laboratized special world, a simulated microcosm of action. This interpretation of the laboratized world as a world in which action is taken necessitates interpretations that do not tell of a digital world of zeros and ones, but rather, for example, as agents who undertake aggressive actions as described in the previous chapters. Only in the form of such a story can the simulation be made socially relevant. Thus, for the simulation to appear socially meaningful, the behaviour of software is here translated into categories of "human differentiation" (Hirschauer, 2017). The social-scientifically usable result of agent-based modelling is thus a story that is, in a strict sense, a fiction, i.e. the construction of its own world with its own rules. Interpreting scenarios thus means a transfer of algorithmic formalism to social reality. Even if agent-based modelling is therefore typically assigned to the procedures of standardized social research, it is, in the form of the protocols it produces, at the same time a procedure that requires rules of interpretative interpretation. The rules of this interpretative interpretation must keep the purpose of modelling in mind, otherwise researchers run the risk of overlooking interpretative possibilities, of reproducing their own prejudices, or of discovering only the already well-known world in the possibility-closing world of the scenario. This reveals an open research gap in the study of social simulation: namely, the translation of modelling into the meaningful-ness of the social world. The category of understanding to be mobilized for this purpose is nevertheless rarely found in modelling purposes. This is even more unfortunate as many modelling purposes explicitly aim at an idiosyn-cratic understanding of an individual case (Gilbert and Ahrweiler, 2009), and the inclusion of qualitative data in the development of model assumptions, i.e. the process of model building, is now a broad field of research in agent-based modelling (Edmonds, 2015). Similarly, the modelling intention to initi-ate social learning[1] would benefit from deciphering agents' understanding of meaning in the field. Last but not least, meaningfulness is a specific charac-teristic of the social world that distinguishes it from, for example, the physical world. Given this desideratum, we propose hermeneutic sequence analysis as a method for interpreting simulation-based scenarios. Hermeneutic sequence analysis lends itself to the interpretation of computer-based scenarios for a variety of reasons. Some of these are general in nature and would be valid for a variety of scenarios. Other reasons are case specific and contribute to why sequence analysis is particularly appropriate for the chosen case of escalating violence in the context of organized crime.

7.2.1 *Presentation of the sequence-analytical procedure*

Probably the most general reason for hermeneutic reconstructions is to arrive at results that are as controlled and intersubjectively comprehensible as pos-sible, which do not simply reflect the already existing presuppositions of the researchers, but at the same time open the possibility of discovering and re-constructing new contexts of meaning. Instead of simply subsuming the data under already pre-formulated theses, at least the chance should be opened to successively develop theses on the case. In the social sciences, sequence analysis is regarded as a central instrument of hermeneutic meaning development. It is "a method of interpretation that attempts to reconstruct the meaning of any kind of human action sequence by sequence i.e., sense unit by sense unit [...]. Sequence analysis is guided by the assumption that in the succession of actions [...] contexts of meaning are realized. The hermeneutic approach of thinking the individual as part of a whole hypothetically spans concrete human action in sequence analysis with a shape of meaning that encompasses all steps of action" (Kurt and Herbrik, 2014: 281).

Sequence analysis as a method is closely linked to the methodologi-cal paradigm of Objective Hermeneutics (cf. Wernet, 2000), which its founder, Ulrich Oevermann, has meanwhile expanded into a comprehen-sive social theoretical model in which *crises and routines* play a key role in constitutional logic (cf. Oevermann, 2016).[2] Accordingly, every social practice is confronted with crises in its execution, with events that call into question a seamless and-so-on. These crises usually remain latent, as they are dealt with through routines. Crisis and routine refer to each other con-ceptually. The concept of crisis indicates that routines are contingent and can in principle become fragile at any time – then the crisis becomes manifest. Routines, in turn, can be understood as stabilized ways of dealing with crises. For sociological observers (and possibly for the actors involved), crises have an enlightening effect. They confront the possibility that things may not continue as they have been used to until now. They question existing routines and provoke the breaking of new ground (Endreß, 2015). Like cracks in the cloud, they allow a clearer view of what was previously hidden. They point to the contingency of social orders and at the same time open the possibility of creating a new order (Folkers and Lim, 2014). Against this background, sequence analysis is also, and especially, a method that promises to reconstruct how actors deal with (manifest and latent) crises (Oevermann, 2002: 9f.).

The procedure of sequence analysis has itself become routine. It is well established in the social sciences, in particular in the tradition of German qualitative research, and has been codified in introductory writings (see, for example, Wernet 2000; Kurt and Herbrik, 2014; Sammet and Erhard, 2018). Therefore, we can limit ourselves here to a concise summary of the rules of interpretation. The first important rule is the eponymous sequential approach. The interpretation is done in the order given by the protocol to be analysed itself. The assumption is that each sequence closes possibilities on the one hand and opens new possibilities on the other. In order to avoid interpreting the text prematurely out of context and thereby possibly only confirming one's own presuppositions, interpretation is carried out context free in the first phases of the analysis. This means, above all, that no contextual knowledge may be used to exclude readings that the text allows. Very well, however, a confrontation of the text analysis with the contextual information can take place in the final determination of structure. In the actual text analysis, however, a protocol is first interpreted literally and extensively. This is done practically by sketching a series of stories in which the particular sequence passage would make sense. The basic question that can be asked of each sequence passage can be summarized as, "Consider who might have addressed this utterance to whom, under what conditions, with what justification, and what purpose?" (Schneider 1995: 140). The answers to these questions are the thought-experimentally designed stories. These stories are examined for commonalities and differences and condensed into readings. A limiting factor here is the rule of parsimony. Readings that require few additional assumptions and that do not assume case-specific exceptionalities without reason are given the benefit of the doubt. By generating readings, certain possibilities of connection to the interpreted sequence passage become visible at the same time. In this sense, each interpretation step sequentially makes spaces of possibility visible and at the same time closes past spaces of possibility. The interpretation of further sequences according to the same pattern then serves to confirm, eliminate, or modify developed readings as well as to generate new possibilities of interpretation. The readings generated so far are carried along as an "inner context" which is enriched sequence by sequence. Finally, the goal of the analysis is the reconstruction of the reading that makes the sequential connection logic of the text comprehensible. This is considered as the case structure of the text under investigation. Hypotheses should be developed as early as possible, which can then be tested during the analysis. As soon as there are no more surprises that would give a reason for completely new interpretations, a faster passage through the material is justified. It is then only a matter of looking specifically for clues in the text that could call the developed theses into question.[3]

Sequence analyses are carried out for a wide variety of data materials (cf. Sammet and Erhard, 2018). They are particularly suitable for reconstructing social processes, since these take place over time, which can be traced through the analysis in its case-specific processuality. The analysis can thus make the contingency of courses of action visible. It reveals not only the course of the case itself, but also and especially the possible alternatives that were not realized in the specific case. In this way, one obtains a reconstruction of a space of "objective possibilities" (Weber, 1968) that goes beyond the specific case. Ulrich Oevermann formulates this as follows: "In every concrete case reconstruction, not only the manifest case embodied in the sequence-analyzed protocol is brought to explication, but beyond it other, further cases are determined, which this case could in principle have become according to its objective possibilities, in its wider historical, cultural, and social environment, its milieu, but did not become. This is because sequence analysis requires that at each sequence point, in the sense of valid rules of generation, the scope of possibilities be concretely explicated in a thought-experimental way, with reference to which the concrete case maps its structural regularity as a recurrent systematics of its decisions and choices" (Oevermann, 2002: 14f.). It is noteworthy at this point that Oevermann considers the generating rules that open certain possibilities as a "set of *algorithmic* generating rules" (Oevermann, 2002: 7, emphasis by the authors). That is, at least in the objective-hermeneutic reading of sequence analysis, human actors are also viewed as agents operating within the framework of rules. These may be syntactic rules of language, for example, or institutions and conventions (such as those of greeting). Oevermann understands these rules as algorithmic because they contain certain potentially explicable rules of action.

7.2.2 *The significance of the model for the hermeneutic interpretation*

The idea of algorithmic generation rules shows an elective affinity to agent-based modelling. This is because the latter now aims precisely at simulating social processes by constructing rule-based sequences of actions. This makes it highly amenable to sequence-analytical interpretations. More than that, agent-based modelling and sequence analysis share a common epistemic goal, namely the construction of "objective possibilities". From the outset, we are not dealing with actual sequences in simulations, but rather with the construction of possibilities, which, as abstractions, of course never correspond to the real sequences to which they refer (and which they seek to model) (Weyer and Roos, 2017: 15). It is a formalized construction of social possibilities. In this context, simulations also open up the opportunity to construct social worlds that have no counterpart in reality but could be possible (or could possibly have been realized).

When sequence analysis is used to interpret such scenarios, it opens up the social meaning of the concretely simulated possibilities as well as of those possibilities that become latently visible through the model – and this is initially independent of the question whether these possibilities could have been chosen by the simulated agents in the socio-technical context of the respective software model. Sequence analysis can thus also help to identify objective possibilities which, according to the interpretation of the "inner context", could have been thought experimentally, but could not have been chosen in the context of the simulation due to the underlying technically realized rules. It can thus also be used to validate and, if necessary, revise a model.

For the reasons given above, hermeneutic sequence analysis thus appears to be a fundamentally fruitful method, which can complement agent-based modelling in its specific function as an evaluation method. Nevertheless, this method has not yet been applied in this way – at least, the authors of this chapter are not aware of any corresponding application cases. This is where this chapter enters the new methodological and methodological territory.

Now we do not want to claim that other reconstructive methods might not be suitable for interpreting computer-based scenarios. Here, too, further explorations are certainly worthwhile. However, the choice of hermeneutic sequence analysis seems particularly instructive for the case of conflict simulation discussed in this book. The simulation model we draw on to demonstrate our methodological considerations in this chapter refers to a real-life escalation of violence within a criminal network discussed in the previous chapters. This social field, which had been operating stably for years, unexpectedly imploded in a spiral of violence without any recognizable external influence. Here, then, the question of the meaningfulness of what happened arises in a particularly pointed way. On the one hand, we are dealing with a case that explicitly deals with the crisis of a social order, namely a crisis that manifested itself in social reality in the outbreak of an escalation of violence. The problem of practice to which the simulations react is thus the problem of a latent crisis that finally became manifest in the form of violence. Thus, the scenarios are protocols of alternative ways of dealing with the latent crisis that led to the spiral of violence that actually took place. The sequence analysis of the scenarios thus promises, on the one hand, to open up these non-actualized possibilities in terms of meaning structure and, on the other hand, to search for the latent crisis that led to the outbreak of uncontrollable violence. In this context, path branching is of particular relevance. Therefore, three experts have discussed which different connecting actions seem plausible in given situation conditions: an

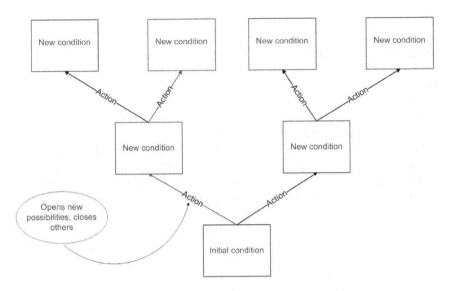

Figure 7.1 Schematic diagram of path branching

expert from the police, a social scientist, and a computer scientist as an expert for the simulation method. The part of a sequence-analytic thought experiment is then taken over by the simulation (based on the discussion of possible ramifications in the creation of the model): to explore the space of possibilities. Here, a simulation supports the thought experiment by allowing, for example, 50 or 100 simulation steps to explore how possibilities open and close.

In Fig. 7.1, for instance, the first box on the left and then the box on the left might be realized in one concrete simulation run, while other possibilities are realized in other simulation runs. However, simulations usually do not capture, or only rudimentarily capture, the sense dimension of the social world. The innovation of generating narratives from simulations makes it possible to open the simulation to the sense dimension. A sequence analysis of the simulation results then enables an investigation of the meaningfulness of the algorithmically generated possibility spaces.

7.3 Interpretating simulations of conflicts in criminal networks

Before we present selected examples of a sequence analysis of the narrative scenarios, let us briefly recap the case: the goal of the modelling and simulation was to develop alternative scenarios of conflict management and its protagonists and antagonists in order to explore, together with the police, the possibility space of the internal dynamics of criminal groups, which remains hidden from the outside view. This enables the police to gain insights into the role and possible actions of the important actors. The data basis are police interrogations from a group of related cases in which more than 200 persons are named. However, the active core consisted of about 20–30 people, some of whom had been personal friends for decades. This network had no fixed organizational structures, such as the Chinese Triads or the Sicilian Mafia, but can rather be described as a loose association of interests. Nevertheless, in the criminal law sense, it is organized crime in which "more than two participants cooperate for a longer or indefinite period ... cooperate" for a "planned commission of criminal acts determined by the pursuit of profit or power ..." (Bundeskriminalamt, 2013: 9). For at least a decade, this network was able to earn triple-digit millions in drug trafficking, which was channelled into the legal market in a highly professional money laundering operation. It was thus a highly professional and successful criminal organization. However, without outside intervention (such as arrests), the network imploded seemingly unpredictably in a spiral of violence. For example, there was a series of three assassinations within a week. Old friends became bitter enemies. In the interrogations, the actors involved literally described the escalation of violence as a "corrupt chaos" or as a "reign of terror" in which "old friends killed each other". On the one hand, these formulations suggest that the escalation of murder and violence was driven by internal dynamics rather than external enemies. On the other hand, they also make clear that from the internal perspective the escalation of violence was no longer understood, but from the subjective point of view was seemingly driven by an invisible hand. The simulation model was developed in cooperation with the police to investigate the question that the actors themselves could not answer: how did the escalation of violence occur? In the following, two scenarios, or exemplary excerpts of scenarios, will be presented and analysed with regard to the mechanisms of conflict regulation. The case-specific interest is the latent crisis that led to the outbreak of uncontrollable violence in the criminal networks. An interpretation of this will be explicated at the end of this chapter.

A word about presentation: in the following presentation of the material, *italicized* text passages are taken directly from the interrogation transcripts, which are assigned to algorithmic rules invoked at the particular point in the simulation process. Non-italic text passages are "hinge points", which already represent first-order interpretations and connect the individual text modules. The names are, of course, fictitious.

Since the simulation model was designed to examine the issue of conflict escalation in a criminal network, the scenarios are each different ways of dealing with conflict. "Routine activities" such as drug trafficking or money laundering are not the subject of the simulation. Both scenarios presented as examples are examples of "successful" conflict management. It should be mentioned here that this corresponds neither to the empirical case nor to the majority of simulation courses. The first scenario is a very short story of successful conflict resolution. It consists of only four steps, i.e. four sequences of situational conditions and follow-up actions. The second example is an excerpt of a longer "story" that ultimately ends with the violent collapse of the network.

However, the episode that will be presented here represents an example of a thoroughly creative conflict resolution.

7.3.1 Scenario

The following passage of a narrative scenario is part of a longer story depicting an interaction between a drug trafficker ("Toby") and a trusted person ("Achim") who had invested the profits from drug trafficking in the legal business world (i.e. engaged in money laundering).

7.3.1.1 Simulation steps 1–4: Initial loss and restoration of trust

At the beginning of this story, Toby began to distrust Achim. He suspected that Achim was embezzling his money, as Toby had *invested a significant amount of black money in Achim's corporate structure.* It remains unclear what happened exactly. However, Toby wanted his money back. *They had a meeting at their lawyer's office to assess the value of his investment,* and Achim complied with the request. Thus, trust was restored, and the groups continued their criminal activities.

7.3.1.2 Sequence analysis

The interpretation starts at the already texted scenario (and initially hides its background of origin). "At the beginning of the story" is reminiscent of a fairy tale, a made-up past, as is indeed the case for counterfactual scenarios. At the same time, it becomes clear that this story is being retold, that we are dealing with a text that paraphrases a story.[4] Only then is the narrative introduced in terms of content: it addresses the conceptual field and how to deal with mistrust. The opposite of mistrust is trust. Trust is a relationship pattern that is linked to the expectation of reciprocity. These are expectations which, however, cannot be demanded. The word "began" makes the situational dynamic clear here: there must have been a relationship of trust, which is now in question.

However, it is not until the following sequence that the substantive basis of the relationship of trust becomes clear: Toby "had invested a considerable amount of black money in Achim's corporate structure". Here the inner context becomes clear. Trust can occur and be of importance in different relationship patterns, each of which allows for completely different options for action: in soccer, a player might trust the coach or vice versa. A love relationship is also often accompanied by trust between the love partners. Otherwise, one would probably not call an erotic relationship a love relationship, even if this rather characterizes the stereotypical ideal image of love. Here, on the other hand, we are dealing with a business relationship. The stereotypical ideal image of a business relationship is the rational calculation: an expectation of mutual profit directed into the future. However, a violation of this expectation does not necessarily have to be linked to distrust of a person, in this case Achim. The violation of an expectation of profit can, for example, be caused by a changed market situation. This can also be detected by rational calculation. Personal distrust, on the other hand, has an emotional component. Why this is so is illustrated by the term "black money". The expectation of reciprocity is to get the money back at some point. Distrust could arise, for example, if Achim were to try to "rip Toby off". In legal business relationships, a court could be involved in this case. However, since it is black money, it is an expectation that cannot be claimed. Toby is susceptible to blackmail because the possession of black money is precisely not a possession that can be claimed in court. Therefore, the actors' relationship is based on personal trust.

How can this situation now be resolved? First, it should be noted that "it is unclear exactly what happened". Toby can only act on circumstantial evidence, not on proof. In this situation, he decides to reclaim his money. In principle, four variants are conceivable here as to how this demand could be implemented: he could threaten Achim in the expectation that this will motivate Achim to comply with his will. He could also obtain a pawn to establish an equivalence relation, for example, stealing something from Achim or kidnapping his daughter. In that case, both actors would have a good of the other actor, which they could exchange. However, since these are only conjectures, a clarifying conversation would also be conceivable. This could be accompanied by a fourth solution of invoking a "substitute leviathan": an authority recognized by both parties. On the one hand, this authority could function as the equivalent of a court, i.e. as an independent third party in the bilateral conflict, or, on the other hand, in connection with a clarifying conversation, it could help to temporarily restore the relationship of trust between Toby and Achim, since both parties in the conflict trust this third person.

So how did the actors in the scenario act? They had "a meeting in their lawyer's office" in which Achim complies with the request. The actors have thus chosen the fourth variant of a non-violent version of conflict management. The role of the lawyer corresponds to the third-party mediating in a clarifying conversation. This allows to avoid a further escalation stage. The contrasting scenario will make clear that, but also how in this fictional story, worse has been prevented.

Sociologically, the role of the lawyer is also interesting because, on the one hand, it suggests a partial legalization of the illegal world, but, on the other hand, it also implies a partial criminalization of the legal world. The very concept of investment refers to the legal world. However, a clarification of conflicts of illegal business relations in a lawyer's office also implies personal relations. A "grey zone" emerges that has characteristics of both legal and illegal socialization. The final sequence, in which it is confirmed that trust has been restored, finally refers to a general pattern of social relations, which can be described with Oevermann as the dialectic of crisis and routine.

7.3.2   Scenario

7.3.2.1   Simulation steps 56–60: Achim strikes back

Although Achim accepted the demands as justified in principle, the intimidation was finally too much. He secretly contacted the police. *He was shocked when he was told by the police that they knew he was on a death list.* Presumably, however, his reaction was not what the police expected. Outraged, *he contacted an outlaw gang and gave them the rest of the money he had to kill his enemies. Many of them hated some members of the gang for a long time.* Therefore, they committed a massacre. On their motorcycles, they went to the gang's favorite club and fired heavy machine guns into the bar until the room was full of blood and bullet holes. It only took a minute for them to drive away at full speed, leaving behind the bodies of Michael, Jason, and Dominik. This was a shock. Never before had such brutal violence been witnessed and all the survivors wondered what had actually happened. Achim, however, cleverly covered all traces: *he remained in contact with the police several times* and *gave a public newspaper interview* in which he fully exposed the group's criminal operations. At the same time, however, he agreed to a deal with Thomas in which he *acquired fictitious rights to a major infrastructure project.* He got a bank loan for this deal. *To feign a prestigious deal, the meeting took place at a lake in Switzerland and Achim came in his own private jet. However, the whole project was purely fictitious.* As a result, Achim managed to maintain his reputation with both the police and the criminal group.

7.3.2.2   Sequence analysis

This scenario begins with a relativization: "although". Here, then, two seemingly contradictory statements are announced. On the one hand, normative agreement with demands is reported: in principle, two readings are conceivable under which an actor accepts demands: for example, someone might have borrowed money from a friend and feel morally obligated to that person to pay it back. This is an informal setting. Second, an employer, for example, might demand sick leave for absenteeism. This would be a formal framework. On the other hand, the manner in which the demand was made seems to violate Achim's normative expectations. In Achim's subjective assessment, therefore, there is a mismatch between the demand and the manner in which it is made, i.e. two conflicting normative expectations.

In any case, the reaction to the contradictory normative expectations remains hidden: Achim "secretly contacts the police". This shows the expectation of the possibility that the counterpart will resort to extra-legal means. This can be, for example, a threat to family members. The police is a third instance for the enforcement of legitimately decided normative claims. This shows that the claim originates from a private actor, i.e. there is an informal framework. In contrast, the information Achim receives from the police, namely that he is on a "death list", points rather to a "bureaucratic" character of the demanding actor. The actor does not act in spontaneous affect but behaves like an organization that creates lists. A list suggests that there are also other people involved. Presumably, there is a unifying motive, because the creation of a list suggests that it is organized around a unifying theme, which is the basis for the death sentences. It could be mafia organizations or warring parties. In any case, the actor is willing to use violence.

Achim's reaction to the information from the police, namely to contact an outlaw gang to commission a murder, suggests that he has the impression that the police will not help him, i.e. cannot solve the problem. Thus, trust in state institutions is weak. This suggests a context of limited statehood in which state institutions have limited capacity to enforce normative expectations. This supports the reading that this is a context of mafia-like organizations. In this context, the word "outraged" suggests that Achim acts in affect. Nevertheless, the action is done in a planned manner: he "contacted an outlaw gang ... to kill his enemies". This shows that he has criminal contacts. Achim is recognized by the Outlaw Gang as an actor who can order a murder. This shows that he is considered a reputable actor. Nevertheless, he is not a "godfather" because he has no command over the gang. Instead, he gives money: it is a situation of a quid pro quo. Achim thus has no problem placing himself outside the state's monopoly on violence and resorting to extra-legal means himself. At the same time, he trusts the gang to carry out the murder contract in exchange for the money. His distrust of state institutions is complemented by a basic trust in the criminal world. He has normative expectations of the criminal world. He thus vacillates between two worlds. On the one hand, he maintains contacts with the police as representatives of the legal world. On the other hand, he maintains contacts with illegal organizations and resorts to methods of problem solving that are highly illegal: commissioning a murder. This is not an ideal type of a fully normatively integrated world in which normative expectations are known to all participants. Nevertheless, it should be clear that from the perspective of the criminal milieu, contacts with the police represent a violation of normative expectations. Thus, Achim has placed himself outside the world, which, on the other hand, he nevertheless resorts to in order to pursue his interests. This explains why he has contacted the police secretly: he does not want to jeopardize his integration into the context of the criminal milieu.

Compared to the first scenario, the order to kill his enemies shows the space of possibilities of alternative forms of conflict management. The fact that Achim has the expectation that this can solve his problems also provides insights into the form of the organization: either, the number of people involved must be relatively small so that a murderer can prevent the execution of his death sentence. After all, in the case of a very large organization (e.g. an army), it would not be possible to kill all members or potential murderers. Or the organization is only weakly integrated so that a murder would not trigger a violent backlash with certainty. In fact, the next sequence confirms that the organization is rather small: in the Outlaw Gang, some members of the gang had been hated for some time. This suggests that people met on the level of personal contacts and had affective, personal relationships with each other. In a large anonymous organization like an army, this would not be very likely because the hatred relates to specific members, not the organization as a whole.

In fact, as the story progresses, it becomes apparent that Achim's trust in the gang was justified: his mission was carried out. "On their motorcycles they (i.e. the Outlaw gang members) drove to the gang's favorite club and fired heavy machine guns haphazardly into the bar until the room was full of blood and bullet holes". The way the order was carried out is quick and effective, but also reveals a semi-public, symbolic level of violence. The execution was not carried out in secret but makes a statement even to the living and the survivors. That the massacre was carried out in the gang's "favorite club" is again a reference to a small organization. "Favorite club" refers to the category of community because there is no clear boundary between work and leisure, and the gang members know each other and have affective relationships. This might suggest that the story ends here. The people killed are presumably those who had threatened Achim. He has thus achieved his goal. So was it a successful form of conflict resolution?

But in fact, the story does not end here. It is now continued from a bird's eye view: with the statement "That was a shock …", it is implied that here there is a breach of normative expectations within this social context. Here it is shown that even the criminal milieu is not so fully integrated that only expected actions would happen. Such a rupture can signify a tipping point at which normative certainties of expectation are overridden. This is underscored by the narrator's highlighting the epistemic problem of imperfect information flows: "all the survivors wondered what had actually happened".

This makes it clear that the story is not yet over. At first, Achim "cleverly covers all traces". This is in contrast to the murder, which was carried out symbolically in public. A terrorist organization, for example, would have claimed responsibility for the deed. Achim, on the other hand, only wants to solve his problem without giving up the possibility of normative ties to the group. The word "skillfully" here indicates that his affect is controlled and that he is following a plan. This plan can be understood as a strategy to keep as many options open as possible: a game with a double bottom. On the one hand, he wants to maintain his normative ties to the legal world despite the murder order: he "stayed in contact with the police several times". Moreover, he "gave an interview" in which he disclosed the group's activities. In doing so, he sends a signal in two directions: to the legal world, to which he reveals inside knowledge of the illegal world. He is posing as a whistle-blower, even though he incriminates himself by revealing the knowledge, making public knowledge that could not be had if he did not also have connections in the illegal world. Last, but not least, it is a signal to the illegal world, namely a public denunciation. This is a breach of trust that cuts normative ties. On the other hand, however, "he agreed to a financial agreement with Thomas". At this point, it should be recalled from the beginning of the story that demands were made on Achim, which he accepted in principle as justified. Towards a selected person, the breach of trust by the newspaper interview is thus taken back. This can be understood as an attempt to divide the group. Towards Thomas, Achim chooses a different strategy of conflict management than commissioning a murder, namely to fulfill the demands. This strengthens the normative ties between him and Thomas and thus implicitly weakens the ties between Thomas and the group he betrayed.

The following conclusion of the story explains how Achim implemented the fulfilment of the demands: he acquired "fictitious rights for a large infrastructure project". Here he shows high professional competence also in dealing with practices of the legal business world. Acquiring rights is a transaction that requires business skills. However, he is only acquiring fictitious rights to a large infrastructure project. Thomas' demands are therefore not met directly, but by transferring legal titles. However, these are merely fictitious rights. Thus, a fraud is implied. On the one hand, this requires knowledge of the legal business world; on the other hand, the fraud makes it clear that its rules are not normatively recognized. However, it remains unclear at first whether the business partner is to be deceived, i.e. the fulfilment of the demands is only apparent, or whether the legal world is to be deceived, i.e. the demands are actually fulfilled, but at the expense of third parties. However, the fact that Achim receives a "bank loan" makes it likely that the loan is intended to serve the fulfilment of Thomas' claims. Presumably, then, it is not Thomas who is to be defrauded, but the bank, i.e. a third (legal) person of the legal world. In the following sequence, it becomes clear that the rules of the legal business world require a fair amount of acting: "The meeting took place at a Swiss lake and Achim came with his private jet". There are no written codified rules, which could possibly also be legally enforceable, to come to a business meeting with a private jet. Just like the quasi-public staging of the murder, the staging of this act is also a symbolic sign, in this case to the legal world. We also see that Achim is a very wealthy person with high social status: few people own their own private jet. Nevertheless, the whole project was purely fictional. So a considerable amount of effort is put into putting on a show, i.e. ostensibly fulfilling normative expectations of the business world, but actually subverting them.

With this, Achim develops a strategy with the aim of maintaining the possibility of normative ties in both the legal and the illegal world. The police, the business world, but also illegal business partners are served with offers that generate normative ties. At the same time, Achim also affects relationship patterns within the illegal group. By behaving differently towards different members, he undermines the integration of the group. Overall, this can be described as a very sophisticated and elaborate strategy that requires long-term planning.

7.3.3 Overall view of the scenarios

The intention of this book is primarily methodological. Therefore, the two scenarios are presented here only as examples to demonstrate the possibility of a sequence-analytic interpretation of narrative simulation scenarios. The two scenarios have been used here because they exemplify the space of objective possibilities of conflict resolution within this criminal group and specifically highlight their different consequences: from peaceful conflict regulation to exemplary violence. In doing so, it becomes clear how decisions in individual sequences exclude and open different possibilities, generating entirely different stories. The tree of path branching can grow in all directions.

What is relevant in both scenarios, however, is that the criminal milieu operates outside the law but within society (Hobbs, 1995). This is evident in both scenarios: the first scenario shows a partial legalization of the criminal milieu. A lawyer is a representative of a conflict resolution institution of the legal world. The second scenario, on the other hand, shows that with a business meeting on a Swiss lake, the legal business world can also be called upon to resolve conflicts that ultimately have their origins in illegal activities. The boundaries of legal and illegal activities are fluid. Thus, of course, the illegal activities can also corrupt the legal world: in the first scenario, the lawyer; in the second scenario, the business world.

It is also striking that the boundaries of perpetrator and victim become blurred: Achim is a victim of an original threat, but in the second scenario he also becomes a perpetrator and the original perpetrators become victims. Although it is known that violence is a common phenomenon in mafia-like organizations (cf. Dickie, 2005; Campana and Varese, 2013), the thematization of criminals not only as perpetrators but also as victims of violence is found rather sparsely. In contrast, the scenarios presented here make it clear that people with a criminal background are even particularly vulnerable to violence.

The central theme of conflict resolution is normative expectations and disappointments in expectations. The world described in the scenarios is rather weakly integrated, and expectation certainties are low. Trust or mistrust is a consistent theme – as are methods of how this trust/mistrust can be generated or manipulated (e.g. by travelling to a fictitious business meeting on a private jet). This is closely linked to the motive of conflict or conflict resolution. Conflict resolution in this context represents the transition from mistrust to trust, although the range of possibilities for conflict resolution also implies murder, i.e. the eradication of a party to the conflict. It is striking that in both cases the negotiation of normative expectations is carried out in front of third parties: a lawyer, the police, an outlaw gang, or even a bank that grants a loan as a third party. This confirms the thesis that the figure of the third party legitimizes the validity of a norm representation (Lindemann, 2014). In this context, very different third-party contexts are invoked, but they are fundamentally not derived from the internal normative context of the group. Peaceful conflict resolution in the first scenario also requires an advocate, i.e. an outside figure, to restore trust.

However, a key difference between first and second scenarios is that in the first scenario the third-party context (the lawyer) is shared by both parties to the conflict. In the violent second scenario, this is not the case: neither the police nor the outlaw gang is shared as a third party by the conflicting parties; Achim contacts them secretly. A central mechanism that fosters an escalation of violence, therefore, seems to be the dissolution of a shared third-party perspective: if there is no commonly shared legitimizing instance of regulating normative expectations, there can no longer be any certainties of expectations.

However, the fact that in both scenarios an outside third party is called in to regulate the conflict suggests that the group was not very integrated. In the classic example of organized crime, the Italian Mafia, one would assume that the "godfather" is the instance of conflict regulation. Although there are indeed rivalries and violent conflicts in the mafia (see, for example, Dickie, 2005), no outside instances are used to regulate conflict. The mafia is an ideal type of a highly integrated organization in which hierarchization solves the coordination problem. The "godfather" thus becomes a substitute for the state's monopoly on the use of force, a quasi-leviathan to whom the legitimacy of internal "law-making" is ascribed. The figure of the third party remains within the organization. The boundaries between inside and outside are clearly drawn. Here, on the other hand, no such intra-group differentiation is apparent, with the result that the boundaries between the internal normative context of the group and the outside world remain fluid. These fluid transitions make the group vulnerable to invoking third-party contexts that are no longer shared by the conflict parties, thus making an escalation of violence more likely.

7.4   What does the hermeneutic evaluation method contribute to social simulations?

In the previous sections, we conducted two exemplary sequence analyses to demonstrate the fruitfulness of the method of sequence-analytic interpretation of narrative simulation scenarios on a specific case. To our knowledge, this path has not yet been followed. The sequence analyses represent the (preliminary) conclusion of a series of translation and interpretation activities. First, a case was studied using the method of consistent conceptual description. This is the first translation activity. It served as a basis for the creation of a simulation model. This is the second translation activity. In the third translation step, this model was then translated into narrative scenarios – and already interpreted in the process. Finally, in the last translation step, this interpretation was the subject of hermeneutic sequence analyses. We conclude with reflections on what we think hermeneutic sequence analyses in general – going beyond the concretely analysed case – can do for social simulations, i.e. what gain this qualitative evaluation procedure offers for a methodological practice that generates its insights through formal modelling. To this end, we will specify the contribution of sequence analyses to the interpretation of agent-based modelling in two ways.

The first contribution of the sequence analysis is the *generation of structural hypotheses* that point beyond the individual scenarios and thus allow for systematic comparisons and make possibilities for future research visible. The above sequence analyses demonstrated different ways a criminal milieu deals with (manifest) crises. The analyses of the simulated crisis situations allow for abductive conclusions that function as structural hypotheses that could prove useful in further analyses of (real or simulated) ways of dealing with conflict in criminal milieus. The interpretations show that the different expressions of the crises and the different ways of dealing with them could be based on the same latent crisis-ness, namely an uncertainty of normative expectations that points to a disintegration of criminal communalization. The likewise common pattern of the path taken out of the crisis is the recourse to an external third instance, which is called upon for (non-violent or violent) conflict regulation. This leads to the thesis that the absence of a hierarchically superior internal authority ("a godfather") acting as a quasi-leviathan is a fundamental structural problem for criminal communities. At the same time, interpretive work allows us to derive the thesis that when a criminal community begins to disintegrate, non-violent conflict management succeeds when mutually recognized actors are involved who have "one foot" in the legal world and bring its norms to bear. In contrast, recourse to external (state or criminal) power structures that lack this mutual recognition brings the risk of violent disintegration of the community. In the first scenario, recognized third parties restabilized the old order. In the second scenario, a new order was created based on violence and fraud.

The second function of the analyses is to *validate* the models. This can be illustrated by the example of the first scenario. This describes a successful, non-violent conflict regulation. It is an example of how the linking of algorithmic rules from the individual parts of the empirical material generates something new. This is because such a mode of conflict regulation was evident in the scenarios, but not in the original empirical case. However, it also shows how the individual pieces of the puzzle of the empirical data material are put together to form a collage that tells a story that makes sense. A sequence that can be interpreted in a meaningful way is produced, as the initial analysis demonstrates. It should be noted, however, that this is a counterfactual sequence. In fact, a significantly different sequence is found in the interrogation transcripts: *Achim was ordered to his lawyer's office. Instead of his lawyer, however, Toby and three thugs were waiting for him. They forced him to his knees and pointed a machine gun at his stomach.* In fact, this was by no means a non-violent form of conflict regulation. However, after Achim (in the real case) was forced to his knees by three thugs and threatened with a machine gun, a peaceful way was hardly open. The sequence generated by the simulation, on the other hand, shows a way how the violence could have been avoided – a way that was not taken by the group in reality. Is this now a "programming error" in the modelling? In the following, we argue in a different direction: the simulation shows that the choice of regulating the conflict by means of machine guns could have been an *adequate cause* of the escalation of violence that actually took place, in the sense of Max Weber. Weber draws on Johannes von Kries' theory of adequate causes to justify the assertion of causal statements in social science in disagreement with the historian Eduard Meyer, without having to refer to historical regularities in the sense of Hegel or Marx (cf. Neumann, 2002). Accidental causes are those that de facto cause an event to occur, but under any other conditions the probability of that event occurring would have been equally likely. If a car goes off the road and is subsequently struck by lightning, this undoubtedly would not have happened if it had not gone off the road. After all, the car would have been somewhere else. But the probability of being struck by lightning is independent of whether the car goes off the path or not. It is an accidental cause (von Kries, 1888). The Battle of Marathon, on the other hand, is of "world-historical" significance in the view of the historians of the time because it decided between two possibilities: a religious-theocratic culture and a rational culture (Weber, 1968). Thus, it is an adequate cause because this event decisively influenced the probability of development in one or the other direction. Now, the fate of the criminal group exemplarily examined here is certainly not of world-historical importance, but from a methodological point of view a comparison of the factual with the counterfactual is instructive: factually, Achim had a machine gun pointed at his stomach. Counterfactually, Achim agreed with Toby on a settlement. From a sequence-analytic perspective, this is a logical conclusion to a story. This does not apply to the factual course of events. Thus, the sequence analysis shows that the simulation here has decided between two possibilities, i.e. has identified an adequate cause of the factual course: a path branching in which possibilities open and others close.

The meaningfulness of the sequences generated by the simulation can be described as an objective possibility in the sense of Max Weber precisely because of their derivation from empirical data: a path branching in the space of the cultural horizon, i.e. a possibility of conflict regulation that would have been accessible in principle to the actors involved. Accessible here means that it seems plausible that possibly in the time before the conflict escalated, and thus in the time when the group was not yet the subject of police investigations, such a form of conflict regulation could have actually been chosen before. Admittedly, such a statement can only be made if one confronts the case structure obtained from the interpretation of the "inner context" of the scenario with the "outer context" of knowledge about the real case. The validity of a narrative is shown by whether 1) a meaningful case structure can be generated at all, or whether the narrative reveals itself as an absurd series of sequence passages from which no rules of action can be reconstructed. 2) It can be tested whether the case structure stands up to a confrontation with the "external context" and can be interpreted as a plausible structural variation. If both are given, scenarios can be read as explorations of the space of cultural possibilities, or of a cultural horizon (in this case, a specific criminal milieu).

The interpretation of the second scenario shows how validation and hypothesis generation can complement each other. While the first scenario shows a possibility that can plausibly be assumed to have already been chosen within the milieu, the second scenario points to an innovation. Here, the sequence analysis reveals a sophisticated strategy in the scenario's narrative. Achim develops a long-term plan to maintain normative ties in various directions and to purposefully undermine just such normative ties within the group. The concept of strategy stands for meaningful action. However, it must be remembered that the scenario was computer generated. The strategy was not implemented in advance but was generated by putting together the pieces of the puzzle as the simulation progressed. It is true that the simulation method is designed to select only action rules that make sense in given situational conditions. However, this is only true microscopically, i.e. it is only related to a single sequence at a time. The development of long-term strategies is not included in the programming. That the sequence of sequences unfolds a strategy is an emergent property of the concatenation of sequences, which becomes clear through the sequence analysis of these concatenations. Meaningfulness, such as strategic action, only becomes visible "through the fact that in the succession of actions [...] contexts of meaning are realized" (Kurt and Herbrik, 2014: 281), and the individual is interpreted as part of a whole. In fact, it is not found in the interrogation transcripts that such a strategy was developed or applied either. The strategy that emerged through the sequence analysis is a virtual innovation that was not envisioned by the real actors or in the programming of the simulation but was latent in the possibility space of the data: a possibility that was not actualized. The analysis showed that a coherent story was told, making the sequences appear as the execution of a strategy. Moreover, it gives hints under which conditions such a strategy could come to fruition – and thus leads to hypotheses on criminal patterns of action that point beyond the real case itself.

Thus, the hermeneutic sequence analysis has already proven its profit in this exemplary test. It generated structural hypotheses which make different scenarios comparable with each other and it served to validate the generated scenarios. Both methods, agent-based modelling and hermeneutic analysis, are methods that do not simply reflect real patterns of development, but always also and especially show alternative courses of action. They are methods of a sociology of possibility, which, by using computer technology on the one hand, or through methodically controlled thought experiments on the other, reveal what – under what conditions – could be. It is not least this epistemic affinity that makes it attractive to further explore the fruitfulness of the methods for each other. In the present case, scenarios were interpreted that already had the form of a narrative themselves. Text passages from qualitatively obtained data were supplemented with narrative hinge points. In a further step, one could, on the one hand, test using sequence analysis itself to construct such hinge points. On the other hand, the generally reconstructed rules of action that emerge from sequence analyses could in turn be translated into algorithmic rules for agent-based modelling or could already be applied in the first translation step of data analysis to decipher the horizon of possibilities that are hidden in a sequence step and thus to hermeneutically secure the programming of the model.

This prospect makes it seem obvious that hermeneutic sequence analyses are not only suitable for the very specific case presented here but could be tested in principle as a method of interpretation, validation, and, if necessary, revision and construction of social simulations. If sequence analyses were already integrated into the development and testing of social simulations in the future, they could become an element of constructive criticism of algorithmic biases and blind spots. In this way, hermeneutic sequence analysis could contribute to shaping digital hermeneutics in social science terms (Capurro, 2010), which is not content with criticizing technological world building from a safe distance but itself enters a "co-laborative" (Klausner et al., 2015) relationship with its object. However, in this book we will abstain from further elaborating these ideas. In fact, the overall research cycle is closed with the hermeneutic interpretation of narrative scenarios. The next chapters are dedicated to epistemologically oriented reflections first on the contribution of the abductive reasoning to generate hypotheses fostered by this methodology to investigative practice in policing. The scenarios provide a virtual experience for the stakeholders. Second, the book concludes with theoretical reflections on the integration of subjective and objective dimensions of sense-making as highlighted by ethnography on the one hand and hermeneutics on the other hand, which is essential for this methodology.

Notes

1 Initiating social learning is particularly intended in so-called participatory modelling approaches, in which scientists develop a model together with actors in the field.
2 In the meantime, it can be stated that the method has emancipated itself from a strict coupling to the Oevermann school. For example, it is now considered an elementary method of methodologically controlled understanding in (sociologically based) social scientific hermeneutics (cf. Kurt and Herbrik 2014: 33ff.) and distanced from Oevermann's Objective Hermeneutics (cf. fundamentally Reichertz 1986). Furthermore, sequence analysis has also been established for some time as a research method of systems theory, which also appears compatible with its social theoretical assumptions (cf. Schneider 1995; Bora 1999). However, most of the literature on sequence analysis is in German language.
3 This description is based on Dickel (2011).
4 We will keep the difference between protocol and "re-narrated" case implicit in the following in order to ensure the readability of the interpretation. That is, we will interpret the story as such and initially hide what type of protocol (namely scenarios artificially generated with the help of a computer simulation) we are dealing with. However, this very thread will be picked up again at the end of the chapter and reflected methodologically.

References

Boero, R. and Squazzoni, F. (2010) 'Agentenbasierte Modelle in der Soziologie', in: Kron, T.; Grund, T. (eds.): *Die Analytische Soziologie in der Diskussion*. Wiesbaden: Springer, pp. 243–264.

Bora, A. (1999) *Differenzierung Und Inklusion. Partizipative Öffentlichkeit im Rechtssystem moderner Gesellschafte On*. Baden-Baden: Nomos.

Bundeskriminalamt. (2013) *Organisierte Kriminalität. Bundeslagebericht*.

Campana, P. and Varese, F. (2013) 'Cooperation in criminal organizations: Kinship and violence as credible commitments', *Rationality and Society*, 25(3), pp. 263–289.

Capurro, R. (2010) 'Digital hermeneutics: An outline', *AI & Society*, 25(1), pp. 35–42.

Dickel, S. (2011) *Enhancement-Utopien: Soziologische Analysen zur Konstruktion des Neuen Menschen*, Baden-Baden: Nomos.

Dickie, J. (2005) *Cosa Nostra. Die Geschichte der Mafia*, Frankfurt/Main: Perlentaucher.

Edmonds, B. (2015) 'Using qualitative evidence to inform the specification of agent-based models', *Journal for Artificial Societies and Social Simulation*, 18(1), http://jasss.soc.surrey.ac.uk/18/1/18.html

Endreß, M. (2015) Routinen der Krise – Krise der Routinen, in: Lessenich, S. (ed..): *Routinen der Krise - Krise der Routinen. Verhandlungen des 37. Kongresses der Deutschen Gesellschaft für Soziologie in Trier 2014*, pp. 15–19.

Folkers, A. and Lim, I.-T. (2014) 'Irrtum und irritation', Für Eine Kleine Soziologie Der Krise Nach Foucault Und Luhmann., *Behemoth*, 7(1), pp. 48–69.

Gilbert, N. and Ahrweiler, P. (2009) 'The epistemologies of social simulation research', in Squazzoni, F. (ed-) *Epistemological Aspects of Computer Simulation in the Social Sciences*. Berlin: Springer, pp. 12–28.

Hirschauer, S.(ed.) (2017) *Un/doing Differences: Praktiken der Humandifferenzierung*. Weilerswist: Velbrück.

Hobbs, D. (1995) *Bad Business: Professional crime in modern Britain*. Oxford: Oxford University Press.

Klausner, M., Bister, M., Niewöhner, J. and Beck, S. (2015) 'Choreografien klinischer und städtischer alltage, in', *Zeitschrift Für Volkskunde*, 111(2), pp. 214–235.

Kries, J. (1888) 'Über den begriff der objectiven möglichkeit und einige anwendung desselben. *Vierteljahrsschrift Für Wissenschaftliche Philosophie*, 12(4), pp. 179–240, 287 – 428.

Kurt, R. and Herbrik, R. (2014) 'Sozialwissenschaftliche Hermeneutik und Hermeneutische Wissenssoziologie, in: Baur, N.; Blasius, J. (eds.): *Handbuch Methoden der empirischen Sozialforschung*. Wiesbaden: Springer, pp. 473–491.

Lindemann, G. (2014) *Weltzugänge. Die mehrdimensionale Ordnung des Sozialen*. Weilerswist: Velbrück.

Maasen, S. and Passoth, J.-H. (eds.) (2020) Soziologie des Digitalen - Digitale Soziologie? *Soziale Welt, Sonderband 23*. Baden-Baden: Nomos.

Neumann, M. (2002) *Die Messung des Unbestimmten. Die Geschichte der Konstruktion und Dekonstruktion eines Gegenstandsbereiches der Wahrscheinlichkeitstheorie*. Frankfurt/Main. Hänsel-Hohenhausen.

Oevermann, U. (2002) *Klinische Soziologie auf der Basis der Methodologie der objektiven Hermeneutik. Manifest der objektiv hermeneutischen Sozialforschung* http://www.ihsk.de/publikationen/Ulrich_Oevermann-Manifest_der_objektiv_hermeneutischen_Sozialforschung.pdf (Download am 27.04.2021).

Oevermann, U. (2016) 'Krise und Routine "als Analytisches Paradigma in Den Sozial-wissenschaften', in: Becker-Lenz, R.; Franzmann, A.; Jansen, A.; Jung, M. (eds.): *Die Methodenschule der Objektiven Hermeneutik*. Wiesbaden: Springer, 43–114.

Reichertz, J. (1986) *Probleme Qualitativer Sozialforschung. Zur Entwicklungsgeschichte der Objektiven Hermeneutik*. Frankfurt, a.M.: Campus.

Sammet, K. and Erhard, F. (2018) 'Methodologische Grundlagen und praktische Ver-fahren der Sequenzanalyse. Eine didaktische Einführung'., in: F. Erhard; K. Sammet (eds.): *Sequenzanalyse praktisch*. Weinheim, Basel: Beltz, pp. 15–71.

Scherer, S., Wimmer, M., Lotzmann, U., Moss, S. and Pinotti, D. (2015) 'An evi-dence-based and conceptual model-driven approach for agent-based policy model-ling', *Journal of Artificial Societies and Social Simulation*, 18(3), 14. http://jasss. soc.surrey.ac.uk/18/3/14.html

Scherer, S., Wimmer, M. and Markisic, S. (2013) 'Briding narrative scenario texts and formal policy modelling through conceptual policy modelling', *AI and Law*, 21(4), pp. 455–484.

Schneider, W. L. (1995) 'Objektive hermeneutik als Forschungsmethode der System-theorie', *Soziale Systeme*, 1(1), pp. 135–158.

Schulz-Schaeffer, I. (2008) 'Deutung und Delegation. Handlungsträgerschaft von Technik als doppeltes Zuschreibungsphänomen', in: Rehberg, K.-S.; Giesecke, D. (eds.): *Die Natur der Gesellschaft. Verhandlungen des 33. Kongresses der Deutschen Gesellschaft für Soziologie in Kassel 2006*, Frankfurt/Main, 3135–3144.

Weber, M. (1968) 'Objektive Möglichkeit Und Adäquate Verursachung in Der His-torischen Kausalbetrachtung', in: Winckelmann, J. (ed.): *Gesammelte Aufsätze zur Wissenschaftslehre*, Tübingen: Mohr, pp. 266–290.

Wernet, A. (2000) *Einführung in die Interpretationstechnik der Objektiven Hermeneu-tik*. Opladen: Leske und Budrich.

Weyer, J. and Roos, M. (2017) 'Agentenbasierte modellierung und simulation', *TATuP - Zeitschrift Für Technikfolgenabschätzung in Theorie Und Praxis*, 26(3), pp. 11–16.

8 Transdisciplinary reflections

Science in context

Martin Neumann and Cornelis van Putten

8.1 Introduction

In the previous chapters, the research process of interpretive agent-based social simulation has been described, starting from ethnographic foundations of model development until the hermeneutic interpretation of simulation results. While referring to the example of the previous chapters, this chapter concentrates more on the transdisciplinary aspects of the research process and its practical implications. For this purpose – and also for the readers of only this chapter – some repetitions occur when referring to the example case in which the research process has been described. It draws on the example presented in the previous chapters. However, the focus of this chapter is on the collaborative work of research and practice. During the GLODERS project (Elsenbroich et al., 2017), which was aimed at simulating extortion racket systems, an intense collaboration between the researchers for the project and law enforcement agencies was initiated. The research questions had previously been formulated in a collaborative manner in order to offer law enforcement agencies solutions to combat and reduce crime. The project succeeded in developing a simulation model of violence and extortion within a criminal group using a hybrid methodology of ethnography, conceptual modelling, and social simulation to provide law enforcement agencies with virtual narratives of counterfactual scenarios.

The core of the participatory simulation consists of the agent-based simulation model of the conflict dynamics among the criminals described in the previous chapters. The focus of this particular chapter is to highlight the analysis of the counterfactual scenarios generated by the simulation model. This enables the study of what-if questions: what might have happened if at some point the actors had made other decisions?

The rest of the chapter is organized as follows: first, the challenge for the investigative practice is formulated, followed by an outline of how this challenge has been met in a transdisciplinary research account. The data and method are briefly recapitulated, as well as a short summary of the central mechanisms of the model. The most detailed part is an outline of the narrative scenarios and a concluding discussion of the what-if questions that have

DOI: 10.4324/9781003393207-8

been posed in the scenario analysis and the style of reasoning and insights that can be gained from this approach.

8.2   The challenge of investigative praxis

One of the major challenges that law enforcement agencies face is how to deal effectively with the scarcity of the people and means needed to achieve their aims. It is not an understatement to say there are more challenges regarding reducing the level of crime than resources available to counter them. This requires both a prudent use of the means and a clear understanding of the effectiveness of the measures taken.

Law enforcement agencies often operate with predefined goals and programmes. For example, one such programme could be to combat organized crime by conducting several criminal investigations of the international drug trade. Usually, these programme are specified with targets, just as a corporation formulates a strategic business plan with specified targets. Such targets in a law enforcement programme could be, among other things, to investigate and prosecute a certain number of wholesale dealers and/or confiscate a specific amount of drugs and the revenues gained by it. Behind such a programme lies the idea that meeting the targets leads to the overall goal of preventing the influence, or mitigating the influence, of organized crime on society, hence leading to a safer and more incorruptible public space. In reality, however, it is often difficult to assess, prior to implementing these measures, what the effects will be. Indeed, it is sometimes difficult enough to measure the effects afterwards.

Therefore, many of the law enforcement programmes that were written on the drawing board face an unruly reality. The actions taken by law enforcement are interventions in a social reality, which leads to a change in its dynamics. Programmes start and run in vivo for a while, and then, the course of action is changed because of a lack of results or due to unanticipated consequences that have caused the situation to deteriorate. The sad reality is that many programmes do not achieve their aims, with a major waste of resources as a consequence. Moreover, from the start, the possible adverse effects of certain measures are often unknown. Nevertheless, these measures shape the social dynamics in unforeseeable ways because they are not executed in isolation. There are many variables that influence reality simply by falling beyond the scope and reach of law enforcement. For example, it is often argued that the "lenient" approach to certain kinds of drugs in the Netherlands, with its policy of tolerance and regulation, has led to the problem of home-grown marijuana on a large professional scale. This leniency towards specific kinds of drugs was a policy born from political compromises. The professionalism of the home-grown marijuana business, as a possible result of these political compromises, has led to all kinds of adverse side effects, such as undermining the integrity of the real estate business in certain parts of the country. This is something that was not anticipated when the policy was introduced. The current level of professionalism of marijuana production in the Netherlands is an example of an adverse side effect. A policy decision, once aimed at managing and regulating a specific problem, instead led to a deterioration of the existing situation. A subsidiary problem is that once a decision has been made to terminate a specific programme, the programme-specific knowledge and experience are often lost. It gets carried away by the humdrum of the day and the new challenges of a changed reality. After a few years, nobody remembers the exact details about why a certain measure was ineffective. Although one programme has concluded, many others are already waiting in the wings to get started.

In light of the above, it becomes clear that there needs to be a more economical way to use scarce resources and, therefore, a better procedure for estimating the consequences of specific policies prior to implementing them. What would be preferable is a decision-making process that enables decision-makers to take into consideration a multitude of variables and to be able to estimate the relevance of their consequences. This, however, requires an enormous amount of qualitative data processing and storage capacity, which simply exceeds the capacity of human decision-making. It is at this stage that the relevance of computer-simulated agent-based modelling (ABM) comes into play.

The world of computer science modelling is promising because the development of systems and techniques shows that computer-based intelligence models simply outperform human capacity when all kinds of variables are being taken into consideration. Moreover, it will enable law enforcement agencies to store specific programmes, thereby building histories and leading to a collective memory of the conditions under which certain measures are effective or ineffective. With hindsight, these measures can be analysed to understand their dynamics, as well as used to assess new opportunities. In order to create this, one needs real-life examples where specific criminal cases or policy programmes on preventing organized crime are built into the system and transformed into models, mimicking the social reality in the most optimal way. With the help of these models, law enforcement agencies can run many alternative scenarios in vitro, before deciding what kind of policy should be introduced in vivo. It will help them to assess the many risks and better equip them to deal with the adverse effects of specific policy decisions.

The GLODERS project, which ran from 2012 to 2015, was a project in which the worlds of law enforcement and science modelling were connected. On the basis of an existing and extensive case file on extortion in organized crime, researchers ran alternative histories on the script of the extortion, and its protagonists and antagonists, leading to different insights on the role of the significant players. This knowledge would never have been obtained if the model had not been built and law enforcement had not opened the possibility for researchers to investigate a historical case file. Although there is still much work to do to produce efficient models guiding the decision-making process, this was at least a promising start. The remainder of this chapter is a clear illustration of this project. As one of the project leaders of Gloders said: "if you start to build a bridge, you first have to make a scale model and calculate the required construction capacity. Then you change variables all the time in order to see whether the calculations made on the drawing board will lead to optimal results in reality. After that, you start building the real bridge". This sounds like common sense. However, the reality of law enforcement is to start building a bridge on the basis of limited calculations and, then, to proceed until the bridge collapses. Then, it simply starts rebuilding the bridge until the process repeats itself. That is why the world of agent-based modelling is welcome assistance in finding effective and economical measures for combatting organized crime.

8.3   Transdisciplinary research process

In the following, it is described how the GLODERS project dealt with the challenges outlined in the previous section through a transdisciplinary research process of participatory simulation (Barreteau et al., 2003). The transdisciplinary collaboration brings together scientific knowledge, on the one hand, which typically entails context-free universal laws or assumptions, and the domain expertise of the stakeholders, on the other hand, which is characterized by context-sensitive skills and in-depth knowledge of concrete cases. In the participatory simulation account, this is reflected by the fact that the decision-making of the agents in the simulation model in fact relies on general rules; these rules, however, are tied to specific contexts that are characteristic of real-life complexity. As Flyvbjerg (2006) points out, context-dependent knowledge is a crucial ingredient for expert activity. Context-independent general theories are of less use in the social domain, in contrast to the mastery of transferring knowledge between contexts: studying the possible side effects of interventions in the social reality requires an awareness of multiple contexts in order to assist a real-life decision-making process that must take into account a multitude of variables. Thus, ultimately, the transdisciplinary collaboration can be characterized as a transformational account for securing the credibility of the scientific inquiry (Cho and Trent, 2006), implying a transformation of practice.

For this purpose, the design of the simulation model also needs to fulfill certain requirements. There are many types of model design at hand: the so-called KISS principle (Axelrod, 1997), which is shorthand for "keep it simple stupid", suggests simple models for easing the analysis of the simulation dynamics and finding generalized context-free, law-like results. The so-called EROS principle (Jager, 2017), which is shorthand for "enhancing realism of simulation", emphasizes the need to secure construct validity by relying on theoretical knowledge of the scientific domains under investigation, whereas the so-called KIDS principle (Edmonds and Moss, 2005), which is shorthand for "keep it descriptive stupid", advocates reliance-descriptive data for model development. Each of the modelling styles has its own legitimacy for specific purposes (Aodha and Edmonds, 2017). For the purpose of transdisciplinary research, a KIDS approach is the most appropriate choice, as only that approach fulfills the requirements of drawing on qualitative data to use computational power to handle real-world complexity and of preserving context sensitivity (see also Edmonds, 2015).

The research design included a mutual exchange between the researchers and the stakeholders. The collaboration included weekly Skype meetings during certain periods of the project and consecutive personal meetings. The stakeholders shared their domain knowledge with the researchers in order for the simulation model to reflect their particular domain knowledge. Even this process of developing the simulation model provided a controlled means for reflecting on the data consisting of the protocols of police interrogations for both the stakeholders and the researchers. Thus, during the process of conceptual modelling, the technique of member checking (Lincoln and Guba, 1985; Creswell and Miller, 2000) was applied to include stakeholder participation to secure the validity of the model design: several consecutive stages of conceptual models were developed and discussed until a stage of theoretical saturation (Corbin and Strauss, 2008) was reached at which the conceptual model reflected the domain knowledge of the stakeholders. The simulation model, in turn, enables the abstraction from the concrete details of particular offences and the drawing of a broader picture of the mechanisms driving the internal dynamics of the social relations within a criminal group. The objective of the simulation can be described as the provision of a virtual experience for police officers as a kind of "think tool" for comprehending the dynamics of the intra-organizational norms in criminal organizations. A counterfactual analysis of the simulation allows for the generation of hypotheses about possible scenarios in complex situations in which many decisions are conceivable, and for this reason, many different pathways are possible.

8.4 Data and method

The motivation for the collaboration between the police and science was that the gang of drug dealers under investigation was extremely successful. Their business was extremely profitable and had made them very rich. For instance, some dealers owned their own private jets. Nevertheless, the group terminated in an outburst of violence. Thus, the puzzle was: why did they kill each other? For instance, in one police interrogation, the friend of a later victim of an assassination testified that he was convinced that nobody will "kill a hen with golden eggs". In fact, this did happen, but why? While an assassination is visible to the police, the motivation for it is not. Generating hypotheses about the possible courses of action that were conceivable for the members of the network was the objective of the development of the simulation model and the subsequent scenario analysis.

The group had no hierarchical structure or formal positions. While certainly some individuals gained more prestige than others, the structure of the group did not consist of positions with managerial authority or a right of command. The group can be described as a network of old friends. For at least a decade, the group operated extremely successfully in the drug market. Presumably formed in the early 1990s, the gang made large sums of money, particularly by ecstasy cooking. They earned a profit equivalent to several hundreds of millions of Euros, which were laundered in highly professional, worldwide financial transactions (Neumann and Sartor, 2016). However, in the early to mid-2000s, the group collapsed in an escalation of violence. An informal network cannot terminate in the same manner as, e.g. a legal company declaring bankruptcy. In this case, the collapse meant that the business relations terminated, either because the group members killed each other or because of a loss of trust, and it was certainly also due to murders and other acts of violence, including kidnapping, intimidation, and extortion. The collapse of trust was essential to the breakdown of the group. A criminal organization needs to rely on the commitment of the members to the organization. For this reason, trust is essential. The collapse can be described as a vicious circle: violence triggers the breakdown of trust, which, in turn, triggers violence. The escalation of violence was described by the involved persons as a "corrupt chaos" governed by a "rule of terror" in which "old friends are killing each other". The notion of "chaos" indicates that seemingly the "terror" was not governed by an individual, such as Nero burning Rome, but – from the perspective from inside – by an invisible hand. The involved persons could not keep track of the complexity of the incidences. This is an emergent phenomenon in which the situational complexity generates a perception of the situation as "corrupt chaos" for the involved individuals. This motivates the research: dissecting the mechanisms that generated the chaos on the level of fine-grained individual interactions.

8.5   Simulation model

In the following, the central mechanisms of the model described in detail in Chapter 6 will be briefly recapitulated. The model consists of three types of agents: the police and two types of criminals, black-collar criminals, responsible for the drug business, and white-collar criminals, undertaking money laundering. The model concentrates on the processes of conflict regulation within the criminal group. It requires a certain amount of cognitive complexity to model this task in a criminal world outside the reach of a Leviathan. In particular, trust and reputation are essential for conflict regulation (Campana and Varese, 2013). The model follows Sabater et al. (2006), who differentiate between image and reputation. While image is a personal assessment of the trustworthiness of a co-offender (i.e. the evaluation of agent x by agent y), reputation is an inter-subjectively valid category within the group. Image can vary between agents and in time: if an agent x observes a norm obedience or norm violation by agent y, then agent x increases or decreases its personal image of agent y. In contrast, reputation is not fully static, but changes only with a much slower dynamic. Agents can build up or lose reputation, but only when a predefined number of agents change their image of the particular agent.

Time is represented by discrete ticks, which denote the period between actions, but no defined time period between ticks is specified.

Figure 8.1 shows the activities that can possibly be performed in a model run, structured in different parts (grey background boxes). The edges represent the control flow, i.e. they show what kinds of activities are triggered by what kinds of preconditions. Some of the edges are labelled in order to improve readability. The diagram can be read as follows.

The dynamics start with an initial normative event (see top left of Fig. 8.1). A randomly selected agent becomes suspect. This event is observed by fellow criminals at the next tick and triggers a decision process on whether and how to perform aggressive actions against the deviating criminal. In the next tick, the possibly many criminals who decided to sanction the norm violation negotiate and, finally, one of them performs a single aggression. Eventually, it might include murder, which causes panic among other members of the criminal network. Otherwise, the victim experiences the aggression and begins an interpretation process. The interpretation begins with distinguishing

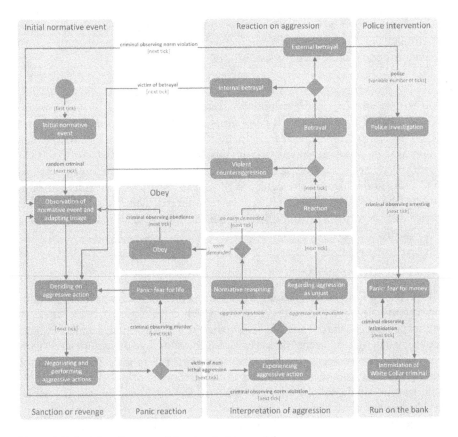

Figure 8.1 Activity diagram of the simulation model

whether the aggressor is reputable or not. In the latter case, the aggression is regarded as unjust, which triggers an aggressive reaction in the next tick. If the aggressor is judged to be reputable, the agent might either judge that a norm is indeed demanded, eventually persuading the criminal to obey to the norm, or the agent might not find a norm that is demanded. In this case, the agent reacts with an aggressive action in the next tick. A decision process is conducted about the actual reaction (taking one more tick), with one of the following results:

- A violent counter-aggression is performed, employing the same activities as for normative sanctioning (as described above), this time, in turn, executed by the reacting agent.
- The criminal who issued the original aggression is betrayed internally, i.e. involving just the two criminals. The victim of this betrayal will decide on a responding aggression in the next tick.
- An external betrayal is performed, which can either be to inform the police or to go to the media and reveal the criminal network (or its members) to the public. Both actions trigger police investigations, while the latter is also recognized as a norm violation, which might be observed by fellow criminals in the next tick and might furthermore lead to the already known consequences of new aggressive actions.

Police investigations are not modelled explicitly, but once initiated they lead to the arrest of some criminals. This can be observed by other members and cause a panic about the potential loss of invested money in the next tick. This fear usually triggers intimidation of the white-collar criminal, which might also be observed by other criminals, starting (with a delay of one tick) a vicious cycle of cascading acts of extortion towards the white-collar criminal in the form of a "run on the bank". If the white-collar criminal runs out of liquidity, the investment can no longer be reimbursed. This is, at the same time, regarded as a norm violation, observable by additional criminals (again with a delay of one tick).

8.6   Narrative scenarios

The intention of the transdisciplinary research collaboration was to start building a repository of the conditions under which certain measures are effective or ineffective. To achieve the goal to provide law enforcement agencies with a tool for analysing different measures and understanding their dynamics, various counterfactual scenarios have been run with the model. These scenarios assist in the assessment of the risks and opportunities of policy decisions. To demonstrate how this objective has been addressed, the scenarios described in Chapter 6 will be briefly recapitulated. However, in order to preserve context-specificity, which is crucial for expert activity, the simulations develop a storyline of a virtual case (Corbin and Strauss, 2008). Thus, the scenarios are a kind of collection of short crime novels, based on a real-world case. The scenarios are a kind of *collage* of the empirical basis of the agent rules, thereby preserving the real-life complexity. They provide the virtual experience for police officers as intended in the participatory modelling approach, offering a "think tool" for investigating the dynamics of possible courses of action from within the worldview of the criminal organization. These scenarios allow for the generation of hypotheses about plausible futures in complex situations in which many decisions are conceivable, and for this reason, many different futures are possible. Thus, the scenarios provide a virtual experience which cannot be directly observed by the police in vivo.

8.6.1 Narrative scenarios: Contextualizing science

In the following, a brief example of a narrative scenario will be provided to demonstrate how context sensitivity is preserved by tracing a simulation back to the empirical evidence. It is part of a longer story in which the white-collar criminal became severely intimidated and extorted. In the last chapter, it has been extensively interpreted. The example shows the rules that were fired as a reaction to the pressure of being extorted.

> While Achim accepted that the demands were justified, finally, the intimidation was too much. He *secretly contacted the police*. ... *He was shocked when he was told by the police that they knew that he was on a death list*. However, presumably, his reaction was not like the police expected. Outraged, he *contacted an outlaw gang and gave them the rest of the money he had to kill his enemies*. As many of them had *hated some members of the gang* for a long time, they undertook a massacre. On their bikes, they drove to the favorite club of the gang, and with heavy machine guns, they fired haphazardly into the pub until the room was full of blood and impact holes. It lasted only a minute, until they drove away at full speed, leaving the dead bodies of Michael, Jason, and Dominik. This was a shock.
>
> However, Achim cleverly erased any traces to him: He remained in *contact with the police several times* and *gave a public interview* in which he completely laid open the criminal operations of the group. However, at the same time, he agreed to a financial deal with Thomas, in which he *bought fictitious rights for a major infrastructure construction*. He got a bank loan for that deal. To mimic a prestigious business, *the meeting was held at a lake in Switzerland, and Achim came on his own private jet*. However, the *whole project was merely fictitious*. Thereby, Achim succeeded in preserving his appearance both to the police and the criminal group.

This brief "crime novel" can be described as a "virtual experience". Tracing the simulation runs back to the open coding of the empirical evidence base enables the development of a storyline of a virtual case that provides a coherent picture (Corbin and Strauss, 2008). First, it shows that Achim seems to be a clever guy in developing strategies to fight against his enemies, but nevertheless takes great pains to preserve his face in all directions: both to the legal world, represented by the police, and to his co-offenders. He might well be described as an individualistic criminal entrepreneur. Nevertheless, the story describes the execution of the rules implemented in the simulation model. However, tracing them back to the empirical evidence generates a sense of verisimilitude insofar as the reader of the story gets the feeling that the events being described could have been experienced. The storyline generates artificial sense making. Thereby, a test of the validity of the rules of the simulation model is provided following the quality criteria in the qualitative research (Denzin 1989; Creswell and Miller, 2000). The narrative scenarios generated by the collage of pieces of empirical evidence can be described as a transfer of evidence between contexts, which is a characteristic skill of domain expertise (Flyfbjerg, 2006).

8.6.2 *Scenarios*

In the following, we show summaries of a few cases that are representative of typical classes of the course of simulation runs. The scenarios explore the path dependency of the simulation runs generated by probabilistic decision rules. The only variation of the parameters is the number of so-called "reputable" and "ordinary" criminals (see the description of the model). While most of the simulation runs resemble the empirical case, the counterfactual scenarios show how different decisions in a complex and non-transparent situation may lead to different courses of action. At certain critical junctures, it is decisive if one certain decision is taken instead of an also possible decision x. This generates new situations that may open up new pathways and close certain others. Here, it is important to note that the development of narrative storylines by tracing simulated facts to the open coding of the empirical data ensures internal consistency and empirical plausibility as well as preserving contextualized meaning.

As intended in the participatory modelling approach, the scenarios explore the space of possible courses of action and plausible futures. The scenarios show possible modes of conflict regulation in a field that is characterized by covertness and the lack of the state monopoly of violence that ensures social order and decides claims among conflicting parties (see Chapter 5). First, a scenario is presented that resembles the central features of the data. This is the most frequent scenario among the simulation runs. Second, this default scenario is contrasted with a simple example of how the escalation of violence could have been avoided. The third scenario represents a case in which the group managed to overcome a severe escalation of violence. These two scenarios are rare but not impossible. Finally, the fourth scenario shows a case of successful police intervention. This is much less likely than the default scenario, but more likely than the two other cases.

1. **Scenario: Eroding of a Criminal Group by Increasing Violence.** The first scenario resembles the empirical data of the violent collapse of the criminal network. The scenario starts with the initial loss of trust of some gang members in a comrade. However, an attempt to sanction him had a very different effect than intended: the dispute escalated to a deadly gunfight. The unexpected violence caused panic, and consequently, the diffusion of mistrust throughout the whole gang. The lack of clear information caused haphazard violence. Some even betrayed the group openly, and others secretly contacted the police. However, it took a while for the police to collect enough evidence for action. For some time, it seemed that the group could return to its ordinary business. However, when one gang member was suddenly arrested, the others feared their money would be lost. In a panic, they wanted to get their money back from the white-collar criminal. Soon, he lost his liquidity and became severely extorted. Finally, *he was like a hunted cat* and started a rampage. He killed several of his former allies. Now, their fear for money turned into a fear for their lives. Others wanted revenge and killed the white-collar criminal. However, the assassination made it impossible to return to the usual business, as the white-collar criminal had privileged access to the legal market for money laundering. Thus, the restoration of the group was not possible, and the gang was dissolved.

2. **Scenario: A Small Irritation.** Some scenarios end quickly and peacefully: a first condition for this simulation result is that the target of the initial loss of trust is the white-collar criminal. The white-collar criminal is the only one who is able to provide compensation, namely by paying a kind of monetary fine. The second condition is that he does so. This mirrors conflict resolution in the legal world: in this case, the loss of trust remains a small irritation in criminal activities, which do not even become known outside. Because, in the simulation, the agents that become suspect are determined by chance, this is a rare event among the simulation runs.

3. **Scenario: The Group Overcomes a Severe Escalation of Violence.** In most scenarios, the gang is destined to a fate of breaking apart in a violent blow-up. However, although it is unlikely, it is possible for trust to be recovered even after severe violence. The particular scenario described here starts with initial severe violence, namely an unexpected assassination. The following panic caused aggressive acts between many gang members and even the betrayal of the group's activities. Consequently, mistrust was diffusing throughout the overall group. The betrayal initiated police investigations, which finally resulted in the imprisonment of a gang member. The arrest fuelled a panic, and the fear of losing money generated a run on the bank. As the liquidity of the white-collar criminal became overstrained, he became the victim of severe extortion. Finally, he struck back with a dual strategy: on the one hand, he contacted a contract killer and secretly contacted

the police. However, he cleverly erased any traces to himself. On the other hand, he made fictitious deals with some of his co-offenders to preserve his face within the gang. Although a further arrest upset his plans, he was able to repay the last of his outstanding debts. Because of this restored trust, and in spite of many assassinations and imprisonments, the group did not break apart and was able to restore the business. Thus, the white-collar criminal rescued the group: first, because he was able to provide compensation, and second, because he applied a clever strategy to stop the run on the bank.

4. **Scenario: Successful Police Operations.** A scenario in which the police could successfully intervene is quite rare among the simulation runs. Nevertheless, it can happen, and conditions could have been identified which would foster such a pathway in the simulation history. A typical simulation run that generates such an outcome starts (as in all the simulations) with an initial loss of trust in one member of the group, triggering a first outbreak of violence. In the particular scenario described here, one gang member decided to execute a death penalty. The murder caused panic in the overall group. As such, this did not determine the further fate of the gang. However, it was decisive for the further development that the panic caused several gang members to change sides and to betray the group, either by making their criminal offence public or by secretly contacting the police. This initiated massive police operations. It was particularly decisive that the police investigations focused on the white-collar criminal, who was later arrested. As the white-collar criminal has a monopoly (in the simulation), once the white-collar criminal was arrested, the business model of the gang was destroyed. The violence did not terminate immediately, and some gang members still decided to collaborate with the police, causing further arrests. Nevertheless, the group faded away quickly. Thus, two elements are important for this particular pathway of the simulation: first, many gang members changed sides, and therefore, the police were able to build up a high pressure of prosecution, and second, the police targeted the white-collar criminal, who has unique features within the group. In terms of network theory (Sparrow, 1991; van Duijn et al., 2014), the white-collar criminal possesses the position of a broker between the legal and the illegal worlds. While targeting the white-collar criminal is a chance event in the simulation, it confirms the assumption that criminal groups are particularly vulnerable when police operations target a broker position (van Duijn et al., 2014).

8.7   Discussion

The transdisciplinary participatory modelling approach presented in this paper is intended to provide a tool for hypothesis generation from known traces of evidence to support police detectives. This is the objective of the narrative scenarios. The factual and counterfactual scenarios demonstrate how the simulation facilitates a what-if analysis. Note that this does not allow for any predictions. Rather, the hypothesis generation can be described as abductive reasoning (Verde and Nurro, 2010): the model instantiates a virtual Sherlock Holmes (Eco and Sebeok, 1985). The counterfactual scenarios explore the space of the actions that are possible from the perspective of the worldview of the criminals. For this purpose, it is necessary to interpret how criminals make sense of complex and non-transparent situations that call for immediate reactions. In terms of a classification of validation strategies as replicative, predictive, and having structural validity (Zeigler et al.,2000; Troitzsch, 2016), the model indeed replicates the data. However, most important for the credibility of counterfactual reasoning is an attempt to approximate structural validity through the traceability of the simulation results to the empirical in vivo codes in the narrative scenarios.

These features of structural validity of meaning structures enable an abductive backward tracing. This is a unique feature of the more descriptive micro-level approach to simulation modelling preserving contextualized meaning. That is to say, it enables the tracing of processes and circumstances that give rise to a particular phenomenon. If the model is built on an analysis of micro scenes in the field, this implies that backward tracing is also possible. Here, the ethnographic approach to model development becomes relevant, as only the ethnographic diagnosis of micro scenes enables a tracing of the processes involved in the field. Process tracing is a method frequently used in political science (Beach and Pedersen, 2013). Similar to the diagnosis of an airplane crash in which the causal chain that ultimately resulted in the event may be traced back to the small defect of a valve, in political science attempts have been made to trace (for instance) the Cuban Missile Crisis back to tiny details of the context in which impactful decisions were made (Allison and Zelikow, 1999). In the same vein, empirically rich descriptive models may be used for crime research.

This process tracing instantiates an abductive reasoning process from given circumstances to an explanatory hypothesis. While inductive reasoning attempts to infer from the individual to the general, and deduction attempts to infer from the general to the individual, abductive reasoning attempts to infer from the result to the case by a hypothetical rule (Douven, 2021). This reasoning process reflects the affordances of police investigative work for which Sherlock Holmes provides a literary role model. For instance, given a murder and certain forensic evidence, police investigators need to infer the murderer. Investigative practice is always idiographic. Note that such process tracing would not be possible with more abstract theoretical models following the KISS style of modelling. Abstract models allow for deductive reasoning to infer hypotheses about general rules. However, abstracting from the specific contexts of the individual case does not allow for abductive reasoning as this exactly requires knowledge of the details of the circumstances of a specific case.

Summarizing these scenarios, it is worth noting that the narratives build on the base of the interrogation transcripts. Thereby, the scenarios enable a systematic exploration of the qualitative data. The scenarios show how different context conditions shape the fate of the criminal group in order to answer questions about what might have happened if at some point the actors had made other decisions. This enables reasoning about questions such as: what kind of sense making and reasoning is conceivable from the perspective of a certain worldview that is found in the interrogations, what kind of action is conceivable in different situations from this perspective, or what effect do particular actions have on other actors' reasoning? This involves the question of how the actors interpret the world, including their interactions with peers. Likewise, the scenarios show what kind of pathways appear to be necessary, likely, or contingent (Levy, 2008), given the background of what is perceived as a possible mode of action by the group members.

For instance, in scenario 3, the clever guy in our initial example of a narrative provides an example of reasoning and sense making in a context outside of the state monopoly of violence. It is an essential element for the success of his strategy to preserve his face before all sides. This is essential because outside the state monopoly of violence, trust built on reputation is crucial for preserving social order. This trust building can be achieved by such behaviour. Nevertheless, factually, he cheated all sides. This is also a likely behaviour in the case of criminals, who already have been willing to leave the safety of the state monopoly of violence to gain an individual advantage (i.e. in the drug market). It is worth noting that with the different cultural backgrounds in the cases of, e.g. the Sicilian Mafia or the Chinese triads, such behaviour might have been much more unlikely. Our clever guy could better be described as an individualistic entrepreneur. A different example of crossing the chains of interaction, in which the actors only partially have control over these interaction chains, is the erosion of trust in scenario 1. Here, the decline of trust is triggered by the side effects of the individual strategies to handle the unexpected violence in the first instance. In particular, the actions caused police operations, i.e. actions taken by a third party outside the control of the individuals in the criminal network. This would be an example of measures (i.e. attempts to gain control over the chains of interaction) intervening in the social reality with many other chains of interaction that are not controlled by the interventions, but have an effect on them nevertheless, and vice versa. The case of the side effects of marijuana legislation is a real-world example. Finally, it shall be noted that Achim, the white-collar criminal, is particularly vulnerable: while not deterministically necessary, many pathways include the possibility that actors with this specific role will become the victims of extortion. Likewise, the central mechanisms of the dynamics that can be found throughout the scenarios are complex and non-transparent situations, which nevertheless call for some kind of immediate reaction. The ambiguity of the violence stimulates it to spread in the group. Only the case of an initial loss of trust (a random event) against the white-collar criminal provides a chance to preserve the operations of the group before the violence gets out of control, as only the white-collar criminal has the resources to restore trust through a generous repayment as compensation for the loss of trust. This enables the encapsulation of the initial mistrust. However, this is a rather unlikely event, as the white-collar criminal is a reputable agent. Moreover, bilateral conflicts may be long-lasting without affecting the overall group. However, they become dangerous when others become involved. This need not be the case immediately. However, in this case, an escalation of violence can easily get out of control. Once the violence spreads, the white-collar criminal is the most vulnerable. In particular, the police interventions rope him into internal conflicts. This stimulates the escalation of conflict. For this reason, police operations directly against the white-collar criminal are the most effective in destroying the business model. Moreover, the police operations are the most successful if a significant number of group members change sides and cooperate with the police (see Chapter 6).

In turn, exploring counterfactual scenarios enables an exploration of what can be called the horizon of the space of the criminal culture (at least for this particular group): as the possibility of decisions is based on the hermeneutics of the first step of the qualitative data analysis, the scenarios provide insight into the motivation for particular actions. This is what the police cannot see in contrast to, e.g. the phenomenology of violence. Therefore, the narrative analysis stands in contrast to an analysis of abstract, simple models, which would not allow for coping with the real-world problem that measures are not executed in isolation, as there are many variables influencing reality. A computer-based intelligence that is grounded in the processing of qualitative data facilitates the exploration of a cultural horizon in-silicio within a simulation run. This, in turn, enables the possibility of a decision-making process that is able to take into consideration a multitude of variables and to estimate their relevance. Therefore, preserving the context sensitivity of domain expertise in a narrative analysis of the simulation scenarios contributes to meeting the challenges of investigative practice.

8.8 Concluding remarks

This chapter is intended to provide a discussion of what research question this approach of interpretive simulation is appropriate. Certainly, this approach is not intended to be the tool for every research question that can be answered appropriately with ABM. The very first ABMs such as Axelrod's model of the evolution of cooperation, or the Schelling model of ethnic segregation, are examples of research questions for which simple and abstract models are fairly adequate. These models attempt to deductively generate general theories of cooperation or segregation by growing such patterns in a simulation (Epstein, 2006). On the other hand, these models do not allow for an idiographic investigation of the particularities of individual cases. This is specifically relevant for transdisciplinary research as the transdisciplinary cooperation is concerned with specific case-based problems. For this purpose, abductive reasoning is necessary. Moreover, specifically for policing reasoning about the meaning which actors assign to human action becomes relevant. This calls for the Weberian concept of a sociological understanding as outlined in Chapter 2. As Weber puts it: "The aim is to understand the social reality that surrounds us in its peculiar character – on the one hand, the contemporary framework and cultural meanings of all the single phenomena we observe now, and on the other hand, the reasons for their historical path that led to their special characteristics" (Weber, 1968: 170f.). The interpretive account to agent-based social simulation is specifically suited for investigating such a research question.

Acknowledgement

The research leading to these results has received funding from the European Union's Seventh Framework Programme (FP7/2007-2013) under grant agreement n° 315874., GLODERS Project.

References

Allison, G. and Zelikow, P. (1999) *Essence of Decision*. New York: Longman.
Aodha, L. and Edmonds, B. (2017) 'Some pitfalls to beware when applying models to issues of policy relevance', in Edmonds B and Meyer R (eds.), *Simulating Social Complexity – A Handbook*. 2nd edn. Cham: Springer, pp. 801–822.
Axelrod, R. (1997) *The Complexity of Cooperation: Agent-Based Models of Competition and Collaboration*. Princeton, NJ: Princeton University Press.
Barreteau, O. et al. (2003) 'Our companion modeling approach', *Journal of Artificial Societies and Social Simulation*, 6(1). http://jasss.soc.surrey.ac.uk/6/2/1.html
Beach, D. and Pedersen, R. (2013) *Process-tracing methods: Foundations and Guidelines*. Ann Arbor: University of Michigan Press.
Campana, P. and Varese, F. (2013) 'Cooperation in criminal organizations. Kinship and violence and credible commitments', *Rationality and Society*, 25(3), pp. 263–289.
Cho, J. and Trent, A. (2006) 'A validity in qualitative research revisited', *Qualitative Research*, 6(3), pp. 319–340.
Corbin, J. and Strauss, A. (2008) *Basics of Qualitative Research*. 3rd edn. Thousand Oaks: Sage.
Creswell, J. and Miller, D. (2000) 'Determining validity in qualitative research', *Theory into Practice*, 39(3), pp. 124–130.
Denzin, N. K. (1989) *The Research Act: A Theoretical Introduction to Sociological Methods*. 3rd edn. New Jersey: Prentice Hall.
Douven, I. (2021) 'Abduction', in Zelta, E. (ed.), *The Stanford Encyclopedia of Philosophy*. https://plato.stanford.edu/archives/sum2021/entries/abduction/
Eco, U. and Sebeok, T. (eds.). (1985) Der Zirkel oder im Zeichen der Drei. Dupin – Holmes – Peirce. Munich: Fink.
Edmonds, B. (2015) 'A context- and scope-sensitive analysis of narrative data to aid the specification of agent behaviour', *Journal of Artificial Societies and Social Simulation*, 18(1). http://jasss.soc.surrey.ac.uk/18/1/17.html
Edmonds, B. and Moss, S. (2005) 'From KISS to KIDS – An "anti-simplistic" modelling approach', in Davidsson P. et al. (eds.), *Multi Agent Based Simulation 2004*. Springer, Lecture Notes in Artificial Intelligence, 3415. Berlin: Springer, pp 130–144.
Elsenbroich, C., Gilbert, N. and Anzola, D. (2017) *Social Dimensions of Organized Crime. Modeling the Dynamics of Extortion Rackets*. Cham: Springer.
Epstein (2006) *Generative Social Science. Studies in Agent-Based Computational Modelling*. Princeton, NJ: Princeton University Press.

Flyvbjerg, B. (2006) 'Five misunderstandings about case-study research', *Qualitative Inquiry*, 12(2), pp. 210–245.

Jager, W. (2017) 'Enhancing the realism of simulation (EROS): On implementing and developing psychological theory in social simulation', *Journal of Artificial Societies and Social Simulation*, 20(3). jasss.soc.surrey.ac.uk/20/3/14.html

Levy, J. (2008) 'Counterfactuals and case studies', in Box-Steffensmeier, J., Brady, H. and Collier, D. (eds.), *The Oxford Handbook of Political Methodology*. Oxford: Oxford University Press, pp. 627–644.

Lincoln, Y. S. and Guba, E. G. (1985) *Naturalistic Inquiry*. Newbury Park, CA: Sage.

Neumann, M. and Sartor, N. (2016) 'A semantic network analysis of laundering drug money', *Journal of Tax Administration*, 2(1), pp. 73–94.

Sabater, J., Paolucci, M. and Conte, R. (2006) 'RePage: Reputation and image among limited autonomous partners', *Journal of Artificial Societies and Social Simulation*, 9(2). http://jasss.soc.surrey.ac.uk/9/2/3.html

Sparrow, M. (1991) 'The application of network analysis to criminal intelligence: An assessment of the prospects', *Social Networks*, 13(3), pp. 251–274.

Troitzsch, K. G. (2016) Can agent-based simulation replicate organized crime? *Trends in Organized Crime*, 20(1), pp. 100–119. doi:10.1007/s12117-016-9298-8.

van Duijn, P., Kashirin, V. and Sloot, P. (2014) The relative ineffectiveness of criminal network disruption. *Nature Scientific Reports* 4. doi:10.1038/srep04238.

Verde, A. and Nurro, A. (2010) 'Criminal profiling as plotting activity based on abductive processes', *International Journal of Offender Therapy and Comparative Criminology*, 54(5), pp. 829–849.

Weber, M. (1968) 'Die Objektivität sozialwissenschaftlicher und sozialpolitischer erkenntnis', in Winckelmann, J. (ed.) *Gesammelte Aufsätze Zur Wissenschaftslehre*. Tübingen: Mohr, pp. 146–204.

Zeigler, B., Praehofer, H. and Kim, T. (eds.). (2000) *Theory of Modelling and Simulation. Integrating discrete event and continuous complex dynamics systems*. 2nd edn. San Diego, CA: Academic Press.

9 On the construction of plausible futures in interpretive agent-based modelling

Martin Neumann, Vanessa Dirksen, and Sascha Dickel

9.1 Introduction

In this book, we explain in detail how we developed a novel approach for combining agent-based modelling (ABM) and qualitative, interpretive research traditions from the social sciences. The previous chapters have described how, at the various stages of the research process, different methods are applied, together making up the methodology referred to as *interpretive simulation modelling* or *interpretive ABM*. As discussed in Chapter 3, at the input side of the simulation, we referred to the methodology as *ethnographic simulation modelling*.

On the output side of the methodology, in Chapter 7 we referred to it as *sequence analysis*, a method that has its origin in the German tradition of objective hermeneutics. On the one hand, the research procedure integrates into a simulation account those elements that distinguish the human from the natural sciences, that is, interpretation and meaning-making (*semiosis*). On the other hand, interpretive social simulation enables the integration of causal understandings of social mechanisms into hermeneutic interpretation. As a consequence, and in line with Max Weber's conception of sociology, the methodology of interpretive ABM is best described as "a science which attempts the interpretive understanding of social action in order thereby to arrive at a causal explanation of its course and effects" (Weber, 1922: 3). The understanding of cause and effects is deemed essential for shedding a light on cultural possibilities, as highlighted in the case of criminology.

Throughout the various chapters of this book, we have shown *how* to generate knowledge on a particular social phenomenon by applying the interpretive approach to ABM. Important in this respect is the difference between method and methodology. *Method*, in Sandra Harding's (cited in Reed, 2011: 3, footnote 2) view, refers to "a technique for (of a way of proceeding in) gathering evidence". *Methodology* refers to "a theory and analysis of how research does or should proceed". *Epistemology*, in her view, is "a theory of knowledge". Whereas in previous chapters we have dealt with the separate methods integrated in interpretive AMB, this chapter concerns the methodology and epistemology as Harding understood the terms, in terms

DOI: 10.4324/9781003393207-9

of how the generated social knowledge by way of interpretive simulation is validated and corrected by experts in the field, referred to as a *community of enquiry* (Lichterman and Reed, 2015). In other words, in this chapter we reflect on how meaning is arrived at by means of the triangulation of methods outlined in this book and how this eventually leads to an idiosyncratic–generalist knowledge claim.

The chapter is organized as follows: in Section 9.2, we discuss the overall research procedure of interpretive simulation modelling. This section zooms in on *how* knowledge about a social phenomenon is established and validated. Section 9.3 concerns the second aspect of Harding's understanding of the methodology and includes "how theory is used and applied" to understand and explain social phenomena (Reed, 2011: 3, footnote 2). Here, we contrast the work of interpretation and meaning-making in objective hermeneutics with how this is done in the Geertzian tradition of semiotic ethnography. Section 9.4 focuses on the nature of the knowledge claim made by way of interpretive ABM. The chapter ends with a reflection on the notion of plausible future narratives, that is, on how to judge the plausibility of simulated counterfactual scenarios.

9.2 The methodology as a research procedure

This section zooms into the *how* of the research procedure; more specifically, we look into how, by means of the research procedure, knowledge about a criminal phenomenon comes into being. This refers to both the input side and the output side of the methodology. The research procedure can be described as a triangulation of methods drawn from a combination of diverse qualitative methodologies by means of computational simulation. The establishment of the social phenomenon is based on ethnographic analysis; as a consequence, the conceptual model is to be regarded as the ethnographic representation of the phenomenon, thickly described. The sequential analysis is the "objective hermeneutic approach to qualitative validation" (Borim-de-Souza et al., 2020). It is important to note, however, that it is a sequential, not a parallel or embedded, design. All research steps build upon each other (Curry et al., 2013); they do not run in parallel. Ethnographic analysis is essential for generating the narratives by means of ABM, which in a subsequent research step is interpreted hermeneutically. Hence, ethnography and objective hermeneutics depend on each other in interpretive simulation modelling. Hermeneutic interpretation would not be possible without the ethnographic data analysis because the generation of narrative scenarios is based on the ethnographic data analysis research step. This step enables one to trace the agent rules that are activated during a simulation to the codes of the data analysis. On the other hand, hermeneutic interpretation validates the counterfactual scenarios and thereby establishes the objective meaningfulness of the ethnographic analysis.

9.2.1   *Ethnographic data analysis*

First, an ethnographic analysis of the micro scenes of evidence is performed; the details of this are described in Chapter 3. To reiterate, ethnography is a microscopic research tradition aimed at deciphering the symbolic world of intersubjective meaning as negotiated in everyday interactions in the field. The data typically are given in the form of unstructured textual data in natural language. In a process of iterative coding, core themes are identified as a number of open codes that are subsumed under higher order codes. The ethnographic analysis provides the categories for a conceptual modelling process that specifies the relations between the categories in the form of condition–action sequences.

9.2.2   *Conceptual modelling*

The process of conceptual modelling is illustrated by the example presented in Chapter 5. The conceptual modelling process links the phase of qualitative data analysis with simulation modelling. The end result of this – the conceptual model made up of the ethnographic input in the form of condition–action sequences *and* the attached annotations that trace the material back to the "intelligible context" (Geertz, 1983) – is to be regarded as a contemporary form of "thick description" (Geertz, 1973). This research step consists of the following elements:

- First, the design of an agent's architecture is needed to specify the elements of the agent's cognition that are necessary for understanding that agent's hopes, fears, and strategies. This agent architecture is derived from the first round of ethnographic data analysis.
- Second, the conceptual model specifies the spaces of the possible action and interaction. Following Coleman's concept of macro–micro–macro schema of a sociological explanation (Coleman, 1990), agents' options for possible actions are captured by condition–action sequences. To be precise, the environment provides certain conditions that trigger certain actions. These, in turn, change the environment, which, then, provides a stimulus for certain follow-up actions.
- Third, a central element of the approach presented in this book is that each rule of the model is linked to the annotations stemming from the ethnographic data analysis. This traceability to the original empirical evidential base preserves the context sensitivity of the model, meaning that throughout the entire research procedure, the model and the simulated narratives remain intelligible in that particular context.

All three elements together – agent architecture, dynamism, and traceability – are at the heart of the conceptual modelling phase of the research procedure. The conceptual modelling specifies the space of possible action and interaction in the field and provides the basis for the implementation of a simulation model.

9.2.3   *Simulation modelling*

The simulation model adds dynamics to the ethnographic representation (or thick description) by way of a temporal dimension, and simulation experiments further enable the generation of counterfactual scenarios. An example of how this is done is discussed in depth in Chapter 6. As mentioned above, a feature that connects ethnography and simulation is the concept of traceability in the development of the rules of the simulation; that is, the rules are equipped with annotations from the open coding from the ethnographic data analysis. Apart from the fact that these annotations provide the empirical justification of the rules, they serve another purpose: the control flow of the model is not specified, which enables a flexible reaction of the agents to situational encounters that are not pre-given by defined sequences of how the programme needs to accomplish its tasks.[1] As a consequence of this feature, when running simulations, the rules are executed at different simulation steps. Because each rule contains the traces back to the empirical codes of the ethnographic analysis, instead of time series, the execution of the simulations generates narrative scenarios, produced by the ordering of the rules that are fired during the simulation run.

9.2.4   *Hermeneutic interpretation*

The final stage of the research procedure consists of the qualitative validation of the simulated narrative scenarios, as outlined in Chapter 7. To interpret the counterfactual scenarios, a sequence analysis is undertaken. Sequence analysis is a method originally developed by Ulrich Oevermann (2002) in the methodological paradigm of objective hermeneutics, even though the method is no longer strictly tied to the Oevermann school. It is "a method of interpretation that attempts to reconstruct the meaning of any kind of human action sequence by sequence i.e., sense unit by sense unit" (Kurt and Herbrik, 2014: 481) that enables an evaluation of the meaningfulness of the digitally generated narratives. For each sense unit, a community of researchers identifies the space of possible follow-up sequences before examining what possibility has factually been realized. Each follow-up sequence opens new possibilities and closes others. In so doing, hermeneutic interpretation increases the trustworthiness of the simulated counterfactual narratives because it provides a methodology for evaluating whether a counterfactual scenario provides a plausible variation of the course of actions found in the data. They describe a space of what is not just logically or physically possible, but – in the field under study – has a plausible future.[2]

Before elaborating on the diverging ways of meaning-making in ethnography and objective hermeneutics, it should be said that, from the perspective of interpretive social research, the combination of objective hermeneutics and ethnography in the methodology of interpretive social simulation is rather remarkable as both methodologies seem to represent opposing camps in the world of qualitative social research, often portrayed as a dichotomy of "subjective" and "objective" meaning-making. Although some have argued that both may be considered as belonging to the domain of interpretive research (Hitzler, 2005), and attempts have already been made to combine or complement both methodologies (Hildenbrand, 2004; Wieser, 2016), reactions range from the claim of forced marriage (Strübing, 2006) and clan liability (Hildenbrand, 2006) to controversies about the clarification of constitutional theory (Loer, 2006).[3] Both camps have perceived each other critically. For instance, the founding father of objective hermeneutics, Ulrich Oevermann, stated that the notion of a "'thick description' (Clifford Geertz) has caused much confusion in recent times" (Oevermann, 2002: 19, own translation). Moreover, the procedures of both methodologies are different. On the ground level of methods, for instance, prominent in ethnographic interpretation is the development of a coding schema whilst staying close to the empirical material and the subsuming of these initial, open codes under overarching codes, or categories, iteratively jumping back and forth in the data (Corbin and Strauss, 2008) in the process of refinement of the codes and categories. The sequential analytic procedure of objective hermeneutics is different: "Jumping around in the protocol, as it is often done in a content analysis (…) is (…) forbidden in the reconstruction-logical approach" (Wenninger, 2015: 57). A sequential analysis takes a sequential stance towards interpretation: interpretation is undertaken sense unit by sense unit in the ordering as they appear in the interpreted text. With the aim of ultimately characterizing the nature of the knowledge claim resulting from this rather unconventional combination of research procedures, the next section will look into meaning-making in both methods separately and how ABM joins the two, working towards the notion of plausible futures.

9.3   Meaning-making in interpretive ABM

This section elaborates on how in interpretive simulation modelling we claim to arrive at the "deeper meaning" of social action. *Deeper meaning* refers to the "[d]eeper set of meanings that inhere in the actions under study" (Reed, 2011: 10). It is distinct from *surface meaning*, that is, those "immediate meanings available in the investigator's evidence" (Ibid.). Interpretive ABM represents a novel take on meaning-making in ethnography comparable to that put forth in the strand of ethnography known as *analytic ethnography*. For the purpose of this chapter, it suffices to say that analytic ethnography, like interpretive simulation modelling, is geared towards developing causal claims (Lichterman and Reed, 2015: 587).

Interpretive ABM thrives on the triangulation of ethnography and sequence analysis by means of ABM. Both ethnography and sequence analysis involve the work of interpretation albeit of different forms. The former results in what can be called *minimal interpretation*, or the reconstruction of surface meaning, whereas the latter results in what can be called *maximal interpretation*, or the "reconstruction of 'deep structures generating action and meaning'" (Flick 2007: 10). Whereas minimal interpretation provides the *what* and the *how* of the social action, maximal interpretation allows one to answer "*how and why what happened*" (Reed, 2017: 118) to arrive at the generalizability and transferability of the findings. This is what in interpretive ABM is done by way of the counterfactual and the sequence analysis of the simulated narrative scenarios. To ultimately understand the kind of knowledge claim arrived at in interpretive simulation modelling, in this section we discuss the following three topics: (1) meaning-making in ethnography, (2) how counterfactual reasoning enabled by ABM enables the move to the third step, and (3) how validation of the simulated narratives by way of sequence analysis results in maximal interpretation.

9.3.1 *Minimal interpretation: The ethnographic establishment of a phenomenon*

As described in a previous section, the first phase of the research procedure is represented by the ethnographic data analysis and results in the empirical establishment of the social (i.e., criminal) phenomenon under study. This is done after the thematic analysis of James Spradley (see Chapter 3). This empirical evidence base is then used to derive the condition–action sequences and related annotations in the subsequent phase of conceptual modelling. We refer to the conceptual model with the related annotations as a form of thick description.[4]

With regard to meaning-making in ethnography, the first thing to understand is that thickly describing a phenomenon does not make it meaningful as such. It is the task of the ethnographic researcher to do the work of interpretation and mediate, as it were, between the ethnographic account of the interactional, the semiotic, and the (historical) contextual information as drawn up from the field (cf. Freeman, 2014: 828) and the world of academia (i.e., the theoretical). Therefore, after the empirical establishment of the phenomenon under study, we have to ask how the ethnographer makes sense of it all (Reed, 2011: 17; Freeman, 2014). To this end, we should comprehend how Geertz himself arrived at the understanding of a thickly described phenomenon, such as Balinese cockfights, as a form of "deep play": as Geertz found, the male gambling game is in essence not about money but "is fundamentally a dramatization of status" (Geertz, 1973: 437). It represents actual social mechanisms of Balinese society and acts as "a mirror image of social relations of masculinity and social power" (Pollock, 2003: 152). Comprehending cockfights as a form of deep play is thus a result of "an intersection between the context of investigation and the context of explanation" (Reed, 2008: 190). The context of investigation refers here to a sense of "being there", that is, in the field, and the context of explanation relates back to the world of academia and scientific theory, that is, "being here". To the ethnographer, theory, and hence explanation, refers to "the sense of understanding what happened at [...] as an instance of a broader phenomenon that can be systematically mapped or construed" (ibid: 192).

For comprehending meaning-making in Geertz's tradition of ethnography, we first point to the prominence of context in ethnography. Contextualization adds layers of meaning to the ethnography (Strathern, 2002) and, thus, is the primary means of meaning-making. Ethnography is, not without reason, referred to as the method that "captures context" (Hansen, 2006: 1055) because it is the ethnographer's primary task to make inferences about how the context in which the action is situated endows it with meaning. Grasping the meaning of cocaine trading by situating the constituents' social actions in the context of reputation-building mechanisms (see Chapter 3), for instance, is signified as an expression of that context. Specific trading actions, then, become symbolic in the context of actors interpreting other actors' doings and reacting accordingly. This is in line with the famous example used by Clifford Geertz (1973): whether an eye movement is an involuntary twitch or a conspiratorial signal depends on the context in which it is situated. Problematic in the Geertzian form of interpretation is to then know what the social act (the twitch) really stands for: is it to make someone feel at ease, or is it a sexual innuendo? As some scholars contend, "Without any evidence he [Geertz] attributes to the Balinese all sorts of experiences, meanings, intentions, motivations, dispositions, and understandings" (Crapanzano, 1986: 72) of which the grounds are wholly unclear.[5] It is for this reason, and because in our research setting there is no way of validating these experiences from the insiders' point of view, that we resort to objective hermeneutics (sequence analysis) to validate the observed mechanisms in the field so as to get to the deeper meaning of the social acts under study, that is, to make the thick description of the conceptual modelling phase meaningful.

Another point of concern in ethnography is the fact that because contextualization as a form of meaning-making and the resultant ethnographic knowledge claim have a strong idiosyncratic character, ethnography is said to be weak when the transferability (aka abstraction/generalizability) of its findings is concerned. Put differently, whilst ethnography is strong when it comes to making generalizations *within* cases, it lacks the tools for theoretical abstraction required for making generalizations *across* cases. In search of the deeper meaning of the mechanisms as represented by way of ethnographic thick description, we want to know the answer to not "only" the *what* and the *how* but also the *why* of the social action (Katz, 2001). The former two are common in ethnography; the latter, however, is often ignored (Reed, 2008). Ethnography typically provides us, then, with what is referred to as *interpretive explanation*: "how the meanings that define the social context of action in a specific way are (…) important in determining *what*, *when*, and *where* certain actions happen, certain social relationships emerge, and certain sorts of community arise as a result of these relationships" (Reed, 2011: 128). Thus, what is needed is the shift from a form of interpretive explanation to "explanations that use law-like generalizations" (Lichterman and Reed, 2015: 596), referring to the distinction between *verstehen* and *erklaeren*, respectively.

The first bridge to enable this move in interpretive simulation modelling is found first in the notion of the counterfactual of ABM and, second, in the notion of meaning structures of objective hermeneutics. The former, the counterfactual of ABM, potentially elevates the ethnography from generalization *within* cases to generalization *across* cases. The latter, the notion of meaning structures, allows us to make the move from idiosyncratic understandings of social phenomena to nomothetic abstractions whilst keeping the interpretive character of the ethnography. Put differently, in interpretive ABM we make the move from thick description to plausible future scenarios. In the next section, we elaborate on the essential role of counterfactual imagination in this.

9.3.2 *ABM as the bridge from interpretation to explanation*

Whereas the first step in constructing an explanation is represented by the first phase of the research procedure as described in the previous section (i.e., the empirical establishment of the phenomenon), this section revolves around the second step of explanation: the role of agent-based simulation and counterfactuals in interpretive ABM. We have to understand the nature of the "why" question or, rather, the nature of the "why" answer into which the counterfactual provides an entrance. Although counterfactual reasoning is not unknown in some forms of ethnography (cf. Hauge, 2021), we elaborate here on counterfactual simulation experiments. This will be done in three steps: first, we consider how the execution of the programme code enables one to take ethnography beyond the descriptive or interpretive explanation and to *theorize* the social instead. Next, we analyse the structure of the explanation provided by the results of an agent-based simulation and examine what kind of explanation the results specifically of an *interpretive* ABM, in contrast to a traditional ABM, provide. This leads us finally to understand the role of counterfactuals in simulation experiments, that is, the structure of counterfactual reasoning during the execution of various simulations.

The first thing to note is that the execution of an agent-based simulation is a chain of rules that are executed consecutively. This comes close to the definition of a mechanism as "a social process that is reliably traceable in multiple locations (or across case studies) and thus can be pictured in abstract language and exhibits some regularity in its tendency to push toward a certain kind of outcome" (Lichterman and Reed, 2015: 613). *Mechanisms* are chains of events in which the prior event causes the latter or, more specifically, the notion that under similar circumstances a similar input X* yields similar outputs Y* (Hedström and Ylkoski, 2010). Indeed, in the past 10 years, mechanistic explanations have been gaining increased attention in the social sciences (Hedström, 2006). Referring back to the classification of social sciences explanations in Chapter 2, it can be stated that an important vehicle in this form of theorizing in ABM (i.e., to make the move from the idiographic to the nomothetic) is the notion of *social mechanisms*. Mechanistic explanations search neither for universal laws nor for statistical regularities between variables. Following a mechanistic style of explanation, a phenomenon is explained by identifying entities and processes that generate the phenomenon to be explained.[6] In agent-based models, the entities are the agents, and the processes are the actions and interactions of the agents. Thus, agent-based models provide the nuts and bolts for the social science (Elster, 1989).

However, while being based on mechanistic explanations, the knowledge claim of agent-based simulation goes one step further than referring merely to the notion of social mechanisms. This leads us to the second step: the structure of the explanation provided by the simulation results of an interpretive agent-based simulation model. One of the most well-known answers to the question of the knowledge claim provided by agent-based social simulation is Joshua Epstein's (2006) notion of *generative explanations*: "If you didn't grow it, you didn't explain it". In agent-based simulations, the interaction of agents generates certain patterns. For instance, drawing on a model structure proposed by Schelling (1971), the interaction of agents might generate patterns of residential segregation (Wilensky, 1997), equilibrium prices (Epstein and Axtell, 1996), or social norms (Conte et al., 2014). In the Schelling model, for instance, agents of two colours (e.g., red and blue) move randomly to a new residential area in a checkerboard world if their neighbourhood does not fulfil certain internal criteria of similarity. As a consequence, on a social macro level, the emergent patterns of segregation are much more pronounced than the internal criteria would suggest at the micro level of the agents. This is but one example of a social macrophenomenon generated by interactions of agents on the micro level. Even though the converse is not true (because other models with different rules of interaction might generate the same patterns), Epstein argued that an explanation of phenomena of sociological interest needs to demonstrate how such patterns are generated, or grown, by processes of agent decision-making and interaction. If a simulation of the interactions at the micro level generates the macrophenomenon of interest, the simulation then provides a candidate explanation of the social phenomenon. This is the basic idea of generative explanations. Thus, a generative explanation in the sense of Epstein relies on a differentiation between a "microlevel" and a "macrolevel". For identifying the explanatory entities, the concept of "levels" needs to be introduced.[7] A generative explanation differentiates between a micro level of the agents as the explanans and a macro level of macroscopic social regularities as the explanandum. Subjects of the explanation are macroscopic social regularities (Epstein, 2006), such as residential segregation, equilibrium prices, or social norms.

Certainly, the model presented in Chapters 5 and 6 of this book as a running example also generates events such as murder. The events are generated in the process of the interaction of the agents. Thus, the simulation model represents a candidate explanation for these events as they are generated during a simulation run. In this respect, it provides a generative explanation. However, whether events such as a murder can be denoted as a social macro level as proposed in Epstein's concept of a generative explanation is questionable.

Subjects of the "generative" explanation of the interpretive account to agent-based social simulation are less macroscopic social regularities and more single events, such as a murder. Here, the idiographic focus of interpretive social science comes into play. In line with Max Weber's concept of sociological explanations, the subjects of the explanation are the courses and effects of a specific social action. This sheds light on the knowledge claim of interpretive ABM: as an agent-based simulation, it offers a generative candidate explanation of social phenomena. In this respect, it does not diverge from more conventional approaches to ABM. However, interpretive ABM does not infer (or does not necessarily infer) a social macro level from a micro level. Whereas ABM usually is concerned with social structure (the macro level), the inference step in interpretive ABM is from interaction to meaning. It explains how meaning emerges in processes of social interaction. Thus, the research focus of interpretive ABM is slightly different from that of conventional ABM: as outlined above, the specific strength of conventional ABM is the explanation of social structure. Social structure need not be meaningful to the actors populating the social world. In contrast, interpretive ABM attempts to understand how the meaningfulness of the social world is generated. We can illustrate this difference with an example: a traditional ABM may generate or "grow" inequality, which might be measured by calculating the Gini Index in the simulation results. An interpretive approach to ABM, on the other hand, may decipher the meaning of poverty, for instance, in the form of schoolchildren bullying classmates in the schoolyard for not wearing the most fashionable sneakers. How this is realized leads us to counterfactuals, paving the way to the final step of simulation experiments that enable the causal analysis of social phenomena.

The puzzle behind growing phenomena such as murder is understanding *why* such events happen when grown in the course of a simulation. To recap the example of criminals killing each other instead of becoming more and more rich, the question is "What the hell is going on here?": why do they kill each other? To answer this question, simulation experiments for studying counterfactual scenarios are essential. If we understand why in counterfactual scenarios events such as murder do *not* happen, we have identified the micro-level units – or sequences – that are essential for understanding why factual events such as murder have happened. Thus, the research process to arrive at such an explanation draws on the concept of counterfactual causal explanations that was proposed by Max Weber. To this end, Weber referred to a theory of objective possibility, the so-called *theory of adequate causation* (see also Chapter 7). This theory relies on a counterfactual theory of causality. It needs to be analysed if another course of events would have been, in Weber's terms, "objectively possible". The rules to undertake such an analysis are abstraction and generalization. First, one needs to disentangle a complex situation into its elementary units. This is the process of the development of a conceptual model as described in Chapter 5. In Clifford Geertz's terms, the condition–action sequences can be described as a generalization within the case (cf. Chapter 3): the sequences are generalizations of the instantiations found in the data; that is, the condition–action sequences represent general event classes. The elementary units of a complex situation can then be imagined away or thought to be different. Counterfactually, one can then examine what course of events would have to be expected if one of these elements is changed or deleted (Levy, 2008). This is what the counterfactual scenarios in the simulation experiments do. If we detect a counterfactual scenario in which the event of a murder is missing, we can investigate which elementary units (i.e., condition–action sequences) are missing or changed compared with the real-world case (Smith, 2016). Counterfactual scenarios do not examine social regularities as ABM traditionally does but instead explore the space of possible variations of a case. Again, in Geertz's terms, this can be denoted as *generalisation across cases*: the counterfactual scenarios explore possible options for courses of action and the effects they would have had if a different course of action had been taken. This enables the detection of critical junctures in a historical causal analysis. Thus, our notion of plausible futures puts into practice Max Weber's notion of objective possibility (see Chapters 3 and 7) as a research methodology for "interpretive *understanding* of social action in order thereby to arrive at a causal explanation of its course and effects" (Weber, 1922: 3).

9.3.3   *Maximal interpretation: Meaning-making in objective hermeneutics*

In interpretive ABM, we make the move from thick description to plausible future scenarios; that is, move from the evidential realm of the social phenomenon to the theoretical realm of the social phenomenon. By integrating ABM into ethnography, we are one step closer to moving from the idiosyncratic reasoning of ethnography to a more general and lawlike nature of causal explanation. Thus, in interpretive ABM, we are after the transferability of particular social mechanisms and social processes. This, however, requires fathoming the *plausibility* of the simulated chains of action and brings us to the last phase of interpretive simulation modelling: the application of sequence analysis. Where ethnographic conceptual modelling denotes the production of data on the input side of the methodology, sequence analysis is applied so as to qualitatively validate the findings on the output side of the methodology (cf. Borim-de-Souza et al., 2020). To arrive at the meaning system of theory in qualitative research,

> The investigator combines bits of theory with bits of evidence, and then these theory–fact pairs are brought together into a meaningful whole. This meaningful whole is the deep interpretation that the investigator constructs, and it gives coherence to her case.
>
> (Reed, 2011: 10)

This is done by way of sequential analysis. Thus, although the simulation establishes the step from evidence to mechanisms, what constitutes *meaningful* mechanisms is determined in the sequential analysis phase, qualitatively validating the possibility that these mechanisms may, in fact, be triggered.

Before understanding how this is done and how, in so doing, the plausi-bility of the future narratives is approached, we first have to understand the specifics of meaning attribution in objective hermeneutics. To facilitate the reasoning, we explain this in comparison to how this is done in ethnography. First, both ethnography and objective hermeneutics are semiotic; that is, they revolve around meaning-making (semiosis). Second, both ethnography and objective hermeneutics maintain that "human behaviour, and interaction is considered to be meaningful and to make sense" (Wodak, 2011: 624). Third, both ethnography and objective hermeneutics seek to reveal the meaning of social behaviour and interaction. Fourth, both objective hermeneutics and ethnography revolve around intersubjective meaning-making (cf. Honer and Hitzler, 2015).

However, despite the fact that on the basis of these grounds they may both be subsumed under the heading of interpretive sociology according to some scholars (Hitzler, 2005), and revolve around intersubjective meaning-making, they do so differently. However, the difference is less in the *how* but more so in the *where* this meaning is reconstructed (Ibid.): in the first two phases of the method (1: genesis of the data and 2: phrasing of the question), there is a considerable similarity with the ethnographic research tradition. The differ-ence with thematic analysis of the ethnographic and grounded theory analysis research tradition "that seek[s] for similarities among the scattered pieces of information" is in the last phase of "interpretation of the text" (Wagner et al., 2010: 11). Sequence analysis takes a sequential stance towards interpretation: interpretation is undertaken sense unit by sense unit in the order in which they appear in the interpreted text. Furthermore, the notion of intersubjectivity in ethnography refers to the ethnographer mediating between the context of the investigation and the context of explanation (for a more elaborate notion of intersubjectivity, see Chapter 3). In objective hermeneutics, however, interpre-tation is done with a so-called community of enquirers. In this case, and again in contrast to ethnography, the work of interpretation done by the researcher is *not* taken into consideration (Wodak, 2011). In doing interpretation inter-subjectively and in text ("follow the sequence"), sequence analysis thrives on the principle of "freedom of context" as opposed to the predominant context-boundedness of interpretation in ethnography: "[O]ne of the key principles of interpretation in Objective Hermeneutics is to temporarily exclude contextual knowledge in order to explore thoroughly the different meanings of the data at hand (Wernet, 2013 quoted in Berli, 2021: 779)". However, as we contend with respect to the context-free theorizing of sequence analysis, decontextual-izing in the final interpretation of an interpretive agent-based social simulation is made possible (or makes sense only) only because ethnography preserves the context in the data-gathering phase to begin with and thus allows for the traceability of the final findings.

In trying to capture the distinctiveness of meaning-making in a sequen-tial analytical approach in objective hermeneutics, we have to turn to the no-tion of *meaning structure*, to provide an entrance into this particular form of interpretation. "'Meaning structure' refers to the set or totality of possible interpretative options opened up by the wording of the text" (Franzmann, 2022: 176). On the topic of meaning, Oevermann maintained that "It is of primary concern to carve out those latent structures of meaning, which are granted a reality of their own (Oevermann, 2002, cited in Wagner et al., 2010: 5)". The first thing to note is that, whereas meaning-making in sequence analysis happens *in* the text (i.e., reconstructing the meaning that inheres in the social interaction as represented by text), meaning-making in ethnography is situation and subject specific (see also Reichertz, 2004). In other words, and in terms of the locus of interpretation, ethnography thrives on the notion of "being there", which equals "the context of investigation" (Reed, 2008: 189), whereas objective hermeneutics departs from the notion of "being here", referring instead to "the context of explanation":

> Unlike phenomenologically-oriented interpretations in the broadest sense, which are directed at reconstructing the typically intended subjective meaning, objective hermeneutics precisely do not regard the subject as being of meaning-constitutive relevance. On the contrary, constitutionally relevant are the structures which Oevermann assumes to be objective: they ultimately carry the meaning in themselves which has to be reconstructed—so to speak by construing right through life experience—by means of the method judged as 'objective' by him.
> (Hitzler, 2005)

A typical example is a greeting. You can return a greeting or not. Both reactions have a meaning that is constituted by the social practice of greeting. Thus, greetings may be said to have an objective structure of meaning, whereas the reactions are conditioned by contingent case structures.

9.4   Plausible futures?

In this final section, we elaborate on the basis on which the methodology of interpretive ABM and its output are to be evaluated. A starting point is provided by the notion of validation. Validation is one of the most discussed and highly controversial issues in ABM. Broadly speaking, "[v]alidity is concerned with the integrity of the conclusions that are generated from a piece of research" (Bryman, 2016: 41). In ABM, *validity* specifically refers to the relation between evidence and simulation (Beisbart and Saam, 2019). The notion of validity denotes, here, whether a simulation is an adequate representation of the target system, albeit the fact that both *adequate* and *representation* are rather ambiguous terms (Knuuttilla, 2011). A number of procedures to determine the credibility of agent-based simulations have been suggested (e.g. Küppers and Lenhard, 2005; Thorngate and Edmonds, 2013; Drchal et al., 2016; Graebner, 2018). However, the potential role of qualitative interpretive methods has not yet been discussed, even though there has been a long debate in the community of qualitative social research on this issue (Creswell and Miller, 2000). Next, we show how qualitative methods contribute to the validation of interpretive ABM.

In ABM, a distinction is commonly made between input and output validation. *Input validation* reflects the degree of realism of the social mechanisms in the model, and *output validation* refers to the match of the simulation results with empirical data. Interpretive ABM provides procedures of both input and output validation: first, the phase of ethnographic model development serves as input validation. At the beginning of the research procedure, it enables one to decipher the elementary units of a complex situation by grounding the model rules on evidence found by the microscopic ethnographic analysis. This is a qualitative account for grounding the model rules on the meanings dissected in the empirical evidence. Ethnography, like any other inductive qualitative research tradition (and grounded theory in particular), is believed to be strong especially when internal validity is concerned because of the strong fit between data and theory. Second, hermeneutic interpretation, standing at the very end of the research procedure, evaluates the external validity of the simulation results by determining the extent to which they create meaningful narratives and – referring to the counterfactual scenarios – are meaningful variations of the mechanisms found in the empirical material. It discloses the latent structures of the meaning of the ethnographically established phenomenon. Hence, its contextlessness hermeneutic interpretation makes up for ethnography's weak spot, the difficulty of transferability as a result of its *context-boundedness*. Thus, the output validation of narrative scenarios does not refer to the positivist notion of the match with empirical data; instead, it takes the feature of agent-based models into account to allow for the investigation of "what if" relations and questions. As such, the ex-ante investigation of possible alternative futures enables the identification of a variety of action alternatives as well as the detection of early warning signals of any eventually undesired effects or developments. For this purpose, counterfactual scenarios are deemed essential in ABM. Because counterfactuals go beyond factual data, their knowledge claim should not be judged in terms of accuracy or correspondence with reality but instead in terms of plausibility. Therefore, we now further explore the notion of plausibility.

The notion of plausibility is strongly linked with the nature of interpretive research on the one hand and with the centrality of counterfactual imagination on the other hand. Assessing the input and output validation is required if one is to understand the output in terms of how knowledge comes about by way of the research procedure of interpretive ABM (i.e., the epistemic mode). Thus, we should question the nature of the larger knowledge claim by asking "What kind of knowledge of the world makes the validated simulated narratives?" As mentioned earlier in this chapter, interpretive ABM is a sequential design consisting of a triangulation of methods. The resultant knowledge claim of the research procedure at large, however, is not a matter of merely adding up the epistemological achievements of those methods separately. We should thus ask, "What is the value of the simulated future scenarios by way of interpretive ABM?" To answer this question, we are concerned with the issue of how to move beyond the theoretical to the plausible. In the words of Hawthorn (1991),

> The possibilities that we consider for the actual [in interpretive ABM, this refers to the counterfactual] (...) start from particular agents in particular sets of circumstances as those agents and sets of circumstances actually were [in interpretive ABM this refers to the empirical establishment of the phenomenon]. Models, theories, or precepts may guide our speculations about what might then follow [in interpretive ABM, this refers to the social, ergo meaningful, mechanisms].
>
> (Hawthorn, 1991: 168)

The plausible, then, takes us beyond the realm of the (purely) theoretical possibility. In interpretive ABM, this refers to the latent structures of meaning. Hence, the integration of ABM into interpretive research such as ethnography and hermeneutics allows one to make the move from *how* to *why* (Katz, 2001). In making judgements about plausible *futures*, the temporal dimension of the causal connections, established by the simulation, is fundamental. The contribution of ABM inheres in the notion of social mechanism as an explanatory concept, whereas the contribution of interpretive social science is the meaningfulness of the social mechanisms deemed essential for the judgement of *plausible* futures. In other words, the notion of plausible futures provides a "rapprochement between interpretation and explanation" (Reed, 2017: 123). Note that this does not imply a dichotomy of "true" or "false", or numerical values of plausibility in terms of, for instance, significance levels in judgements about statistical hypotheses, as is common in the quantitative tradition. Instead, plausibility in interpretive ABM is "essentially a measure of sensemaking" (Alsharari and Al-Shboul, 2019: 52) and carries the meaning of "convincingness of interpretive research" (Ibid.). In other words, plausibility in interpretive ABM has to do with "how we reason and how we construct a convincing argument" (van der Helm, 2006, quoted in Uruena, 2019: 20). This implies the relevance of criteria regarding the coherence of the narrative on the one hand and of conformity to prevailing theoretical insights on the other (cf. Fischer and Dannenberg, 2021). Hence, interpretive ABM realizes the research agenda of "the interpretive understanding of social action in order thereby to arrive at a causal explanation of its course and effects" (Weber, 1922: 3). In this sense, its knowledge claim has the potential to reveal plausible futures.

Notes

1 This already corresponds to the claim of Ulrich Oevermann, the founder of objective hermeneutics, that a finite number of rules generates an infinite space of possible results (Oevermann, 2002).
2 For instance, in the case described in this book, it was a conceivable option to threaten people with machine guns, which would be less conceivable for children

playing in, say, a Danish schoolyard (taking school shootings into account, this might not be a valid argument in a worldwide context). For schoolchildren, however, coming to blows might be a plausible option, but a less plausible option in, say, parliamentary debates in the US Congress.

3 In part, the differences between the two approaches can be traced back to the different background traditions of the two methodologies: hermeneutics goes back to the German philosophy of history of the 19th century, and the roots of ethnography can be found in the semiotic account of pragmatism and symbolic interactionism.

4 "It is the interpretive characteristic of description rather than detail per se that makes it thick" (Schwandt 2007, in Freeman, 2014: 827).

5 Crapanzano continued: "Cockfights are surely cockfights for the Balinese—and not images, fictions, models, and metaphors. They are not marked as such, though they may be read as such by a foreigner for whom 'images, fictions, models, and metaphors' have interpretive value" (p. 73).

6 What should be noted in this respect, to begin with, is that "[t]he search for social mechanisms produces partial, not totalizing, explanations" (Lichterman and Reed, 2015: 620). Second, it is about the *potential* transferability of social mechanisms and processes.

7 The differentiation between levels is rooted in emergentist philosophy (Emmeche et al., 1997). For instance, emergentist explanations of life differentiate between a level of the physical world; a chemical level emerging from the physical level; and the level of biological life, emerging from the chemical level. Likewise, emergentist explanations of society claim that the social level emerges from the individual level. Because the notion of emergence is central also in ABM and distributed artificial intelligence, it is not surprising to find the notion of levels in the concept of generative explanations.

References

Alsharari, N. and Al-Shboul, M. (2019) 'Evaluating qualitative research in management accounting using the criteria of "convincingness"', *Pacific Accounting Review*, 31(1), pp. 43–62.

Beisbart, C. and Saam, N. (eds.) (2019) *Computer Simulation Validation: Fundamental Concepts, Methodological Frameworks, and Philosophical Perspectives*. Cham: Springer.

Berli, O. (2021) '"Maybe this is speculative now" negotiating and valuing interpretations in qualitative research', *Human Studies*, 44, pp. 765–790.

Borim-de-Souza, R., Travis, E., Munck, L. and Galleli, B. (2020) 'An objective hermeneutic approach to qualitative validation, *qualitative research in organizations and management*', An International Journal, 15(4), pp. 523–541.

Bryman, A. (2016) *Social Research Methods*. 5th edn. Oxford: Oxford University Press.

Coleman, J. (1990) *Foundations of Social Theory*. Cambridge MA: Harvard University Press.

Conte, R., Andrighetto, G. and Campenni, M. (eds.) (2014) *Minding Norms: Mechanisms and Dynamics of Social Order in Agent Societies*. Oxford, England: Oxford University Press.

Corbin, J. and Strauss, A. (2008). *Basics of Qualitative Research*. 3rd edn. Thousand Oaks, CA: Sage.

Crapanzano, V. (1986) 'Hermes' dilemma: The masking of subversion in ethnographic description', in Clifford, J. and Marcus, G. (eds.) *Writing Culture: The Poetics and Politics of Ethnography*. Berkley, CA: University of California Press, pp. 51–76.

Creswell, J. and Miller, D. (2000) 'Determining validity in qualitative research', *Theory into Practice*, 39(3), pp. 124–130.

Curry, L., Krumholz, H., O'Cathain, A., Plano Clark, V., Cherlin, E. and Bradley, E., et al. (2013) 'Mixed methods in biomedical and health services research', *Circulation: Cardiovascular Quality and Outcomes*, 6(1), pp. 119–123.

Drchal, J., Certicky, M. and Jacob, M. (2016) 'VALFRAM: Validation framework for activity-based models', *Journal of Artificial Societies and Social Simulation*, 19(3), https://www.jasss.org/19/3/5/5.pdf

Elster, J. (1989) *Nuts and Bolts for the Social Scientists*. Cambridge, England: Cambridge University Press.

Emmeche, C., Køppe, S. and Stjernfelt, F. (1997) 'Explaining emergence: Towards an ontology of levels', *Journal for General Philosophy of Science*, 28(1), pp. 83–119.

Epstein, J. (2006) *Generative Social Science. Studies in Agent-Based Computational Modelling*. Princeton, NJ: Princeton University Press.

Epstein, J. and Axtell, R. (1996) *Growing Artificial Societies: Social Science from the Bottom-up*. Cambridge MA: MIT Press.

Fischer, N. and Dannenberg, S. (2021) 'The social construction of futures: Proposing plausibility as a semiotic approach for critical futures studies', *Futures*, 129. 102729. https://www-sciencedirect-com.proxy1-bib.sdu.dk/science/article/pii/S0016328721000380

Flick, U. (2007) *Designing Qualitative Research*. London: Sage.

Franzmann, A. (2022) The method of sequence analysis within the framework of objective hermeneutics—Origins and exemplification, *Gesprächsforschung - Online-Zeitschrift zur verbalen Interaktion*, 23(2022), pp. 167–189. http://www.gespraechsforschung-online.de/fileadmin/dateien/heft2022/si-franzmann.pdf

Freeman, M. (2014) 'The hermeneutical aesthetics of thick description', *Qualitative Inquiry*, 20(6), pp. 827–833. https://doi-org.ezproxy.elib11.ub.unimaas.nl/10.1177/1077800414530267

Geertz, C. (1973) *The Interpretation of Cultures*. New York: Basic Books.

Geertz, C. (1983) *Local Knowledge: Further Essays in Interpretive Anthropology*. New York: Basic Books.

Graebner, C. (2018) 'How to relate models to reality? An epistemological framework for the validation and verification of computational models', *Journal of Artificial Societies and Social Simulation*, 21(3). https://www.jasss.org/21/3/8.html

Hansen, H. (2006). The ethnonarrative approach. *Human Relations*, 59(8), pp. 1049–1075.

Hauge, A. M. (2021) 'How to take sides: On the challenges of managing positionality', *Journal of Organizational Ethnography*, 10(1), pp. 95–111.

Hawthorn, G. (1991) *Plausible Worlds: Possibility and Understanding in History and the Social Sciences*. Cambridge, England: Cambridge University Press.

Hedström, P. (2006) *Dissecting the Social. On the Principles of Analytic Sociology*. Cambridge: Cambridge University Press.

Hedström, P. and Ylkoski, P. (2010) 'Causal mechanisms in the social sciences', *Annual Review of Sociology*, 36, pp. 49–67.

Hildenbrand, B. (2004) 'Gemeinsames Ziel, verschiedene Wege: Grounded theory und Objektive Hermeneutik im Vergleich', *Sozialer Sinn*, 5(2), pp. 177–194.

Hildenbrand, B. (2006) 'Wider die Sippenhaft. Eine Antwort auf Jörg Stilibing', *Sozialer Sinn*, 7(1), pp. 159–167.

Hitzler, R. (2005). 'The reconstruction of meaning: Notes on German interpretive sociology, forum', *Qualitative Social Research*, 6(3). https://doi.org/10.17169/fqs-6.3.7.

Honer, A. and Hitzler, R. (2015) 'Life-world-analytical ethnography: A phenomenology-based research approach', *Contemporary Ethnography*, 44(5), pp. 544–562.

Katz, J. (2001) 'From how to why: On luminous description and causal inference in ethnography (part I)', *Ethnography*, 2(4), pp. 443–473.

Knuuttilla, T. (2011) 'Modelling and representing: An artefactual approach to model-based representation', *Studies in History and Philosophy of Science Part A*, 42(2), pp. 262–271.

Küppers, G. and Lenhard, J. (2005) 'Validation of simulation: Patterns in the natural and social sciences', *Journal of Artificial Societies and Social Simulation*, 8(4). https://www.jasss.org/8/4/3.html.

Kurt, R. and Herbrik, R. (2014) 'Sozialwissenschaftliche Hermeneutik und hermeneutische Wissenssoziologie', in Baur, N. and Blasius, J. (eds.) *Handbuch Methoden der empirischen Sozialforschung*. Wiesbaden: Springer VS, pp. 473–491.

Levy, J. (2008) 'Counterfactuals and case studies', in Box-Steffensmeier, J., Brady, H. and Collier, D. (eds.) *The Oxford Handbook of Political Methodology*. Oxford, England: Oxford University Press, pp. 627–643.

Lichterman, P. and Reed, I. A. (2015) 'Theory and contrastive explanation in ethnography', *Sociological Methods & Research*, 44(4), pp. 585–635.

Loer, T. (2006) 'Streit statt Haft und Zwang—Objektive Hermeneutik in der Diskussion. Methodologische und konstitutionstheoretische Klärungen, methodische Folgerungen und eine Marginalie zum Thomas-Theorem', *Sozialer Sinn*, 7(2), pp. 345–374.

Oevermann, U. (2002) *Klinische Soziologie auf der Basis der Methodologie der objektiven Hermeneutik. Manifest der objektiv hermeneutischen Sozialforschung*. Frankfurt am Main: Institut für hermeneutische Sozialforschung.

Pollock, G. (2003) 'Cockfights and other parades: Gesture, difference, and the staging of meaning in three paintings by Zoffany, Pollock, and Krasner', *Oxford Art Journal*, 26(2): 141–165. https://www.jstor.org/stable/3600394

Reed, I. (2008) 'Maximal interpretation in Clifford Geertz and the Strong Program in cultural sociology: Towards a new epistemology', *Cultural Sociology*, 2(2), pp. 187–200.

Reed, I. A. (2011) *Interpretation and Social Knowledge: On the Use of Theory in the Human Sciences*. Chicago: University of Chicago Press.

Reed, I. A. (2017) 'Ethnography, theory, and sociology as a human science: An interlocution', *Ethnography*, 18(1), pp. 107–129.

Reichertz, J. (2004) 'Objective hermeneutic and hermeneutic sociology of knowledge', in Flick, U., von Kardor, E. and Steinke, I. (eds.) *A Companion to Qualitative Research*. London: Sage, pp. 570–582.

Schelling, T. (1971) 'Dynamic models of segregation', *The Journal of Mathematical Sociology*, 1(2), pp. 143–186.

Smith, R. C. (2016) 'What's a life worth? Ethnographic counterfactual analysis, undocumented status and sociological autopsy in a wrongful death lawsuit', *Ethnography*, 17(4), pp. 419–439.

Strathern, M. (2002) 'Abstraction and decontextualization: An anthropological Comment', in Woolgar, S. (ed.), *Virtual Society? Technology, Cyberbole, Reality*. Oxford: Oxford University Press, pp. 303–13.

Strübing, I. (2006) 'Wider die Zwangsverheiratung von Grounded Theory und Objektiver Hermeneutik', *Sozialer Sinn*, 7(1), pp. 147–157.

Thorngate, W. and Edmonds, B. (2013) 'Measuring simulation-observation fit: An introduction to ordinal pattern analysis', *Journal of Artificial Societies and Social Simulation*, 16(2). https://jasss.soc.surrey.ac.uk/16/2/4.html

Uruena, S. (2019) 'Understanding "plausibility": A relational approach to the anticipatory heuristics of future scenarios', *Futures: The Journal of Policy Planning and Futures Studies*, 111, pp. 15–25.

Wagner, S. M., Lukassen, P. and Mahlendorf, M. (2010) 'Misused and missed use— Grounded theory and objective hermeneutics as methods for research in industrial marketing', *Industrial Marketing Management*, 39(1), pp. 5–15.

Weber, M. (1922) *Wirtschaft und Gesellschaft*. Tübingen: Mohr.

Wenninger, A. (2015) 'Hermeneutische Analysen neuer Kommunikationsformen im Internet. Methodologische und methodische Erörterungen am Beispiel eines wissenschaftlichen Blogportals', in Schirmer, D., Sander, N. and Wenninger, A. (eds.) *Die Qualitative Analyse internetbasierter Daten*. Wiesbaden: Springer, pp. 51–87.

Wernet, A. (2013) 'Hermeneutics and objective hermeneutics', in Flick, U. (ed.) *The Sage Handbook of Qualitative Data Analysis*. Los Angeles: Sage, pp. 234–246.

Wieser, C. (2016) 'Verschiedene Fokussierungen, gemeinsame Möglichkeiten. Perspektiven der komplementären Nutzung von Strategien der Grounded Theory Methodologie und der objektiven Hermeneutik', *Sozialer Sinn*, 16(2), pp. 199–221.

Wilensky, U. (1997). *NetLogo Segregation Model*. Center for Connected Learning and Computer-Based Modeling. Evanston, IL: Northwestern University. http://ccl.northwestern.edu/netlogo/models/Segregation

Wodak, R. (2011) 'Complex texts: Analysing, understanding, explaining and interpreting meanings', *Discourse Studies*, 13(5), pp. 628–629.

10 Outlook on potential further directions

Martin Neumann and Bruce Edmonds

10.1 Introduction

Throughout the book, we used the example of criminology to illustrate the methodology of interpretive ABM. It is hoped that constantly referring back to the one example of criminal culture fosters a reuse of this methodology in the community as the reference to just one case allows to explicate the research process in detail step by step from the beginning to the end. Hopefully, it also became clear throughout the different chapters that criminal culture is an appropriate example to highlight the specific insights that can be gained by this approach: understanding criminal culture calls for a contextualized hermeneutic interpretation of a world outside the state monopoly of violence which fosters specific codes of conduct, a criminal culture.

In fact, current digital technologies in policing and criminal justice such as predictive policing (Perry et al., 2013) or forecasting criminal behaviour (Dressel and Farid, 2018) are in danger of losing sight of the intelligible frame of criminal acts (see Chapter 3) and in turn might not always generate meaningful evidence. Statistical analysis of big data certainly generates patterns of correlations. However, it need not necessarily represent the meaning assigned to actions in the field. In fact, it has been questioned whether machine learning technologies replicate human biases and prejudices in the digital realm. For instance, it has been argued that it fosters racial discrimination (Angwin et al., 2016; Flores et al., 2016). Algorithms might just reflect human bias. Therefore, it is important to note that criminal acts are meaningful actions. To arrive at meaningful evidence, it is necessary to preserve the context of an action by a detailed description and analysis of the micro level of local practices (see Chapter 3). Taking into account the meaning of actions fosters dissecting the potential variety of alternative courses of action and thus possible futures (see Chapter 7). At the same time, preserving context in narrative scenarios enables hermeneutic interpretation of their meaning (see Chapter 7) and fosters an abductive diagnosis of potential reasons for certain courses of action by backtracking processes for identifying relevant events that shaped the further history of follow-up events (see Chapters 7 and 8). Understanding criminal practice

DOI: 10.4324/9781003393207-10

is also of practical use as understanding this culture potentially enables more targeted interventions, as simulation allows for investigating scenarios which provide virtual experiences for criminal investigators.

While these features make criminal culture a fruitful and practically useful case for exploring the potential of an interpretive account to ABM, the central focus of the book is on methodology. Criminal culture is but one example of an application domain in which the choice of an interpretive ABM as a research methodology provides fruitful insights. However, there are certainly many other domains as well in which the choice of this methodology is appropriate. Understanding where and why applying this approach might be appropriate to gain insights that otherwise would hardly be possible calls for reflections on a more abstract level in what kind of research fields this approach might be promising before we provide at least an outlook to one example of a potential different application in the hope that providing an example facilitates a transfer also to other contexts.

10.2   The framework of research questions for interpretive ABM

The first thing to note is that there is no doubt that there are also research questions for which this approach might not be the best choice. There exists no tool which is the one and only for each and every question. Such a claim would lead to dogmatism. ABM is specifically well known for its generative explanations, explaining social macro phenomena by interacting agents on the micro level (see Chapter 9). This feature makes traditional ABM a well-suited tool to investigate the micro-macro link in sociological theory: following Coleman's (1990) classical concept of a sociological explanation, ABM allows for explaining macro phenomena by situated agents, i.e. a micro level which is embedded in a macro level system of action. Thereby traditional ABM revealed its potential for answering questions about the development of the social structure. Examples include the development of demographic characteristics of societies (Harland et al., 2012; Silverman et al., 2013), the development of the income distribution in societies (Yang and Zhou 2022), and also, for instance, the number of fatalities in armed conflicts (Bennett 2008; Geller and Alaam, 2010). Moreover, ABM allows the examination of not only the macrostructural properties of societies but also how these properties are generated. The past decades have proven that ABM can provide insights that would not have been gained otherwise in numerous application domains, even in research fields beyond classical development of social structure. It can be asked, for instance, how many people adopt certain norms or when whole groups of a society start to rebel (Epstein, 2002; Cioffi-Revilla and Rouleau, 2010) or undertake massacres (Bhavnani, 2006). Following norms and also the willingness to make existential decisions as starting to rebel includes a dimension of free will in human decision-making. There need to be reasons for these decisions. Usually, people can give an answer to why they do so. However, the approach of ABM to these dimensions remains restricted to the investigation of the macrostructural level: for instance, how many people adopt norms or start rebelling.

There are research questions which call for numbers as an answer and traditional ABM reveals such numbers as an output. Examples range from macroeconomic indicators to the number of voters or epidemiological incidences. The methodology of interpretive ABM proposed here is less suited to provide numerical answers to such questions. Thus, there are large domains of research fields in which this approach is not recommended. However, numbers as such do not make sense. Without interpretation, there cannot be meaning attributed to numbers. Even macroeconomic indicators need to be interpreted as wealth or prosperity. Traditionally, the interpretation of simulation results is an informal, rather unstructured process which relies on the tacit knowledge and experience of the researcher. In this book, a much more systematic process of interpretation has been described.

Under what circumstances is interpretation particularly necessary? This question refers back to Chapter 2 on the epistemological foundations. Certain research questions call for deciphering the meaning of certain actions or events. In the case of the example used in this book, the question is to understand why people started killing each other instead of becoming richer and richer. At first sight, this is a puzzle: nobody gains from it. It does not make sense. To put it in terms of Clifford Geertz: what the hell is going on? This is the question with which the police were struggling. Sometimes the question of *why* did this happen at all is more important than the exact number of people who have been killed. For such questions, the approach of interpretive ABM becomes relevant. It allows for asking why something happens, what are in specific cultural settings possible modes to interpret and react to actions of others, and how people negotiate meaning in this process of their interaction. That is to say, how culture emerges in the web of interactions and in turn shapes this web of interactions. This is important for understanding how people make sense of their world and lives – including their potential failure. Referring back to the question of norms or rebellion, interpretive ABM does allow for investigating why people follow norms or start rebelling. Understanding why people act in a certain way provides the basis to explore the space of cultural development, that is, possible alternatives that are conceivable from the perspective of the actors in the field and how alternatives could potentially be realized. For such problems which are often of high practical, social relevance, typically beginning with a "why", interpretive ABM provides a new alternative to gain new insights. Next, we provide an example of such a question.

10.3   Example application: Narrative identities

One of these puzzling sociocultural problems is the question of identity which people ascribe to oneselves or others. Identities are important for the question of well-being and decisively shape individual and collective decision-making. Examples range from genocide to behaviour change towards more sustainable behaviour. For instance, in the former Yugoslavia or Rwanda, identity conflicts were a major factor in the escalating spiral of violence. On the other hand, social context decisively shapes environmental behaviour. For instance, farmers may come in conflict with environmentalists. However, interests may be mediated by identities to foster more sustainable environmental behaviour (Fielding and Hornsey, 2016). Thus, understanding how identities are constituted and why and how they change is important for understanding society and potentially influencing its future, be it for the good or bad.

The Social Identity Approach (SIA) is a socio-cognitive account of group identity – to which groupings we associate ourselves with and when we do so (Reicher et al., 2010). It is an integration of Social Identity Theory (Tajfel and Turner, 1979) and Self-Categorization Theory (Turner et al., 1987). This is a relatively rich theory which explains how such associations may affect our behaviour and our attitudes towards those we perceive as being "in our group" and "those not in our group". The SIA framework resulted from a merging of social psychological and sociological viewpoints. However, it leaves the processes by which groupings emerge as largely implicit – focusing more on how social structure influences and constrains the individual. It does not specify how the groupings are constituted and reproduced. Here ABM has a role, as it is an ideal tool for representing and exploring such processes. ABM can incorporate SIA in the cognitive model of its agents but then can add the missing social dynamics (e.g. Pires and Crooks, 2017). This combination results in simulations whose agents (when you follow them around in simulation runs) are more interpretable in terms of recognizable social behaviour.

However powerful this combination of SIA + ABM is, it still misses out on many important aspects, for example: why an individual might choose a particular association rather than another in a given context, the strength of any such association, or why they might wish to change their associations. If you ask people why they associate themselves with any of their groupings, they are likely to respond with a narrative; for example: "because I was born in the area", "I am worried about the future of the planet", "my parents were working class", or "I became a lawyer to fight injustice". These narratives are central to how we perceive our identity choices and give them meaning.

These aspects of identity have, together, been called "Narrative Identity" (summarized in Singer, 2004). That is, narrative identity explains *why* we are as we are – both to ourselves and to others. Narrative identity is the story we tell about ourselves. It is built up and changes over a lifetime, as a result of complex constitutive influences rooted in specific cultural and historical matrices, integrating the subjectively experienced past, present, and imagined future of a life course into a coherent story. That is to say, narratives are shaped by the characteristics of storytelling: they consist of themes, episodes, and characters and follow a storyline plot including a beginning, a middle part, and an end, i.e. elements which make a life course a meaningful whole (McAdams, 2001). These narratives can be personally constructed or socially spread, highly elaborate or nothing more than a slogan, and can have a variety of origins, including class, nation, geography, or occupation. These narratives affect our decision-making, particularly in how we might choose reference points and background assumptions for such choices.

Many of these stories have a social origin – stories that the individual has heard and then uses to understand their identity. However, even when these stories are highly individualized, their full meaning and impact are only clear in their social context. Thus, narrative identity is one of these phenomena which arises out of the interaction between the individual and the social – the micro and macro levels, highly mediated by the immediate social structures (meso level) that the individual participates in (e.g. a criminal gang).

Following on from the example of criminal culture, one might think about imprisoned criminals: the experience of being sentenced to a prison term might trigger a process of conversion for some persons in which they become convinced that they did something wrong. This creates a conflict between a past criminal life experience and the newly adopted convictions. A need arises to integrate the self which committed the crime into a larger concept of the self. Religious conversion may be a tangible way of handling this process. A conversion narrative may function as a shame management and coping strategy and allows a sense of control over an unknown future (Maruna et al., 2006. Note, however, that this characterization of a conversion narrative as "shame management" and "control mechanism" is purely from the perspective of the individual. It is a highly individualized description. However, at the same time, the narrative involves concepts such as "God" and "crime" and happens under the constraining circumstances of a prison. Concepts such as "sentence" or "crime" cannot be fully understood without taking the social dimension into account. While the physical act of the crime (may it be beating up an old lady or fraud in the cryptosphere) may be undertaken by an individual, the word "crime" is a complex move in a sociocultural language game involving sentencing authorities and prison bars. A full understanding of the narrative needs to take into account the dialectics between the individual and society: while narrative identities are expressions of the personal self, they are at the same time instantiations of the social structures the individual participates in.

A second, and important case, is the use of narrative identity in politics. In politics, narratives are a crucial element whose introduction can decisively shift political outcomes. One interpretation of why Brexit happened includes the mobilization of disaffected voters using the populist narrative that this was substantially the fault of a "Brussels-loving elite" who did not care about "normal people" but rather wanted to reduce Britain's sovereignty and allow high levels of immigration (Calhoun, 2017). Whilst this is just one strand of the complex of factors that lead to the event, it illustrates both the power and the complexity of narrative identity. The populist narrative does not stand alone but is related to many nationalist narratives (e.g. Britain "standing alone" against Nazi Germany in WWII). Furthermore, the populist narrative is only accepted by some people – presumably when it helps to make sense of their experience and fits with their own narrative identity. There is a lot of political research about the various factors and attitudes that might influence voting behaviour but the strands that concentrate on formal modelling and quantitative data are largely separate from each other. Accounts that integrate the role of narratives with those of attitudes and party policies would enable a more complete exploration of such political events – enabling richer understandings.

10.4   How interpretive ABM can help understand narrative identity

Understanding narrative identity poses special challenges for any methodology. It ineluctably involves both the individual and the social. The stories an individual chooses to characterize themselves shape how they interact with and choose social groupings – playing a part in their constitution. However, these stories only have meaning within the wider set of social stories which may act as more or less constraining templates for them and against which they will be judged – the stories are central to the social justification of their choices. Also, they involve both static and dynamic aspects. They must have some temporal continuity if they are to have a significant influence on the person's evolution, but it is the times when they change that mark the most significant turning points for many people.

The approach described in this book is well positioned to address these challenges. Narrative ABM provides narratives as simulation results which is an outcome that obviously resonates with narrative identities: both are presented as meaningful stories. Furthermore, a hermeneutic interpretation of counterfactual narratives enables an assessment of whether they can be regarded as plausible variations of a factual course of action. Such a counterfactual analysis reveals more of the latent meaning structures hidden in the cultural matrix. Thus an approach to ABM which produces narrative scenarios as simulation results that are hermeneutically interpreted obviously converges with a narrative approach to identity that perceives humans as storytelling animals and hermeneutically attempts to interpret these stories.

Applying the interpretive account to ABM, as described in this book, for the study of narrative identities is not without difficulties, of course. Without claiming completeness, a few pitfalls may be mentioned here:

- First thing to note is that the timescales in the criminological examples sketched here differ vastly from the timescales of the formation of a narrative identity. For instance, biographical interviews in narrative identity research cover a whole life span, whereas the condition-action sequences in the examples in this book mostly are concerned with immediate follow-up actions to certain events. While they may include a certain period of planning of days or weeks, they may also be just direct affective reactions.
- This difference is amplified by the fact that the formation of narrative identities may involve a process of putting together different phases of life to a coherent whole. Such a process includes a kind of backward tracing: prior

phases of a life are retrospectively evaluated to make them meaningful in the present. Such an evaluation need not take into account the causal ordering of events. For instance, former dissidents in the GDR may re-evaluate their experience with the state apparatus after the fall of the Berlin Wall (Andrews et al., 2004). This is only possible retrospectively. It could have been possible that the fall of the Berlin Wall had not taken place, which would have resulted in a quite different evaluation. In contrast, the condition-action sequences of the examples in this book are always of a strictly linear temporal order. There is no reason why backward-looking re-evaluations should not be built into an ABM. However, that obviously adds considerable complication to their programming.

- The notion of an evaluation refers to another difference between the data utilized in this book and the kind of data necessary for research on narrative identities. Namely, that evaluation includes an element of valuation. An episode of a lifetime is not just presented as a historical event as perhaps historically critical historiography would do. Rather, the event is merely the material for valuation from the perspective of certain values. This is different in the data and the data analysis presented in this book. The criminological research on the norms and values guiding criminal organizations needs to abstain from any valuation of these norms and values. Here a strictly descriptive account is applied. Personal narratives can be compared to a wider set of narratives that are around in society, but more interpretation and innate human social expertise (not all of which can be exposed) are needed.

- Finally, eventually the data basis and method of data gathering in narrative research might be reconsidered for being utilized in an interpretive ABM. The counterfactual scenarios that we presented in this book are based on police interrogations. Thus, they are based on events that have factually taken place. It is the reordering of these events which in the end generates a completely different story. It can only be explored by conducting research on narrative identities by means of interpretive ABM whether the data is sufficient for generating *meaningful* counterfactuals.

Thus, the methodology cannot be transferred in a one-to-one manner. The book cannot be read like a recipe in a cookbook. Further efforts and also creativity might be needed for resolving these pitfalls. Here we used the case of narrative identities merely as an example. However, the approach seems also to be quite promising for such research.

- If possible, it would allow for investigating the combination of attending to, and recording, individual narratives at points in time, whilst at the same time developing wider social and dynamic meta-narratives developed via ABMs. This allows for a more holistic, dynamic, and narrative-based understanding to be developed. In this case, the ABM allows for a kind of narrative interpolation, filling in the possible dynamics between ethnographic snapshots and facilitating simultaneously multi-level accounts.

- Such a holistic view on narrative identities may also help understanding on a more abstract level the processes denoted as immergence (Conte et al., 2014): the constraint or influence from the macro to the micro completing the recursive feedback loop from micro to the macro and back again also known as cycle structuration (Giddens, 1984). Understanding how macrosocial events shape individual identity formation facilitates understanding this complex feedback loop in the constitution of society. Thus, studying narrative identities in a holistic manner which takes the social dimension of the self fully into account might provide insights also into the development of cultural narratives on a societal level and how the individual and cultural narratives are interwoven.
- In particular the scenario-based approach of simulation experiments by generating counterfactual narrative scenarios might provide novel insights for research on narrative identities. The generation of a counterfactual life course can stimulate reasoning about alternatives and how these might have been realized. This fosters an identification of critical junctures of a life course, consisting of both an individual and a social dimension. We already noted the fall of the Berlin Wall as a decisive event for many dissidents. This is a social dimension that is out of control of the individual, at least the dissidents themselves had less or no immediate agency in this event. However, how such events are mentally processed is shaped by the individual and their history of experiences. Likewise, there are events during an individual's life course which are decisive for opening possibilities or closing others. The counterfactual approach for studying causality (see Chapters 8 and 9) enables us to integrate a causal understanding of the critical events that decisively shaped a life course with an interpretive understanding of how these events shape the story we tell ourselves, that is: how individuals make sense of these events and why these events are decisive in the narrative of ourselves. It might enable deciphering the making of the plot of this story.
- The approach can allow us to extend our understanding to cases where the narrative is crucial – at both societal and individual levels – such as in the politics or personal transformation examples briefly described above. At the moment, the approaches for exploring their role are limited, so narrative ABM has the potential to help deepen our representations, explorations, and hence understanding of these cases.

10.5   A final note

Here we outlined a possible direction for applying the approach presented in this book in future research. Certainly, this is just one example. Other applications are imaginable as well. For instance, ethnic conflicts provide an example closely related to narrative identity, as ethnic conflicts are also based on identities. While narrative identity is focused on the individual, the theory of ethnic conflict takes a view on the macrosocial implications of identity formations, in this case identity conflicts. A further example may be research on resilience to change at the workplace in management science. This research might benefit from the account of narrative scenarios as narrative scenarios might provide an inside view of how actors negotiate the meaning of their work environment. This might help an understanding of the conditions which foster such resistance, or under which conditions on the contrary change might be successful. A further at first sight not so obvious example may be the investigation of human trafficking. Human trafficking involves the interaction of many actors: perpetrators and victims, who mutually interact with each other. In Chapter 3, we already outlined how a model of reputation building in the cocaine trade might look using the approach of ethnographic simulation in the process of model development, the first step of the interpretive ABM account. The negotiation of meaning might even be more complicated when the interaction of perpetrators and victims has to be taken into account as the interpretation of actions and their sense-making may be quite different on both sides.

In more general terms, ABM is often applied in fields which cross-cut the disciplinary boundaries of natural and social sciences. Environmental research provides an example which includes natural science aspects ranging from physics to biology but in which obviously also social aspects are relevant. However, often it remains an open issue of how to integrate the social aspects in the positivist research tradition of the natural sciences. Within such a framework, social aspects are in danger to remain a mere add-on such as a rough estimation of parameters. It might be worthwhile to examine whether the methodology presented in this book might provide a new approach for the integration of the two very different research traditions which does justice to both the natural and the social sciences: the positivist character of the natural sciences and the interpretive traditions in the social sciences. Such a coupling might build on another feature of condition-action sequences which has been less emphasized throughout this book: namely, that it is an event-based approach. While the model of the social world may remain based on an interpretive account, this model may generate events which can trigger a simulation tick in a natural science model when agents generate actions that have an impact on the environment. For instance, they may take fish out of the sea. Why agents do so may be based on an interpretive understanding. However, this event may provide an input for a purely scientific (i.e. natural science based) model of fish population. Thus, events could provide a coupling for two models based on natural and social sciences.

In this chapter, we concentrated on just one area (narrative identity), and, certainly, we outlined only a brief sketch of a field of application for the approach outlined in this book which is different from (but intersects with) criminology. It has to be proven by future research that applying this methodology for studying narrative identities reveals fresh and novel insights. Moreover, science is a collective enterprise. We hope that this example stimulates readers to extend and apply the approach in directions that eventually we cannot even imagine.

References

Andrews, M., Sclater, S., Squire, C. and Tamboukou, M. (2004) 'Narrative research', in Seale, C., Gobo, G., Gubrium, J. and Silverman, D. (eds.) *Qualitative Research Practice*. London: Sage, pp. 97–112.

Angwin, J., Larson, J., Mattu, S. and Kirchner, L. (2016) Machine bias: There's software used across the country to predict future criminals. And it's biased against blacks. *ProPublica* [online]. 23 May 2016. Available from: www.propublica.org/article/machine-bias-risk-assessmentsin-criminal-sentencing

Bennett, S. (2008) 'Governments, civilians, and the evolution of insurgency: Modeling the early dynamics of insurgencies', *Journal of Artificial Societies and Social Simulation*, 11(4). https://www.jasss.org/11/4/7.html

Bhavnani, R. (2006) 'Ethnic norms and interethnic violence: Accounting for mass participation in the Rwandan genocide', *Journal of Peace Research*, 43(6), pp. 651–666.

Calhoun, C. (2017) 'Populism, nationalism and Brexit', in Outhwaite, W. (ed.) *Brexit: Sociological Responses*. Anthem Press: London, pp. 57–76.

Cioffi-Revilla, C. and Rouleau, M. (2010) 'MASON RebeLand: An agent-based model of politics, environment, and insurgency', *International Studies Review*, 12(1), pp. 31–52.

Coleman, J. (1990). *Foundations of social theory*. Harvard: Harvard University Press.

Conte, R., Andrighetto, G. and Campenni, M. (eds.). (2014). *Minding Norms. Mechanisms and Dynamics of Social Order in Agent Societies*. Oxford: Oxford University Press.

Dressel, J. and Farid, H. (2018) 'The accuracy, fairness, and limits of predicting recidivism', *Science Advances*, 4(1), pp. 1–5.

Epstein, J. (2002) 'Modeling civil violence: An agent-based computational approach', *PNAS*, 99(3), pp. 7243–7250.

Fielding, K. and Hornsey, M. (2016) 'A social identity analysis of climate change and environmental attitudes and behaviors: Insights and opportunities', *Frontiers in Psychology*, 7. https://doi.org/10.3389/fpsyg.2016.00121

Flores, A. W., Bechtel, K. and Lowenkamp, C. T. (2016) 'False positives, false negatives, and false analyses: A rejoinder to "machine bias: There's software used across the country to predict future criminals. And it's biased against blacks"', *Federal Probation*, 80(2), pp. 38–46.

Geller, A. and Alam, S. J. (2010) 'A socio-political and-cultural model of the war in Afghanistan', *International Studies Review*, 12(1), pp. 8–30.

Giddens, A. (1984) *The Constitution of Society: Outline of the Theory of Structuration*. Cambridge: Polity Press.

Harland, K., Heppenstall, A., Smith, D. and Birkin, M. (2012) Creating realistic synthetic populations at varying spatial scales: A comparative critique of population synthesis techniques *Journal of Artificial Societies and Social Simulation* 15(1). https://jasss.soc.surrey.ac.uk/15/1/1.html

Maruna, S., Wilson, L. and Curran, K. (2006) 'Why God is often found behind bars: Prison conversions and the crisis of self narrative', *Research in Human Development*, 3(2/3), pp. 161–184.

McAdams, D. (2001) 'The psychology of life stories', *Review of General Psychology*, 5(2), pp. 100–122.

Perry, W. L., McInnis, B., Price, C. C., Smith, S. and Hollywood, J. S. (2013) *Predictive Policing. The Role of Forecast in Law Enforcement Operations*. Santa Monica, CA: RAND.

Pires, B. and Crooks, A. T. (2017) 'Modeling the emergence of riots: A geosimulation approach', *Computers, Environment and Urban Systems*, 61, pp. 66–80.

Reicher, S., Spears, R. and Haslam, S. A. (2010). 'The Social Identity Approach in Social Psychology'. In: Wetherell, M. and Mohanty, C. (eds.) *Sage Identities Handbook*, London: Sage, pp. 45–62.

Silverman, E., Bijak, J., Hilton, J., Dung Cao, V. and Noble, J. (2013) 'When demography met social simulation: A tale of two modelling approaches', *Journal of Artificial Societies and Social Simulation*, 16(4). https://www.jasss.org/16/4/9.html

Singer, J. A. (2004) 'Narrative identity and meaning making across the adult lifespan: An introduction', *Journal of Personality*, 72(3), pp. 437–460.

Tajfel, H. and Turner, J. (1979). An interpretive theory of intergroup conflict. *The Social Psychology of Intergroup Relations*. Monterey, CA: Brooks Cole.

Turner, J. C., Hogg, M. A., Oakes, P. J., Reicher, S. D. and Wetherell, M. S. (1987) *Rediscovering the Social Group: A Self-Categorization Theory*. Basil Blackwell.

Yang, X. and Zhou, P. (2022) 'Wealth inequality and social mobility: A simulation-based modelling approach', *Journal of Economic Behavior and Organization*, 196, pp. 307–329.

List of key terms

This list of key terms attempts to explain in simple terms the technical terminology that has been used throughout this book, trying to avoid specialist terms as much as possible. Sometimes this might come at the cost of precision when terms are embedded in specialist terminology. However, it is hoped that readers of various disciplinary backgrounds get an idea of what is meant by the terms and that thereby this explanatory list of key terms helps a comprehension of this book which delves into various disciplines throughout the different chapters.

Abduction Abduction is an epistemological concept developed by Charles Sanders Peirce in delimitation to induction and deduction. It serves to generate hypotheses about the causation of phenomena. Peirce described the abductive inference as follows: "The surprising fact C is observed; but if A were true, C would be a given; consequently, there is reason to suspect that A is true". This is hypothetical reasoning to infer an unknown rule. Abduction is often discussed in the context of inference to the best explanation.

Action diagram An action diagram is the result of the conceptual modelling of a simulation program. It is the sum of condition-action sequences which describe the flow of events in the simulation model.

Activity diagram In Software engineering activity, diagrams are used for a graphical representation of workflows of stepwise activities or actions. It is part of the developmental modelling language, unified modelling language (UML), for the graphical representation of software design.

Agent Agents are software units that are capable of acting autonomously in a virtual environment. Autonomous action means that the actions performed by individual agents are not controlled top-down by a central processing unit but that agents decide for themselves. Central features of agents are reactivity (reacting to stimuli from the environment), proactivity (pursuing goals), and sociality (interacting with other software units).

Agent-based social simulation (ABM) Agent-based social simulation is a scientific discipline concerned with the simulation of social phenomena, using heterogeneous agents in computer-based models. In agent-based social simulation, many software units denoted as agents act and interact with each other in a virtual environment.

Codes In qualitative content analysis, codes stand for classes of objects, events, or actions that are found in the data which have some major properties in common. Relevant text passages are subsumed under a list of codes.

Conceptual modelling Conceptual modelling denotes the phase of the development of the rules of a simulation model prior to the implementation of these rules in the program code of a simulation model. In the approach of interpretive ABM, conceptual modelling follows a specific modelling approach denoted as condition-action sequences.

Condition-action sequence Condition-action sequences are an a priori methodological device to identify social mechanisms on a micro level of individual (inter)action. A sequence is initiated by a certain condition which triggers a certain action. This action in turn generates a new state of the world which is again a condition for further action. Whereas the data describes individual instantiations, the condition-action sequences represent general event classes.

Counterfactuals Scenario analysis in simulation experiments includes counterfactual results. Counterfactual results explore outcomes that did *not* actually occur, but *could* have occurred under different conditions. It is a *"what-if"* analysis for testing *cause-and-effect* relationships.

Culture Culture is used here as in social sciences and humanities, denoting social behaviour, norms, and institutions of a society or group (not restricted to "high" culture such as music or arts).

Emic The notion of emic denotes research that attempts to uncover the first person perspective, i.e. the perspective of the researched subjects.

Epistemology Epistemology is a philosophical term for the theory of knowledge. Epistemology encompasses the analysis of truth and justification of knowledge claims, sources of justified beliefs, and the structure of the body of knowledge.

Ethnography Ethnography is a branch of anthropology for studying cultures, mostly using qualitative methods. Ethnography studies cultural phenomena from the perspective of the subjects of study. It attempts at interpreting the meaning negotiated among the subjects in the fields by situating social actions in the semiotic, historical, and situational context.

Generative explanation (generative social science) Generative explanations are a way of explaining social phenomena by agent-based simulation models. Agent-based models enable to generate macro-social patterns through the local interaction of individual, heterogeneous agents. The models "grow" the social phenomenon from the bottom-up. This demonstrates that the rules implemented can produce the social phenomenon.

Hermeneutics Hermeneutics studies the interpretation of texts or signs. It can be found in many disciplines such as theology, philosophy, law, as well as social sciences. It became prominent in the 19th century in the philosophy of history. In the social sciences, the methodology of hermeneutics attempts to interpret processes of interaction and communication.

Idiographic   Idiographic research is a research field in which the aim is the comprehensive analysis of concrete, i.e. temporally and spatially unique objects.

Implementation   Implementation denotes the process of programming a computer code, in this case a simulation model.

Inner context   Within the framework of the method of sequence analysis, the notion of inner context denotes the principle to interpret only the text without taking context information into account. The text is regarded as the inner context.

Intelligible frame   In ethnography the concept of an intelligible frame, introduced by Clifford Geertz, characterizes the context that is capable to be understood as a symbolic system by the subjects in the field.

Interpretation   Interpretation denotes a methodological approach in the humanities and social sciences in which an interpreter attempts to understand the meaning attributed to actions and cultural objects.

KIDS   "Keep it descriptive, stupid" (KIDS) is a principle for developing agent-based models. It suggests to include in a model as much evidence as possible, taking into account the widest range of sources of evidence. The goal is to keep the model a valid representation of the target system.

KISS   "Keep it simple, stupid" (KISS) is a principle for developing agent-based models. It suggests to program the model as simple as possible. The aim is to generate complex behaviour (in a simulation) from simple rules in order to keep the model comprehensible.

Meaning (meaningfulness)   The meaning of an action, including a speech act, becomes visible through the context of other actors interpreting the action and reacting and responding accordingly. Therefore, meaning is an emergent property of linguistic practices, that is to say, it is negotiated between actors and groups of actors.

Meaning structure   The term meaning structure denotes a concept in objective hermeneutics which refers to the totality of interpretive options opened by the wordings of a text. The meaning structure is a property of the text independent of the subjects involved in the field.

Mixed methods   Mixed methods denotes the combination of different research methods, typically qualitative and quantitative methods.

Narrative scenario   Narrative scenarios are the simulation results of interpretive ABM. Different simulation runs generate different scenarios, i.e. different results. The results are not presented as numerical time series but as stories that can be meaningfully interpreted.

Nomothetic   The term nomothetic characterizes a research direction in which the goal of scientific work is universally valid laws. Their methods are experimental, often reductionist, and the data collected quantitative. Nomothetic theories abstract from the phenomena.

Objective hermeneutics Objective hermeneutics is a qualitative method of empirical social research. Objective hermeneutics perceives the social world as a text and attempts to reconstruct meaning structures inherent in the text. The methodological approach for reconstructing the meaning structure is sequence analysis. Objective hermeneutics is embedded in a social theory which perceives social practice as a continuation of routine and crisis.

Open coding Open coding is a method in qualitative content analysis. It is the first step in the development of categories to compare and contrast events in the data. Open codings are annotations of characteristic text passages that have certain themes in common.

Phenomenology Phenomenology is the study of the structures of experiences. It attempts to study objectively topics regarded as subjective such as experience or consciousness. Experience is regarded as being shaped by intentionality; that is, experience is directed towards something which is perceived as meaningful by the experiencing subject. Phenomenological studies in the social sciences often focus on the emic (i.e. first person) perspective of the subjects under investigation.

Process tracing (backward tracing) Process tracing is a research method which attempts to infer mechanisms that potentially caused a certain event. It is a method to find out (by various methods) likely reasons why something happened. Often this is complemented by comparative case studies.

Scenario Scenarios are possible actions of events. The scenario technique is used for strategic planning in science and policy to explore hypothetical alternative situations. In simulation experiments, scenarios describe a variety of simulation results, for instance, by varying parameters of the simulation model. A scenario analysis shows how sensitive a model is to certain parameter constellations.

Simulation experiments Simulation models enable simulation experiments to investigate in multiple simulation runs the space of possible simulation results.

Simulation run Simulation run denotes the execution of a simulation model until a somehow defined termination point. Typically this represents a process in time. The whole process from the start to the end is one run of the simulation.

Semiotics Semiotics is the science of signs. The notion of signs includes also non-linguistic sign systems. Semiotics studies how signs communicate meaning to an interpreter. Typically it is differentiated between a) the material sign, b) the object to which the sign relates, and c) the interpreter of the sign as well as between different types of signs. They can be iconic, indexical, or symbolic. Semiotics is applied in various disciplines, ranging from literature studies to social and cultural sciences.

Sense unit In a sequence analysis, a sense unit denotes the minimal meaning bearing element in a protocol that can be interpreted in isolation.

Sequence analysis   Sequence analysis is a method of interpretation developed by the approach of objective hermeneutics. The first rule is that the interpretation is done in the order given by the protocol. Interpretation is carried out context-free in the first phases of the analysis. This is done practically by sketching a series of stories in which the particular sequence passage would make sense. Each interpretation step sequentially makes spaces of possibility visible and at the same time closes past spaces of possibility.

Social mechanism   A mechanism is a relation that transforms an input X into an output Y. A further condition is a certain degree of abstraction, which becomes evident in a certain degree of regularity, i.e., under similar circumstances a similar input X* yields similar outputs Y*. In the social world, this is typically an action which relates X and Y.

Stakeholder   Stakeholders are persons or groups which have a legitimate interest in a certain course of events or the outcome of a process.

Structural variation   Structural variation is a term in the hermeneutic interpretation of narratives. It denotes a possible variation of a narrative that can be meaningfully interpreted. Structural variations are counterfactual scenarios which demonstrate possible alternatives to the case structure.

Thick description   Thick description is an ethnographic method. The term describes the intentional, communicative meaning of a behaviour. As a method, a thick description is a detailed report which mediates between the ethnographic information from the field and the scientific interpretation of the meaning of this information.

Tick   The notion of a tick denotes one step in the execution of a simulation.

Traceability   Traceability denotes a method in ABM to endow the rules of a simulation model with annotations from the empirical evidence base that justify the rules. The annotations enable traceability of simulation results to the evidence base as each rule that is executed during a simulation can be traced back to its annotation.

Understanding   The term understanding ("Verstehen") has been coined by Max Weber to denote a sociological methodology that attempts at deciphering the context of the meaning of social actions.

Validation   Validation denotes the examination of the correctness of scientific results. In the case of simulation modelling, validation confirms that within the range of accuracy, the model is a correct representation of the modelled system with respect to the intended application.

Verisimilitude   Verisimilitude denotes statements that produce for the readers the feeling that they have experienced, or could experience, the events being described in a study.

What-if analysis (ex-ante)   What-if analysis are simulation experiments to experimentally assess questions of interventions in a system within the virtual environment of the simulation model, where the aim is to identify development scenarios and design options for possible "futures", but also, in the sense of an early warning system, undesirable developments.

Index

Note: Page numbers followed by "n" refer to notes; and page numbers in **Bold** refer to tables; and page numbers in italics refer to figures

Printed in the USA
CPSIA information can be obtained
at www.ICGtesting.com
LVHW020919301023
762360LV00007B/546